Gridiron Gumshoe

My Life in and out of
the
NFL Films'
Vault

Ace Cacchiotti

iUniverse LLC
Bloomington

GRIDIRON GUMSHOE
MY LIFE IN AND OUT OF THE NFL FILMS' VAULT

iUniverse books may be ordered through booksellers or by contacting:

iUniverse LLC
1663 Liberty Drive
Bloomington, IN 47403
www.iuniverse.com
1-800-Authors (1-800-288-4677)

ISBN: 978-1-4917-0379-3 (sc)
ISBN: 978-1-4917-0380-9 (hc)
ISBN: 978-1-4917-0381-6 (e)

Library of Congress Control Number: 2013914788

Printed in the United States of America.

iUniverse rev. date: 12/03/2013

"They talk about Heaven and I don't know what is up there but it could never be any better than what I have down here."

NFL Films' President Steve Sabol relayed those feelings to Sports Illustrated writer Peter King a few months after Doctors discovered a brain tumor after Steve had suffered a seizure in February, 2011 in Kansas City. Eventually after eighteen months my friend passed away saying goodbye to his NFL Family and friends and that is just what it was and still is – a family and that is why I believe I am reaching out to the fans of the game of Pro Football and more importantly NFL Films. There are no doubts - those that have felt the visceral effects of my former employer's incredible work. I wanted all that have flattered me with their interest in **"Gridiron Gumshoe"** to understand that I wrote my life story as if I was writing a letter to each NFL Films' fan and that is why I decided to use *italics as my font because it is my way of letting all know that it was as if I wrote this in my own handwriting for I have that wonderful feeling for those that loved and still love the game but most important NFL Films and their late President and that is why I am leaving an email to anyone that wants to express his or her heartfelt memories of what it was like and still is being part of that wonderful family known as NFL Films. So and I apologize for the cliché "With that said" read on.*

Always sincere,

acecacchiotti@yahoo.com

In Memory:

My Sister Paula:

October 15th, 1950 – November 19th, 2010

Who saw the good in all until she could see no more.

Remember Me?

Many of you do but for those that don't:

*I **am** the person, who made any visit to my home most memorable,*

And when any believed that re – assurance was not needed,

*I **assured** each, they were correct in his or her belief,*

When the topic of self doubt crept into our conversation,

I doubted any needed to converse on the latter following our talk.

Remember me?

*I **am** the person whose smile served as a beacon of light so that others could find their way*

*I **am** the person, who saw the good in all,*

*Because I had the good fortune to make it possible **to see the good in all**.*

And although I'm sure no one would want to visit me today at my new place of residence,

*I have **assurance** that my new home will be most memorable.*

Remember me:

*Of course you do; my name is **Paula and she forever is my sister**.*

To my mother Carolina, my father "Joe Cash", my sisters' Teresa and Paula my brother in laws whom have been so supportive, Richard and Gregg and my wife Susan, thank you.

Special thanks to Colleen Smith Grubb from NFL Films who throughout was and always will be a friend.

Foreword

By the late Steve Sabol

President of NFL Films and the "Guts and Glory of Pro Football":

"In March of 2011, doctors discovered a tumor in my brain and unfortunately its location made it inoperable. I knew my time here on what I liked to say "The one hundred yard field of life" was soon to end but prior to the inevitable, Ace had asked if I would write the foreword to his autobiography as he felt I was the only person he believed could give insight to his NFL Films' life. I agreed but as the days turned into weeks that turned into months my ability to transfer my thoughts into documentation form became near impossible so what follows I believe has not only ever been done before but has never been attempted before as well: I will do my best to relay to you what it was like having Ace Cacchiotti work for my Dad and I and what it was like having him as a friend. It is difficult to express considering I have passed on to retirement as I said Goodbye to the game I loved on September 18th, 2012".

"I first heard of Ace when the Media Service Department which was headed by Don Thompson, Billy Driber and Scott Scharf, told me of "This nut" who was driving from Rhode Island to NFL Films and living in a motel selling jewelry at night but knew everything not just about Pro Football but NFL Films as well. Well; I had always said that if I believed someone came across my desk whom I felt could help the company, I would hire him and I did. It was one of the best moves I ever made. Not only did Ace know Football but his passion for the sport and more importantly the history of the game rivaled mine for the game but Ace was not your normal employee: He has strange work habits: Ace was like Dracula; I only saw him at night and he never ate but that is what made Ace so unique so when he decided to move into the vault, I thought it wasn't that crazy because I always appreciated the eccentrics and the weirdoes maybe because I was one myself. I used to think that I watched more Football Film than any man alive but I passed that banner on to Ace and I believe he has a photographic memory but you know how you would hear that a certain job is someone's destiny? Well, Ace Cacchiotti was born to be the "Director of Archives" for NFL Films. It's too bad we didn't get him when we started in the sixties but we're glad we have him now"!*

---

* *Sabol expressed those Sentiments in 2002 when he was Interviewed for the* **NFL Beat** *and the Production of* **"Gridiron Gumshoe".**

Introduction

From 1989 to 2008, I was the Director of Archives for NFL Films. My title was given to me by NFL Films' President Steve Sabol. For nearly twenty years I immersed myself in my work and in that time I was able to meet some of the greatest to have played Professional Football. My years with the company also enabled me to work with some of the finest film producers. Each possessed his and her own style with a creative approach leaving everlasting impressions with millions of fans who loved - and continue to love the game. No one thing or for that matter; any number of things could ever compare to the personal feeling of accomplishment whenever I worked on a major historical project as was 1994's **"75 Seasons"**: **"The Story of the National Football League***" or on our* **"Greatest Games***" series for* **ESPN** *when I would physically place back the original film in chronological order of every camera angle of any Super Bowl or other post season game such as the 1967 NFL Championship;* **"The Ice Bowl".** *To be able to "track" down the original film of any signature footage became a trek. Thus, the moniker* **"Gridiron Gumshoe***" given to me by producer Dave Swain fit as in perfect. I was also given wonderful opportunities to travel; working at eight Super Bowls, in major cities across the country. Pro Football's "Greatest Weekend" was just that when I visited Canton, Ohio during the induction weekend. I was responsible for the writing, producing and directing the two and a half minute highlight feature for each new member as he became part of a wonderful fraternity. Life as the* **"Gridiron Gumshoe***" also taught me valuable lessons in life as;* **"To pay attention to detail and finish like a pro".** *It was Sabol's father; Ed the founder of NFL Films who believed in that mantra - as do I continue to.*

Since the 1963 NFL season that culminated with the Chicago Bears' Larry Morris causing injury to New York Giants' Y.A. Tittle's leg in the Chicago Bears' head coach's George Halas's last NFL Championship, to the Giants' Eli Manning's touchdown pass to Plaxico Burress at Super Bowl **XLII,** *I have followed the game of Pro Football but enjoyed it immensely looking through the camera eye of NFL Films. I hope to express those moments in the following reliving as it was as the* **"Gridiron Gumshoe".**

Chapter One: "Retirement" and "I'll be Ace".

Following the New York Giants stunning 17 – 14 victory over the previously unbeaten New England Patriots in Super Bowl XLII , Home Box Office decided not to renew the contract with NFL Films for the production of **"Inside the NFL"** *ending a partnership of 31 years since 1977. The loss was worth a sum of five and a half million dollars to Films, a substantial amount that* ***more*** *than covered operating expenses for the company each year. It was no secret that NFL Films would have to scramble to fill that now financial void and with no immediate prospects in the future, changes would have to be made.*

I decided to stop in on NFL Films' President Steve Sabol to speak with him and hear what his take was on what would be a major financial problem. Steve always the optimist: "Ace the news ruined my breakfast but not my lunch". With that said I decided to help in the only way I thought I could by offering to take a pay cut. Steve assured me it would not come to that. He was right - ***it didn't.***

Thursday, March Sixth, 2008 1:05 P.M.

I had just finished putting together a proposal which would utilize the NFL Films' Vault to its fullest potential by "bringing to life" those original produced shows so they could air on The NFL Network when I received a phone call from Vice President Bill Driber asking me to come to his office. Before I did, I dropped off the information on Steve's desk. When I entered Billy's room I was looking at the "Big Three": Steve, Billy and Barry Wolper: "Okay give me the bad news".

Steve as only he can expressed his deepest regrets on informing me that after twenty seasons I was being released and that I was the last of the 21 being let go. After the numbness subsided, I was actually able to hear what was being said to me and spoke with Steve alone in his room 15 minutes later. The "Boss" as I had and still do refer to him, informed me that this was not the end and I would be brought back for numerous historical productions continuing as the "Director of Archives" for the company. A very generous severance pay, a sincere embrace with the "Boss" and a chance to continue my work for two more weeks eased the transition from employment to what was now unemployment. Those heartfelt moments I experienced as a fan and as an employee of NFL Films are something I will always cherish. However, I knew that things would never be the same and it was time to move on.

Although I now was officially "unemployed", I continued to work at NFL Films for the next two weeks as I finished research projects for many of the producers. Like many former athletes who announce the current year; would be their last - unless you are Brett Favre, those two weeks were something of a farewell tour.

My departure was bittersweet: As mentioned earlier, a generous severance pay helped the transition and saying goodbye to my peers was genuine and sincere. Many were more than just acquaintances.

March 21st, Friday 6:00 P.M.: *as I left the 200,000 square foot state of the art's facility at One NFL Plaza in Mt. Laurel, N.J., I thought back to my childhood and the game of football:*

I was born August 7, 1953 in Providence, Rhode Island: the six pound eleven ounce boy to Caroline and Joseph "Joe Cash" Cacchiotti. My older sister Paula was ecstatic when mom brought her new brother home: "Paula, look at your new baby brother Joey", my mom glowed. "He's nice". "Can I go out and play"? Life on 85 Hudson Street was simple and for me without wanting. My biggest concern was the monumental decision whether or not to spend my last 10 cents on a **Drake's Ring Ding** *or* **Devil Dog**. *With milk the dog was better but in later years the* **Ring Ding** *was a good side dish for Smirnoff Vodka. Friends were many and sports minded. Whether we shoveled and removed the snow from some court to play basketball during the winter, wrapped adhesive tape the size of a quarter in diameters for stick ball in the spring and summer or turning our street into a "roped off" crime scene to play touch football in the fall, we all found a way to compete. The competition at times was downright nasty. Trades of one player for another were executed many times without the prime subject(s) being notified. Although I resided on Hudson Street, the majority of "athletes" came from one street south: Wood Street possessed some of the more established players. The Rinaldi brothers were as talented as any family. Each was unique and yet different as was his liking for certain baseball players. David the youngest was a southpaw who had good hands and was a big Sandy Koufax fan. Kevin could run like the wind and loved Rocky Colavito. Dan the middle child of Fred and Gloria was the most competitive and Willie Mays could do no wrong. Mays was my favorite player also and maybe the reason why Danny and I would become the best of*

*friends. Dennis did everything well and would always argue with brothers'
Kevin, Danny and oldest Ken on whether Colavito, Mays, and Hank Aaron
could equal the play of Mickey Mantle. Ken as mentioned revered Aaron and
had a great arm. Rounding up the other "athletes" was Biagio Michelletti
his younger brother Joey, Kenny Campagnone, Bob Dinafrio whose father
ironically would pass away on the same date as my father on December 27th,
2001, and Jeff Alexander also a left hander, who could only "go" to that
side. Later, we would refer to him as the southpaw John Havilcek; the Boston
Celtics' Hall of Fame player. On the west side of Wood Street was Mike
Ruggierio, Joe Capuano, Vinnie Escoli, brothers' Steve and Sal Loporchio,
and Mark Del Deo. Mark although a good all around player had a D.N.A.
makeup more of that of the opposite sex. He would later in life have a sex
change. I have not seen Sarah since. As for me; I was the best football player on
the west side. I could run faster than the speed of a sun dial (no, actually I was
fast) and would catch anything and everything that was thrown in my direction.
However, we were no match for the east side. They would regularly beat up on
us. Finally, a "trade" was made for me and I became a teammate of the east
squad. In return the west received a "player to be named later". Both groups
have yet to name that player. Prior to that trade, it was on Saturdays that the
east side with regularity had their way with us. The Loporchios lived next
door to the Cacchiottis on 89 Hudson Street. Joe Capuano lived nearby on
Messer Street. The four of us would meet in the driveway of Sal and Steve's
house planning some type of strategic maneuvers to combat the east side. We
also read a comic book titled;* **"Challengers of the Unknown".** *The
main characters numbered four and survived a plane crash that was piloted by
World War II flying ace Kyle Morgan, who was nicknamed appropriately;
"Ace". The other three heroes were wrestling champion; Leslie "Rocky" Davis,
deep sea skin diving researcher; Mathew "Red" Ryan and mountain climber
and scientist; Walter Mark "Prof" Haley. By walking away from the crash,
the four now believed to be "living on borrowed time". Now it is a well known
conclusion that whenever anyone walks away from a plane crash he or she
must fight evil for the good of mankind. The four did just that until the original
series ended in 1971. In October of 1962 my three friends and I were reading
episode 14;* **"Captives of the Alien Beasts"** *when we decided to adopt
the nicknames of the four. Since I was nine years old and the eldest of the four,
I said "I'll be Ace" the leader of the group. Sal Loporchio wanted to be known
as "Rocky" and Joe Capuano as "Red". That left Sal's younger brother Steve
to now own the nickname of Professor Haley or "Prof" for short. However, we
all thought the pronunciation sounded like proof. Joe Capuano would become a*

*success in real estate, Sal Loporchio is one of the top ophthalmologists in Rhode Island and Steve "Proof" Loporchio did some work in Hollywood and now resides in his home state; the lead singer in the music group; "Steve Anthony and the Persuasions". I continue to refer to Steve as "Proof" after all these years and make it a point to see him whenever I return home and wherever he is performing requesting a certain song; "Hey Proof, "Play that "***Funky Music****" by the group "****Wild Cherry****" and his response; "Is that you Ace"? Yeah, for 48 years, it still is.*

Chapter Two: "What's the line"?

Although physically very active in the game of football, I never really knew much about the National Football League or for that matter what was to be the fourth season of the American Football League. Saturday night; August 2nd was a big day for me: I would be ten years old in five days and to celebrate had a "sleep over" at Rocky and "Proof's" house who now resided at 28 Wood Street. It was also the very first time I would see a "Professional" Football game: The College All – Star game was played between the defending NFL Champions and a group of all star collegians who finished their careers the previous year. It was the 30th anniversary of the game that began in 1934 when sports editor of the Chicago Tribune; Arch Ward arranged a game between the NFL Champions' Chicago Bears who had defeated the New York Giants 23 – 21 six months earlier in the NFL Title Game to play against the College All Stars. Although no one knew at the time but this anniversary game in 1963 would be the last time the College All Stars would defeat the NFL Champions: Vince Lombardi's Green Bay Packers who had lost only once during the 1962 season were upset by head coach Otto Graham's All Stars 17 – 16. The last game; between the Pittsburgh Steelers and the College All Stars ended on July 23rd, 1976. Torrential rains and a serious threat of lightning called an end at 1:22 remaining in the third quarter -- and an end to the traditional series.

Now introduced to "Professional" Football, I could not wait to see my favorite teams on television again. However, at the time my favorites were the Green Bay Packers and the College All Stars! The Columbia Broadcasting System televised the NFL and the American Broadcasting Company the AFL. WPRO in Providence, Rhode Island was the television home to New York Giants' Football and Sundays became my favorite day of the week except for Fridays when school would let out in early afternoon. Actually, Saturday was my favorite day but the first day of the week came in a close second (or third).

Teams in the NFL would play five exhibition games before the regular season schedule and in 1970, the first year of the merger between the two leagues, the number increased to six. However, the word exhibition did not sit well with the owners and those "exhibitions" in later years changed to pre season games. However, in 1963 teams would play their starters for almost four quarters and fans would really get their "monies worth". Today; four games are the norm and there is talk that the league may drop that number to two if the NFL adopts an 18 game regular season. On September 2nd, Monday night, just twenty six days north or is south of my tenth birthday, the Giants traveled to Green Bay for their fourth exhibition game against the Packers. Once again, I had a sleep over at Norma and Sal's; the parents of my comic book character friends. It was a great night: pizza, cold cut sandwiches, Coca Cola, and Pro Football. The Giants who had won the last two Eastern Divisions only to lose to the Packers in the Championship Games possessed some all – stars of their own. Quarterback Yelberton Abraham Tittle or Y.A. as he was called had set an NFL record for most touchdowns in a regular season with thirty three in 1962. Incredibly, seven came in one game against the Washington Redskins and another six in the last game against the Dallas Cowboys. Tittle's favorite target was Del Shofner, a six foot three 185 pound speedster from Baylor University. The Giants possessed a good backfield with Phil King and Alex Webster. 36 years later, I with Kyle Rote, Roosevelt Brown, Ordell Braase, Jim Mutscheller, Art Donovan, Gino Marchetti, John Unitas, and Webster were part of the entertainment aboard the Norway, the largest ship in the Norwegian Cruise line. I asked Alex why he was called "Big Red". "Because my hair was red, Ace"! It took me over three and a half decades to "figure" that out!

That Giants' team of 1963 would have six players inducted to Canton, Ohio in later years: Tittle, flanker Frank Gifford, offensive lineman Brown, defensive end Andy Robustelli, middle linebacker Sam Huff and former 49ers' Hugh the "King" McElhenny, who was a teammate of Tittle for nine seasons at San Francisco.

The Green Bay Packers, who would win five NFL Championships in seven seasons and the first two Super Bowls, did not lack in talent: Quarterback Bart Starr, running backs; Paul Hornung and Jim Taylor, cornerback Herb Adderley, safety Willie Wood, defensive linemen; Willie Davis, Henry Jordan, offensive center Jim Ringo, offensive lineman Forrest Gregg and head coach Vince Lombardi would also be inducted into the Pro Football Hall of Fame. It was Jordan who was quoted; "Lombardi treats us all the same": "Like dogs"!

The Packers defeated the Giants 24 – 17 on that early autumn summer's night, just as I finished my fifth piece of pizza. Now that may not seem like too many pieces for a growing boy but you have to take in consideration that the two cold cut "sangweeches" and the full liter of Coke might have filled me up. The next day, I walked home which was a full block and a half to 85 Hudson Street from the Loporchios when my father asked if I had a good time. I did but was a "little down" because the Giants had lost the night before. With that said my father replied; "Son it doesn't matter because the Giants covered the line". "What does it mean; "what's the line"? By the time my mom set down the macaroni, meat balls, Italian sweet sausage, pork, and braciolla, (pronounced bra-zhall) we were ready to have Sunday dinner when I asked my dad again; "What's the line"?

My dad was always "showing me off" to his friends; urging me to name all the capitals of the fifty states or in chronological order of all 35 presidents at the time. I would debate the number by explaining that although there have been 35 individual presidencies the number of men that have served as our "Commander in Chief" is one less. Grover Cleveland served two individual terms at numbers 22 and 24 with Benjamin Harrison interrupting the "streak".

The last hurrah for the New York Giants came in that season of 1963. It would not be until 1981 that the team would reach post season play again. In that season of 1963, New York had to "fight off" the Cleveland Browns with arguably the greatest runner ever; Jim Brown, the St. Louis Cardinals with the aerial attack of quarterback Charlie Johnson and receivers' Ulmo Shannon Jr. "Sonny" Randle and Bobby Joe Conrad, who led the NFL in receptions that year with 73 and the Pittsburgh Steelers who possessed the hard running of John Henry Johnson and the very aggressive defense led by Ernie Stautner. Late in that 1963 season one of the few sports' magazines did a feature on the soon to be retired 38 year old veteran. A huge close up of number 70 became my very first portrait I ever drew having acquired the same artistic gene qualities of my dad. It would not be the last: Twenty nine years later; I drew a portrait of Ed Sabol and gave it to his son Steve to give to his dad. One year followed, when I discovered the picture tucked and hidden away: Steve informed me his dad didn't like the way I drew his teeth. That framed portrait now hangs downstairs in my sports bar next to the Steelers' legendary defensive lineman. Going into week fourteen the Giants had won 10 games and lost only three, while both the Browns and Cardinals were at 9 and 4. However, the Steelers had the best chance of winning the Eastern Division: Earlier they had shutout the Giants 31 – 0 when Tittle did not play because of an injury he suffered against the Baltimore Colts in week one. Pittsburgh at 7 wins 3 losses and three ties could win the division with a win over New York because of having a better record by percentage. In front of 63, 240 at Yankee Stadium, the Giants jumped out to a 16 – 0 lead on Tittle's 34th and 35th touchdown passes to Shofner and Joe Morrison respectively. However, the Steelers' defense stiffened and Pittsburgh trailed by just six late in the third quarter, when the Giants faced a "3rd and long" deep in their own territory. Tittle dropped back to pass and threw over the middle to Gifford. The USC graduate extended his right hand a made the grab. The **"Velcro"** catch enabled the Giants to keep the drive alive and when Tittle connected with Morrison for his 36th touchdown pass of the season, New York had wrapped up the Eastern Division. The 33 – 17 victory enabled the team to win their third straight Division Title and once again would play for the NFL Championship: This time at the Chicago Bears' home field; Wrigley Field.

The Bears had won the Western Division for the first time since 1956; the year they lost to the New York Giants 47 – 7 in the Championship Game. The Bears had "de thrown" the two time defending NFL Champions' Green Bay Packers by defeating them twice during the regular season by scores of 10 – 3 at Green Bay on the opening weekend and then again in week ten; 26 – 7 at Wrigley. Those two losses by Green Bay were the difference as the "Pack" finished one/half game behind the 11 win one loss and two ties record of head coach George Halas' team.

I was a little afraid of the "Monsters of the Midway": They did instill fear in me and as I would learn later in the opposition, working for NFL Films. The offense of the Bears that season took a back seat to their defense and with good reason: While the Giants led the league in points scored with 448, the Bears allowed the least amount with just over ten per game at 144. Chicago's secondary of Dave Whitsell, Bennie McRae, Roosevelt Taylor, Richie Pettitbon and J.C. Caroline intercepted 36 passes, a league high. Linebackers' Joe Fortunato, Larry Morris and Future Hall of Fame Inductee Bill George were as good as any linebacker core in the NFL. On the defensive line; tackles' Earl Legget, Fred Williams, Stan Jones, defensive ends Ed O'Bradovich and Doug Atkins allowed the least amount of rushing yards at 1,442. Middle linebacker George was inducted to the Professional Football Hall of Fame in 1974 and 8 years later teammate Atkins. At six foot eight and 265 pounds, Atkins was the largest man to be inducted to Canton, until 1990 when San Francisco 49ers' offensive lineman Bob St. Clair at six foot nine inches claimed that distinction. One year later in 1991, Jones would become a member of that exclusive fraternity. On December 29th, of that 1963 season, with temperatures hovering around zero all day, New York scored first when Tittle connected with Gifford in the right corner of the end zone to give the Giants a 7 – 0 lead. The Giants had a chance to increase their lead late in the first quarter but a wide open Shofner could not hold on to a Tittle pass in the back of the end zone. It was an opportunity missed as Giants' placekicker Don Chandler could not convert on a 32 yard field goal attempt. Late in the 1st *quarter, the first of five interceptions Y.A. would throw that day was snatched by linebacker Morris who returned it 61 yards. Later Morris quoted; "For the first 30 yards I was hoping no one would catch me, for the last thirty I was afraid no one would"! Bears' quarterback Bill Wade sneaked in from the two and the game was tied. Late in the second quarter, disaster struck the Giants and for everyone else at 28 Wood Street: While attempting a pass to Gifford down the right sidelines, Bears' linebacker Morris while on the ground tried to "get" to Tittle. As the Giants' QB released his throw, number 33 rolled up and onto his lower left leg. The 16 year veteran who had began his career in 1948 with the Baltimore Colts of the defunct All America Conference, 14 year veteran of both the 49ers and Giants and one of the very best to play the position; tried to walk off the field. High above from a top camera position and with Tittle's back to us, Blair Motion Pictures' that soon would become NFL Films' camera man Walter Dombrow captured what was one of the most memorable Pro Football moments on film: While Tittle limped back to the Giants' bench, teammate Hugh McElhenny, helped his buddy off the field.*

"Back up" Giants' quarterback Glynn Griffing who would only play one season in the NFL, replaced Tittle and even though the Giants would lead at halftime 10 – 7, we all believed that without the Giants' "Field Leader" there was little hope to defeat the Bears. The mood at Rocky and "Proof's" house was a somber one but we all did our best to assure one another that all was not lost. Suddenly he appeared: At the start of the third quarter; wrapped and heavily bandaged returned our savior! In later years, in the final game of the 1970 NBA Championship, the New York Knicks' Willis Reed came limping on to the court hitting his 1ˢᵗ two shots as his team defeated the Los Angeles Lakers. At Pasadena in Super Bowl XIV, the Rams' Jack Youngblood suited up against the Pittsburgh Steelers, despite a broken bone in his leg and in 2008 at Torrey Pines, San Diego; Tiger Woods somehow kept it together winning the United States Open; playing 91 holes winning in a playoff against Rocco Mediate despite playing with a left knee that would require surgery immediately after. But that was later; and in the second half hobbled by the injury to his left knee, the knee needed to plant and throw, Tittle was intercepted three more times, including one by defensive end O'Bradovich that led to Wade's second quarterback sneak for a touchdown. For the third straight year, the Giants and their inspirational leader were defeated in the NFL Championship Game. The sound of the car horn informed me my Dad was here to pick me up. The skies were cloudy and the rain steady which seemed to be the imperfect ending to an imperfect day. My Dad realized how heartbroken I was and said little. Through my tears I made it clear; "Dad, I don't care what the line was".

Chapter Three: November 22nd
"Big Ed" and Blair Motion Pictures

In an earlier reference, the year of 1963 was the last season of the eight since 1956 the Giants would dominate the NFL's Eastern Division. In that time, they played in six NFL Championship Games albeit winning just once in 1956. New York fans would have to wait 18 years for another playoff team.

1963 was also the year America would tragically and unexpectedly say goodbye to our 35th President: On Friday November 22nd, at 12:30 P.M. Central Standard Time, John Fitzgerald Kennedy was struck down by an assassin's bullet in his motorcade car in Dallas, Texas. Ironically, no radio or television station broadcasted the infamous moment in United States history because many of the local affiliates were waiting for the President and the first lady; Jackie to arrive at the Dallas Trade Mart. I remember our teacher Miss Kennedy (yes that was her name) receiving a phone call a little after 2:00 p.m. (E.S.T) and asking; "Is he dead"? Thirty eight minutes later, as all were tuned to the television, CBS's Walter Cronkite, while removing his eye glasses relayed what we feared most; "The President has died". Our school decided to let out early; and as a nation mourned, I was "kinda" happy that we had a head start on the weekend ahead.

Pete Rozelle in his fourth year as Commissioner of the National Football League faced a monumental decision: Should he call off the upcoming games on Sunday while America grieved or allow the seven games to be played: In a decision that he called "the worst decision I ever made," the NFL would resume its regular season schedule. The "other league" however, did suspend all games until Thanksgiving Day when the Oakland Raiders defeated the Denver Broncos 26 – 10. Meanwhile, the Giants traveled to St. Louis to face the Cardinals: CBS made the decision: not to broadcast any game that Sunday and covered the events in Dallas, Texas. With my Sunday routine interrupted; "Mom, I am going out for awhile". What followed was one of the two most indelible events caught live; on television. While the alleged assassin of the President; Lee Harvey Oswald was being transferred to a maximum security jail, local Dallas resident and night club owner Jack Ruby emerged from the right of the television screen, shot and killed Oswald. My mom shouted "Oh my God, did you see that"? I didn't. I was outside throwing the football around. 38 years later on September 11, 2001, my wife Susan cried out; "Ace they are attacking the World Trade Center" seconds after a second plane hit the south tower. I missed that too: I was in the bathroom. The Giants lost 24 – 17

Gridiron Gumshoe

following the Oswald assassination and the loss knocked the Giants out of first place in the division and in the process - ruined my day.

A little less than eleven months later; on October 25th, 1964 in a game played at San Francisco; the 49ers' Bill Kilmer caught a pass from quarterback George Mira and fumbled after being hit by the Minnesota Vikings' Karl Kassulke. Vikings' defensive lineman Jim Marshall scooped up the ball and darted towards the goal line - in the wrong direction! After crossing his own goal line he heaved the ball into the stands. Marshall had committed the all time blunder! Five years later, his dubious achievement would be categorized as a folly by National Football League Films.

In 1962, Ed Sabol, who loved movies and the game of Professional Football approached NFL Commissioner Rozelle and offered him and the NFL $3,000.00 for the film rights to the NFL Championship Game. Rozelle agreed and on December 30th of that year, Blair Motion pictures (Blair was Sabol's daughter's name) set out to film the game played between the defending NFL Champions' Green Bay Packers and the New York Giants at the Giants' home field; Yankee Stadium. The weather conditions were brutal: Added to the freezing cold was a bitter wind that made passing near impossible and affected the Giants' quarterback Y.A. Tittle much more than his counterpart Bart Starr. As difficult as it was for the two teams to play it was tenfold more difficult for Sabol and his camera crew to film. On what he called "Pro Football's Longest Day", Sabol's team somehow was able to salvage enough film to create a highlight of the Championship Game. Later, it was shown to Rozelle and others receiving accolades. My first year with the company, I would meet "Big Ed" and discover why he was called that: It seems he was a tremendous swimmer and at times would display his aquatic talent on different occasions donning nothing but Ed Sabol. Although able to produce two highlight films for the 1962 and 1963 Championship Games, Sabol wanted more and decided to "pitch" an idea to the commissioner and the fourteen NFL owners in Miami in 1964 at the NFL's yearly meetings. What transpired has been documented many times: After being denied with his first request the league later agreed: For the amount of $12,000.00 per team, Blair Motion Pictures would be granted a license from the NFL, to film every regular season game, the NFL Championship and produce a highlight film for all 14 teams. An interesting note to the 1964 season: Prior to Blair Motion Pictures, the company that had filmed the NFL on a regular season basis was Tel – Ra, which "shot" with negative black and white film stock. Tel – Ra since 1949 had also produced a highlight package each week narrated by

Harry Wismer and later Jim Leaming. The company also covered the 1964 season. However, the choice to film in color by Blair Motion Pictures was one of the deciding factors why the NFL decided to keep Sabol's company. Ed's son Steve also loved Professional Football, the movies and attended Colorado College. A self made promoter; "the tiny tot from Pottsville trot" was "hired" by his dad to work with him with the new company, since according to his father; "after looking at your grades at college, it seems you have done nothing but play football and have gone to the movies; and this makes you perfect for the job". In 1965, Blair Motion Pictures became NFL Films and continued to produce team highlights and now feeling comfortable with its new employer created interesting features following the 1965 and 1966 football seasons:
The Rookies, The Receivers, The Runners and 10,000 to One, *were some of the early pieces produced by the newly named company; NFL Films. However, following the "Runner up Bowl", which was played by the Eastern and Western Division second place finishers in Miami, one week **after** the NFL Championship Game, Films began the production of;* **"They called it Pro Football".** *The show focused on every aspect of the game and for the first time viewers could listen to a head coach during a game. On January 8ᵗʰ, 1967 Films had Philadelphia Eagles' head coach Joe Kuharich wear a microphone so all could see and hear exactly what went on during a Pro Football Game from a coach's perspective. The Colts won a game of not much significance but what was significant was NFL Films' use of the wiring.*
Months later after viewing **"They Called it Pro Football.",** *Rozelle said; "It was the greatest football movie he had ever seen". Making his debut was John Facenda, who would narrate for NFL Films for 18 years until his death at the age of 71 in September, 1984 leaving more of an impact with me than my divorce to my first wife Debbie which happened earlier that year. I do apologize to Debbie but I have always kept my priorities in order.*

Chapter Four: "Non Contact Sports" and "Mom, are they going to kill Dad"?

*Although I loved to play and watch football, I was also very active in other sports: At the age of twelve, I made the Little League's all – star team and received a great honor: I was switched from seventh in the batting order to fourth; the "clean up" spot right before my team Federal Hill Dairy, was buried 12 – 2 in the last Little League Game I ever played. Another "sport" we participated in: was our version of stick ball: We use the handle of a broom for a bat and would try to hit rolled up tape the diameters of a quarter. Our "field" was located on any street, usually with the pitcher having his back against some house that had many windows. In one of the greatest pitching performances ever; one that rivaled Koufax's perfect game against the Chicago Cubs on September 9th, 1965, Dennis Rinaldi struck out all 27 batters he faced in a game and won - one to nothing. It was during stickball I became very familiar with the word "run"! which was always shouted any and every time someone drilled one through a house window. Every week it seemed that one of us was headed to the hospital for some emergency. As a matter of fact, I was such a regular at Rhode Island Hospital that the Cacchiottis had a wing named in their honor for "donations" to the hospital. One time "Proof" "button hooked", caught the ball, turned and BAM! Right into the back fin of a Cadillac! The good news: The car was parked. The bad news: Bam, right into the back fin of a Cadillac! We all carried the crimson covered 8 years old to the fire station that was only three blocks away. After we assured them there was no fire, they "cleaned" him up and put a band aid over his right eye. Another "non contact" sport we played was handball. We would relocate to a basketball/tennis court. There were no tennis nets, just the iron poles coming out of the cement where one time nets had been attached. The object was for the batter with the ball in his opposite hand, to toss it about three feet over his head and make contact, where and when he would run the bases. Three players defended. Once, while Dave Rinaldi was playing third base; he chased a popup, turned and **smacked** right into one of those unforgiving iron poles! The good news: The pole wasn't moving. The bad news: The pole wasn't moving. David's face looked like the colors of the NBC peacock. The next day after dropping a foul ball that gave another "life" to Mike Ruggerio, while chasing a popup, I turned and well by now you know what happened. It was as if I decided to take up the profession of dentistry.*

In the autumn seasons of 1965 and 1966, just around eleven o'clock each Sunday morning, my dad would take me to Depasquale Avenue in Federal Hill to the "club". Angelo "Pic" Piccone ran the "establishment". It was a scene something right from a **"Goodfellas"** movie and everyone there wanted to know "What's the line?". "Pic" always seemed to be on the phone: "Yeah, the Giants are getting 14". Actually, it seemed that the Giants were always getting fourteen. They gave up 501 points that 1966 season in a fourteen game schedule, including an incredible 72 against the Redskins. (Read on). "The line is three and are you going to parlay that with the four o'clock game"? I always saw the handling of tens and twenties throughout the morning. Somehow though, all the "patrons" left by one o'clock. Finally I asked; "Dad, was "Pic" talking about what the line was"? It was answered with a history lesson that included mention at that time of New England Crime Boss, Raymond L.S Patriarca. My dad during the spring of 1967 took me to meet **"Mister Patriarca"**. In Chapter Two I touched upon that my dad was a very talented artist and portraits were his specialty. So much so that he drew one for the New England Crime Czar. I did not want to go with my Dad and watch my father hand it to L.S. because "what if he doesn't like it"? I thought the L.S was his nickname because he smoked Lucky Strike unfiltered cigarettes. Actually the L.S. stood for Loreda Salvatore. Once the history lesson was over and no immediate quiz in sight, I replied; "Oh, that's why Willie Marfeo was killed": On July 13, 1966 at the Corner Kitchen restaurant on Atwells Avenue, in Providence, William "Willie" Marfeo was gunned down. It seemed that Patriarca was not happy with Marfeo running an "unauthorized" dice game and when he sent the "number two" man Henry Tameleo to tell him to stop, according to reports; Tameleo was slapped in the face by the now soon to be late "Willie" Marfeo. I remember that night when the local news reported the "hit", I turned to my Mom and asked in tears; "Mom are they going to kill Dad"! My mom wanted to know why I thought such a thing. "Because he is always up the "Hill", wondering what the line was"? After all it had become a known fact that many believed; all Italians were related to the mob and could cook. My mom assured me, that in both cases concerning my dad neither was true.

I began to become somewhat of an authority on "hitting" on NFL Games, although I did enjoy watching that "other league". Following the Giants' broadcast, NBC who had offered 10 million in 1964 to televise the American Football League, usually would broadcast a game played on the west coast. The very 1st AFL game I watched was when ABC had the contract: The

Gridiron Gumshoe

Oakland Raiders 52 – 49 win over the Houston Oilers in the last game of the regular season in 1963. In that game Raiders' quarterback Tom Flores threw for six touchdowns, which was a club high that was tied by Daryle Lamonica when he threw for the same number against the Buffalo Bills on October 19th, 1969. Incredibly, Lamonica's were all thrown in the first half and another interesting sidebar: With seconds remaining in the first half Lamonica was deprived of his seventh touchdown pass when wide receiver Dre Buie caught what could have been historic number seven but ran out of bounds at the two yard line trying to stop the clock. Unfortunately Lamonica came up just short.

I guess when I really started to become "full of myself" was following the week of October 10th, 1966. As was our routine following church services, my dad took me to the club. Once again the patrons wanted to know, what teams "Joe Cash's kid" liked. Although the Giants were in the midst of the worst season in their history, I felt they could play the Cardinals tough. The Cards were a seven point favorite. Another game I "liked" was the Dallas Cowboys to cover against the Eagles. Dallas was giving fourteen. New York lost to St. Louis 24 – 19 and the Cowboys buried Philadelphia 56 – 7. Come Monday; those who parlayed both games won some money. I was given ten bucks for my "cut". I can honestly say I won more than my share for my Dad and his friends but it came to an end in week eleven. The Giants who had defeated the Redskins earlier in the season 13 – 10 for what was to be their only win that year traveled to our Nation's capital to play Washington for the second time. Now we all know, except for in Las Vegas, gambling on Professional Football, is illegal and no one does it, but beside the "line", there is something called the "under and over" or the "over and under". By taking the two combined scores and "laying" down a bet one can win if he or she wins by picking "over or under". Simple! That particular November 27th, the number was right around forty eight points and although the Giants would give up the most points in league history for one season, I felt that based on the first game between the two teams, I advised; "take the under". When Giants' quarterback Gary Wood connected with Joe Morrison for a 41 yard score early into the third quarter, it "shaved" the Redskins' lead to 34 – 21. Another 58 points later, I decided to stay home on Sundays.

Chapter Five: Frank Bosco,
Bobby Argenti and "Where is Vietnam"?

*Following that NFL season of 1966 after the Packers had defeated the Dallas Cowboys 34 – 27 for their second consecutive NFL Championship, we moved to 291 Mt. Pleasant Avenue. Although still living in Providence, it was an important move for the family. Since 1948, the Cacchiottis lived on the second floor of a five room flat above my Mom's parents. I loved it; especially following "suppa" when I would go down stairs to visit "gramps". Saverio would read to me a certain comic strip titled ***"Henry"*** in the Providence Evening Journal. Although I could read, I had trouble understanding this particular strip because there weren't any words but my grandfather told his own story. Also, it was the time for my sisters' Paula and Teresa and I to have our 1st taste of homemade wine. My grandfather had his own wine press down in the basement. We called it the "cella" when basements were scary. I never went down alone unless I had to but then I remembered that's where the home made wine was. Every night was special on the first floor at 85 Hudson Street but my favorite visit was at Xmas Eve: The time Italians celebrated the birth of Christ with the "seven fishes" dinner. Grandmother Rose would make spaghetti with clam sauce, smelts and "baccala" which is the Italian word for codfish. I know that's only three dishes but what the heck; at least we had homemade wine. My dad never ate with us because growing up in a family with nine siblings, fish was a staple at his parents' house so seven fishes were the last food he wanted or for that matter the three fishes we had. From there the night continued next door to the second floor at 89 Hudson Street to visit my Dad's parents. They too had the "seven fishes", which was made up of spaghetti with clam sauce, smelts and "baccala".*

After the move to Mt. Pleasant Avenue, I attended George J. West Junior High school and decided that my nickname Ace would be no more and I would go throughout life as Joe Cash Jr. Following my first day at the new school, I heard "Hey Ace"; bellowed by a new friend; Joe Gemma. His cousin Janet Spaziano, whom I attended school with back home at Asa Messer Elementary School had given me a second chance with my old, "new" nickname.

Immediately I became well liked because I was "cute". I think the girls thought that because I was still four inches shy of five feet and eight pounds south of 90. I remember when we took our eighth grade class picture in front of the school; the smaller children would be sitting in the front row. I was so small, I had my own row. In spite of my intimidating and imposing "being" I participated in two organized sports at the school: baseball and basketball. My sister Paula and I "hung out" at the park across the street from the school. Our group was inseparable and we did anything and everything together. Whether it was twelve of us going to see Jane Fonda who appeared in the 41ˢᵗ century as **"Barbarella"** *at the movies, swimming at "Twin Rivers" or renting a bus for a field trip, we did it together. One of the other "activities" we focused our attention on was gang fighting. Although at my height and weight, my peers thought it was better if I just stayed back and hang out with the girls. My first thought was to "carry my own weight" but once I saw the damage that was inflicted upon my guys, I became the best babysitter I possibly could be. My sister was dating Frank Bosco. The Bosco clan was tough "sunsabitches"! Frank, the middle child of three boys was our leader and no one wanted to "f---k" with him! Frank really liked me because "I was cute" and the brother of the girl he was seeing. I never really hung out with anyone in particular but would rather hide in the shadows except when I wanted to be noticed which was all the time. (What?) Another one of our gang leaders was Bobby Argenti; who at 18 years old was a six foot three blond blue eyed eccentric fellow - to put it nicely. Back in the sixties he was referred to as a "nut job". Bobby was always trying to "one up" us. One particular time when we would throw rocks at cars, he would wait for a car to stop at a light, run right up to it and then throw some two handed boulder in its direction. 15 minutes later we all would be confronted by the "To Protect and Serve" units who were looking for a six foot three, blue eyed blond haired kid who was extremely strong. Bobby could never understand why he was always singled out. When I wasn't "participating" in improvisation of sports' activities, I focused my attention on my second greatest passion; the opposite sex. Being cute could take you just so far with the young ladies so I had to devise other ways to get noticed. I usually would plead for a date and after awhile, I would get one. I really didn't look for sympathy but I was good at it. I had a good foundation; my height and weight. I loved Elaine Balasco because she "kinda" liked me "sought of" or as Rhode Islanders would say "sorta". She had light brown hair, green eyes and Angelina Jolie type lips. Back then they were just called big. I would dream of what it would be like to kiss her. Today, I still dream of what it would be like to kiss her.*

In the fall of 1967, I continued to watch Pro Football but I loved watching NFL Films' productions of "This Week in the East" and "This Week in the West". 1967 was also the only year that NFL Films would eliminate "special" rolls of the game by date and game number. All the highlights would be incorporated in highlight reels for each team at the end of the season. Years later when we produced America's Game, which was a look back at the 1ˢᵗ forty years of the Super Bowl Champions, the 1967 Packers' season highlights was hard to find until I informed producer Steve Seidman of the unique storage of film that season. In 1968 we reverted to our old style of "special" rolls.

My father's interest in Pro Football was as mentioned earlier strictly from a betting perspective. Whenever "Joe Cash" bet on a game and "things weren't going his way", he would change the channel thinking when he returned to watch, his team would "cover the line". I could never watch a full game with him. Luckily, we had two televisions and when he would ask "What's the score?" I couldn't tell him because I too had changed the channel. The NFL season of 1967 had divided the league into four divisions: The Capitol Division, which consisted of the Dallas Cowboys, Philadelphia Eagles, Washington Redskins and New Orleans' Saints. The Century Division comprised of the Cleveland Browns, New York Giants, St. Louis Cardinals and Pittsburgh Steelers. The Costal division had the Los Angeles Rams, Baltimore Colts, San Francisco 49ers and the Atlanta Falcons while the Central Division was made up of the Green Bay Packers, Chicago Bears, Minnesota Vikings and Detroit Lions. In the playoffs, the Dallas Cowboys defeated the Cleveland Browns 52 – 14 and would face Vince Lombardi's Packers; 28 – 7 winners over the Los Angeles Rams. The Championship Game would be played on New Year's Eve. It would be the first and last time two NFL Championship Games would be played in the same calendar year; the 1966 game was played on January 1ˢᵗ, 1967.

In bitter cold with a temperature of 15 below at kickoff, the Packers scored the first fourteen points on two touchdown passes from quarterback Bart Starr to split end Boyd Dowler. However, the Cowboys battled back and took the lead on the very 1ˢᵗ play of the fourth quarter when halfback Dan Reeves rolled to his left and threw a 50 yard touchdown pass to Lance Rentzel to give Dallas a 17 – 14 lead. Although I was still a New York Giants' fan I wanted the Packers to win: Green Bay had won the previous two NFL Championship Games and with a win could and would become the first team in NFL history to win the title three straight years. Another reason: I wanted Dallas to lose because they shot John Kennedy! With four minutes and fifty seconds remaining, the Packers got the ball back with 68 yards ahead of them. Bart Starr and company and in particular Chuck Mercein, who had come to Green Bay from the Giants that season, maneuvered the ball to the Cowboys' one yard line. With 13 seconds remaining the Packers won their third straight

*NFL Championship when their QB sneaked in. Later, NFL Films produced the "**Chilling Championship**" which was narrated not by the soon to be legendary John Facenda, but by William Woodson. The opening piece of music was called "**Veiled Threat**" an ominous piece that would be used later in the **Spider Man** cartoon episode titled; "**Revolt in the Fifth Dimension**" in1968 and 40 years later in the movie "**Ocean's 13**". The "**Chilling Championship**" would be referred to as the "**Ice Bowl**" in later years with Facenda doing that narration. An interesting sidebar to this story: My parents had celebrated New Year's Eve early by going out to dinner with my Uncle John and Auntie Carmela. My two sisters had gone to a New Year's Eve party that began sometime in mid afternoon, which left me alone in the house to watch one of the most memorable games in Championship history. The final drive by the Packers was an extension of the team's head coach; Vince Lombardi, who had driven his team to a place, none had ever been before and who would die two and a half years later in 1970 at the age of 57. For me; I would always remember that last drive by watching NFL Films' Bob Ryan's production of the "**Chilling Championship**" because I never saw the last drive live while it was happening: I changed the channel hoping the Packers would win if I didn't watch.*

1968 was a tumultuous year in United States History: Two leaders with the same message of hope and understanding for our fellow man were tragically gunned down: Civil Rights' movement leader Martin Luther King on April fourth in Memphis and democratic presidential hopeful candidate and the brother of the late President John F. Kennedy; Bobby in Los Angeles on June 4th. The assassin of Bobby Kennedy was Sirhan Sirhan an Arab nationalist, who was upset with Kennedy because he felt betrayed by the support that the younger Kennedy had for Israel during the six day war in 1967. The assassin was subdued and disarmed by many, including Los Angeles Rams' defensive lineman Roosevelt Grier and 1960's Olympic Decathlon Champion Rafer Johnson. Johnson's brother Jimmy was inducted into the Pro Football Hall of Fame in 1994 and I produced the highlight feature that was shown that weekend at the Civic Auditorium's dinner. The following day, Rafer approached me and thanked me for the two and a half minute production and one week later, I received a letter from the gold medal winner thanking me again. It is one of my most cherished possessions.

Our country was still involved in the Vietnam War and in August our gang got the news that both Frank Bosco and Bobby Argenti had been drafted. "Where's Vietnam"? I asked. "I'm not really sure", I remember Bobby replying. "But we'll be back"! Why shouldn't they be? Frank was one tough "sunsabitch" and Bobby was six foot three and an eccentric fellow. We had a going away party for the two before they embarked on the one way trek: Frank Bosco died when the helicopter he was aboard was shot down and Bobby Argenti two months later in an ambush. My sister Paula cried as we all felt the loss. My two years at 291 Mt. Pleasant Ave and in particular the summer of 1968 left an indelible mark on me as did Frank Bosco and Bobby Argenti on "our gang".

Chapter Six: "Fast Eddie", "Heidi" and Super Bowl III

Before the autumn season of 1968, our family moved for the second time in less than two years; this time to 129 Legion Way in Cranston, Rhode Island. It was the very first house that my parents owned. My father at the age of 43 finally had fulfilled one of his lifelong dreams. Ironically, twenty eight years later I too would own my first home at the same age. The Cacchiotti home was a two story, three bedrooms and one bathroom house resting on the corner adjacent to main drag Reservoir Avenue, nicely situated next to a car wash. We had a relatively good size back yard half the size of an NFL red zone area. My favorite room at our new home was the bathroom because the toilet was situated next to a window that overlooked Reservoir Avenue and many times I would spend many a summer night looking at the lights at some of the city of Cranston's landmarks; Christy Liquors and Thalls' Pharmacy as life passed. The bathroom was where I literally memorized all 6,000 questions and answers of the first edition of Trivial Pursuit and won first place in a Rhode Island contest in 1984, worth $100 of gift certificates, losing my amateur status forever. The bathroom is still today my favorite place for sanctuary. I even read Tolstoy's **War and Peace** *in one sitting. The times that I actually left Nirvana, I attended Cranston High School east and immediately became friends with Bobby Stravato, Richard Merlino and Larry Gibson. It was Bobby who introduced me to the game of ten pin bowling at Lang's Bowlarama. Located at 225 Niantic Avenue in Cranston, R.I. Lang's would be my home away from the bathroom and I made it to the concourse area just about every night during the months throughout high school. I was infatuated with the game. Bobby, Richard, Larry and I joined a winter league in the Rhode Island Junior Bowlers' Association. The most accomplished at the sport was Bobby who was referred to as "stroker" which I always thought he was called because of his hand release. Well, at least that's what we thought. Richard's mindset was to throw the ball as far down the lane as possible without hitting the alley and as hard as he could hoping for what he called a "bomb back". Larry who was to become one of my best high school friends and an all around athlete at Cranston High School east would bend his elbow prior to releasing the ball. He was called the lobster and my "backswing" was very similar and so I was called the crab. It was just easier to call us the crustacean brothers. Despite our awkward deliveries Larry and I won many awards that included the Rhode Island State Doubles. I also was the first place winner in the State's; All Events contest. Professional Bowling was able to showcase* *the game's best with ABC coverage on Saturday afternoon hosted by Chris Schenkel with former Professional Billy Welu. It was the bowlers' take on Monday Night Football: A ritual that could not be missed. On Friday Night, bowlers from other "houses" would come down to participate in "pot games". Some of the best from New England would try to take the locals down. Future PBS stars' Larry Lichstein, Paul Moser, George LeCain, from Connecticut, Buddy Sequin, Dick Furtado and George Webb from Massachusetts would face off against Lang's best; Bobby's brother Richie Stravato, Johnny Beard, Mike Lubera and my favorite "Fast Eddie" Skovron. Although small in stature; "Fast Eddie" who had adopted that moniker while watching the movie* **"The Hustler"** *starring Paul Newman as "Fast Eddie" Felson a pool shark and Jackie Gleason as Minnesota Fats, was someone I looked up to. Eddie was seven years older than I and took a liking to me in a way a big brother would watch out for his own. Eddie would take me to bowling tournaments throughout New England watching him compete in "well known" cities across New England, such as Windsor Locks, Connecticut, Wickford, Rhode Island and Chicopee, Massachusetts. On the back of Eddie's tournament bowling shirts read "Fast Eddie" Skovron. I wanted to be so much like Eddie that later when I competed in tournament play the back of my shirt would read Ace "Fast Cash". On some occasions I did.*

Being able to smuggle any alcohol for intake was another of way of "passing time" with my high school buddies. Warm beer seemed to be the "beverage of choice" for all of us. In one of the many satirical moments involving that "beverage of choice", Bobby drank enough to alter his walk to put in nicely and fell over his front porch into bushes that were as high as six feet. We never found Bobby until the next day when the mailman rang Mrs. Stravato's doorbell and informed her that someone was sleeping in her front bushes. I was never interested in achieving academically in high school: My study periods mainly consisted of writing down bowling scores. For instance; each of the first two frames was strikes: Followed by a solid ten, which I dumped in the "channel". The fourth frame was a 3 − 10 baby split which I hit the three pin too solid for back to back opens. So as of now I was 66 in the fourth. Frames five through eight, I struck for a four bagger which is now referred to as a "hambone" on ESPN. I left a soft ten in the ninth and once again missed it. In the tenth I got lucky and avoided a split after going through the "nose". I made the 4 − 7 and filled with ten for a 203. Not bad. 10 more minutes and study period is over.

Gridiron Gumshoe

1968 was also the year NFL Films began to film American Football League games. Two years earlier in June of 1966 both the NFL and AFL agreed to merge and decided for an NFL – AFL Championship game following the 1966 season, pre-season games in 1967 and regular season games between the National and American Conferences in 1970, which then would make up the NFL. NFL Films, the production company of the NFL, now would be filming the regular season games from the "other league". The league required Ed Sabol's company to wear shirts that read AFL Films and during that season of 1968 produced a weekly review and preview series appropriately named AFL Films. The weekly series was narrated by Charlie Jones. I always connected Charlie to the AFL and that weekly series. In 1997 at "Pro Football's Greatest Weekend" in Canton, Ohio I told Charlie, how I felt like crying when the late Sunday afternoon game between the league's west coast teams had ended and school was the next day. Charlie asked why and I replied; "Because it had ended and school was the next day". Those highlights would air on our NBC affiliate WJAR TV Providence, Rhode Island on Saturdays. It was there I became familiar with the AFL stars: The Oakland Raiders' Daryle Lamonica who was nicknamed the "Mad Bomber", the Kansas City Chiefs' Len Dawson, known as "Lenny the Cool", the San Diego Chargers' wide receiver Lance Alworth who did not like his "Bambi" nickname and the Jets' "Broadway Joe" Namath. Namath was perfect for the "Big Apple" with his on an off the field swagger, on occasion Fu Manchu mustache and his white spikes. The one time Alabama quarterback one year earlier in 1967 set a Pro Football record by throwing for 4,007 yards in a season. Namath's team would face the Oakland Raiders for the AFL Championship on December 29th at Shea Stadium. The two teams had met earlier that season at the Oakland Coliseum on November 17th. With one minute and five seconds left in the fourth quarter, the Jets' placekicker Jim Turner connected from 26 yards out to give his team a 32 – 29 lead. Following the ensuing kickoff, NBC went to commercial and never came back to the game. Instead, **"Heidi"** *the title character of Johanna Spyri's 1880 little Swiss girl aired. The NBC switchboard became inundated and* **literally** *blew up because of all the calls of irate fans who wanted the game to continue to air according to NBC executive Chet Simmons. Official reports told the following: With seven minutes left in the game, people began to call into NBC asking the network to stay with the soon to be exciting finish. NBC broadcasting operations' supervisor Dick Cline had been given orders to air the children's fairy tale at seven. With so many calls coming in prior to the top of the hour, NBC executives decided to stay with the game but were not able to get through to*

Cline because of all the calls coming in. Thus, he never got the word and followed his initial order to switch to **"Heidi"** *at seven.*

The rest of the nation missed an incredible ending. From their own 23 yard line, the Raiders gained 20 on a pass completion from Lamonica to halfback Charlie Smith. A face mask penalty put the ball on the Jets' 43 yard line. On the very next play, Lamonica and Smith teamed up again for the remaining distance and after George Blanda's extra point, Oakland led 36 – 32. The Raiders kicked off and after the Jets' couldn't find the handle, Preston Ridlehuber, who two years earlier had played for the NFL's Atlanta Falcons returned the fumble from the two yard line and Oakland had won 43 – 32. 20 minutes following the game NBC "crab crawled" the score at the bottom of the television screen during **"Heidi".** *NBC issued an apology 90 minutes later and from that day on all major games in major markets are shown in its entirety. For me - I felt like crying because school was the next day.*

The Jets defeated the Raiders 27 – 23 to win the AFL Championship and two weeks later would play the NFL's Baltimore Colts. The Colts were heavily favored to win what was now being called the Super Bowl. Vince Lombardi's Green Bay Packers had handled the AFL's first two champions' Kansas City Chiefs and Oakland Raiders in the AFL – NFL Championship games. On Thursday January 9th, Joe Namath was being honored at the Miami Touchdown Club where he was chosen as "The Outstanding Professional Football Player" of 1968. It was here that the Jets' quarterback issued the "guarantee". After recognizing that the award he received should be in actuality an award given to his teammates and coaches he said; "You can be the greatest athlete in the world but if you don't win those football games, it doesn't mean anything. And we're going to win Sunday, I'll guarantee you". Namath backed up his word and was voted the game's Most Valuable Player as the Jets' stunned the world of Professional Football with their 16 – 7 win over the Colts. Trivia question: Who was the first man to rush for 100 yards in a Super Bowl? The answer may surprise you: Many believe it was the Jets' Matt Snell with 121 when actually it was the Colts' Tom Matte who although rushed for five yards less with 116 reached the 100 yard mark earlier in the fourth quarter before Snell had.

Sometime later, Steve Sabol would write and produce NFL Films' highlight of Super Bowl III. During the feature it was quite clear that Steve was an "NFL guy" and had a tough time giving the Jets' their due. With the game clearly in the hands of New York the producer gave the NFL and its fans hope as their hero John Unitas attempted to bring his team to victory in what else but heroic fashion. With the narration of John Facenda and the music from composer Sam Spence, many believed the Colts' quarterback could "save the day" for the NFL. But it was not to be and as both Unitas and Namath left the field, Facenda could be heard reciting the lines; "Two champions on a Sunday afternoon; a new one as a quarterback, an old one as a man". The Jets would not win another playoff game until the season of 1982 while the Colts two years later after Super Bowl III on January 17th, 1971 would be victorious at Super Bowl V in Miami the same year I would graduate from high school and spend all my time bowling and being in love with something other than Pro Football.

Chapter Seven: "This Week in Pro Football"; "The New Breed" and Mary Testoni.

Officially according to the Gregorian calendar, since 1752, January 1ˢᵗ begins our new year. But for me the first week of September signified the first monthly start of a new season. There was and still is nothing like the aesthetically picturesque quality of a New England Autumn and in the first week of the ninth month but my first, I entered my senior year at high school in 1970. 1970 also was the start of the NFL's 51ˢᵗ season and now the league would be made up of both National and American Conferences totaling 26 teams. On September 21ˢᵗ, ABC broadcasted their first ever Monday Night Pro Football game between the Cleveland Browns and New York Jets and it continues to be one of the most watched prime time series in television history now televised by ESPN. An earlier attempt by both CBS and NBC at a national televised Monday Night game; however, was not as successful: Beginning with Halloween night in 1966 between the Chicago Bears and St. Louis Cardinals; one year later on October 30th between the Cardinals and Green Bay Packers; two games from 1968; September 16ᵗʰ, the Los Angeles Rams and the Cardinals; October 20ᵗʰ; the Packers and Detroit Lions and in 1969 between the Houston Oilers and New York Jets on October 20ᵗʰ; all failed. CBS did not want to lose their **"Gunsmoke"** *and* **"The Lucy Show"** *fans and NBC wanted to keep their following of the* **Rowan and Martin's' "Laugh In Celebrity Variety Hour"**. *The first year of the 70's decade also gave us once again the NFL Films' production of* **"This Week in Pro Football"**. *In 1969 Pat Summerall and Charlie Jones co – hosted the one hour review and preview weekly series in its first year. One year later, Jones was replaced by Summerall's great friend Tom Brookshier who had played for the Philadelphia Eagles for seven seasons and also with Summerall had worked previously for the company that was based in Philadelphia at 13th and Vine Streets above a Chinese Laundromat. Each week the 48 minute of Pro Football content would take a look back at the previous weekend's games; courtesy of NFL Films' footage. Prior to the show ending both hosts would give their opinions on which team they "liked" to win their upcoming games. Summerall played in one game with the 1952 NFL Champions' Detroit Lions, five years with the Chicago Cardinals and four with the New York Giants before calling it quits after 1961. Each would do his best not to be so obviously partial to his former team and in week four of that 1970 season both teams at no wins and three losses played each other at the Giants' home field Yankee Stadium. Now was the time for both to give their opinions. It went something* *like this: Brookshier: "Well Pat; the Eagles despite their 0 and 3 record have been playing well of late. In last week's loss to the Washington Redskins they did play better losing a hard fought 33 – 21 contest. I like the Eagles to win their first of the season against the Giants on Sunday". Pat responded; "I like the Giants". For the record; New York won 30 – 23 which was the beginning of a six game winning streak that came to an end on ABC's Monday Night Football against; you guessed it; the Eagles at Philadelphia, which would be the team's last year at Franklin Field. TWIPF aired on Saturday's at 11:30 a.m. It would have taken an act of God for me to miss the show and one Saturday it almost did: My mom asked me to do the unthinkable; cut the grass but then remembered TWIPF was about to come on. Our grass doing the football season usually could be mistaken for Golf's U.S. Open's rough on steroids. Both Summerall and "Brookie" would do the voice over the segments' footage but what really made me a fan of the show was the music composed by Sam Spence. Later I always would reflect; "how music was instrumental to the mood". I came up with that line I think one day when while visiting Nirvana was looking at some of the city of Cranston's landmarks outside my bathroom window. I just could not get enough of the music and would literally take my tape recorder and put it in front of the kitchen's television so I could record the songs titled;* **"The Over the Hill Gang", "Let's Go Big O", "March to the Trenches"** *and my all time favorite* **"Roundup".** *I also for some reason liked the opening of the show when "Brookie" would say* **"This Week in Pro Football"** *is brought to you by Haggar Slacks. I thought wearing those slacks would be one of the two coolest things in the world to achieve: The other: being able to be driven in one of those golf carts through a major airport. Years later while working for NFL Films, I achieved the latter.*

Although my grades in school were to be kind; average, my scores in bowling were above the grade and I began to compete in the Independent Bowling Association. The I.B.A was a sanctioned monthly tournament governed by the Rhode Island Bowling Association. I did not initially cash like the name on the back of my shirt would have you think until later, but traveling with "Fast Eddie" to different bowling sites was something I looked so forward to. I also looked forward to Lang's Classic scratch league which was the most competitive in the state. Eddie's team was made up of Richie Stravato, John Beard and he. I would keep score and reacted after every "pitch". I also couldn't wait for Friday because Eddie's fiancée, the soon to be former Nadine Gravelle would accompany him during those three games each week. It was no secret that I had a crush on Nadine Gravelle and I just loved that name - Gravelle. The trio would finish on top at the end of the season and I was given a percentage of the team's winnings for keeping score for every game and for keeping Eddie's fiancée company. I never thought I would be rewarded just for staring.

Following The Baltimore Colts 16 – 13 win over the Dallas Cowboys in Miami at Super Bowl V; NFL produced their one half hour highlight show reviewing the game. Some of Sam Spence's best music was used as other music from other companies: Following Mike Clark's field goal that gave the Cowboys a 6 – 0 lead, the scene switched to defensive lineman Larry Cole who was standing at the end of the Cowboys' bench and from above was an airplane made cloud formation. John Facenda could be heard: "Once in a great while, the clouds of chance will overshadow the plans of man". "Such was the case in Super Bowl V, when John Unitas dropped back to pass early in the second quarter": This was the controversial 75 yard touchdown pass to the Colts' tight end John Mackey who caught a deflected ball off the finger tips of teammate Eddie Hinton and then the Cowboys' Mel Renfro. Prior to 1978 passes could not be successfully completed after being deflected from one offensive player to another and Dallas's rookie defensive safety Charlie Waters argued vehemently. The play stood and Baltimore tied the score before Jim O'Brien's extra point was blocked. The piece used for the background music score was titled **"The Artful Dodger"** *which was produced by KPM music performed in London, England. The first time I had ever heard that song was in the year end production of NFL 70 by Films during Facenda's narration of the Cardinals not being able to beat the Giants that season losing twice to their NFC Eastern Division foes. With Super Bowl V tied at 13, Dallas's Craig Morton's pass was intercepted by the Colts' Mike Curtis after Dan Reeves could not make the catch. Films had a microphone on the Colts' sidelines and you could hear the team scamper to bring out the "field goal team" including one familiar voice of Ed Sabol's son Steve incorporated in post production. Baltimore was ready to attempt what would be the game winning field goal as Facenda again was heard: "All the money, all the glory and all that is Pro Football rested on the right foot of Colts' rookie place kicker Jim O'Brien". The screen went silent until you could hear a manufactured thud. The ball "soared" through the up rights and all "Hell broke loose". The next shot cut to a leaping O'Brien in perfect synchronization with a new piece of music titled* **"Open Prairie"** *produced by Sylvestri records. As the Colts left the field in jubilation the top shot of the team leaving the field was damaged in the post production of the feature. The best way I can describe what that film looked like: I mistook the ektachrome film for parmesan cheese while grating over* *pasta. I loved the production however, and although the final ground shot of the game winning field goal was an actual extra point attempt used by the company for the climatic kick, it remains one of my favorite NFL Films' productions.*

Films had produced many wonderful features that gave millions a different perspective than what was seen from a television broadcast. In 1971, **"Glorious Game"** *was written and directed by NFL Films producer Bob Ryan. Many of the greatest lines ever read by Facenda came from this production including "On Sunday the game comes alive", a two and a half hour carnival of colors for the ears and the eyes". Two decades later with a little improvisation we would change his narration and time of the game to "a three hour" and so forth. Two years before in early 1969, 26 year old Steve Sabol produced* **"Big Game America"** *paralleling the industrial growth of America with that of Pro Football. The show is my all time best and was narrated by the actor Burt Lancaster, who had some football ties of his own portraying the legendary Jim Thorpe in the movie titled* **"Jim Thorpe All American"** *in 1951. The company also produced* **"Try and Catch the Wind"** *in 1969 focusing on young boys' dreams of becoming a receiver. Great music complimented the Facenda narration including* **KPM's 'Hell's Kitchen'** *used during the Cleveland Browns' tight end Milt Moran's wild ride to the one yard line. NFL Films also kept up with the times and in 1971 produced the* **"New Breed".** *The feature took an on the field but also an off the field look at some of Pro Football's more interesting characters, including the San Diego Chargers' "Dickie" Post, the Oakland Raiders' Ben Davidson and the Philadelphia Eagles' Tim Rossovich. The Rossovich feature was the last and the most unusual. Rossovich's Eagles' teammate Gary Pettigrew and NFL Films' soon to be president of the company Steve Sabol were roommates. Sabol would relate some of the most hard to believe stories about "Rosso" to others: Tim would sleep on the floor at times facing a certain direction because the earth's magnetic field of energy was more attainable in his prone position. Another "gem": While Steve and others were waiting for the future movie actor to appear at a party, "Rosso" finally appears setting him on fire and other times just for kicks would chew glass. None however would "top" the wild display of this "eccentric fellow" the time he was being filmed making candles at the shore. NFL Films' cameramen being directed by Sabol captured every outlandish act. In the produced segment which included his actions at the beach, Films also incorporated the Rossovich wiring at the last NFL game ever played at Franklin Field. Viewers were able to see and hear many of the Eagles' linebacker's actions, thoughts and comments including* *his lifelong wish: To play in the Super Bowl and make the game saving tackle for his team and in the process die and go to heaven! While we hear this, the song, once again from* **KPM's** *library;* **"Summer Rain"** *is being played. This particular piece of music is soothing and we can see Rossovich running with his back to us towards the ocean before the film freezes and the credits are rolled. On July 11ᵗʰ, 1996* **ESPN's** *Roy Firestone who was to be the master of ceremonies at Ed Sabol's retirement party hummed a few bars of a song he loved growing up for Steve and myself hoping I would know what song it was so he could get a cassette of it. No problem; "I can" and did name that tune;* **"Summer Rain"** *in three notes. The production of* **"The New Breed"** *was uncomfortable for the stuffed shirts at the NFL Office and as uncomfortable as a woman trying to fit into her prom dress at a 25 years reunion, (Sorry about the metaphor) noting that type of behavior sends a negative message to NFL fans. As for me, I sleep comfortably in my bed which faces magnetic north.*

The PBA's winter tour of 1971 was winding up with the Firestone **"Tournament of Champions"** *in Akron, Ohio, on April 1ˢᵗ. The winner was Johnny Petraglia who defeated the defending champion Don Johnson 245 – 169. The win for the Brooklyn born native was his fourth of the year and third straight. The $25,000 1ˢᵗ place money brought his total earnings for the year to $85,000, the most in PBA history. While Petraglia was enjoying his* **"Bowler of the Year"** *award, I was looking to early June for my graduation of high school. However on May 28ᵗʰ, my life would change forever: On that Friday Evening, I once again was "hanging out" at Lang's, when I spotted four young women on lane eleven. One lady had thrown a strike and was feeling pretty good about it, when I informed her that she "crossed over" to the Brooklyn side which is the left side of the head pin for a right hander. Mary Testoni had just turned 20 years old on April 12ᵗʰ and was a junior at Rhode Island College. The brown hair, brown eyed beauty was wearing cut off jeans' shorts, which accentuated her long lovely legs that seem to reach as high as her chin! "Wow" what a doll"! We began a relationship, albeit a short one that began that day and unofficially ended on July 12, which happens to be the date of my wedding anniversary to my wife Susan which took place in 1996. Although I was only seventeen and still a senior in high school, we "clicked". Mary gave me her phone number which was 401 739 3431. Oh, I mean 555 739 3431, and her address; 3 Hayes Street, Warwick Rhode Island. She drove her dad's car with the license plate VT 27 and introduced me to the culinary delight; tomato and grilled cheese sandwiches, which I really* *didn't like but her legs reached as high as her chin! We had planned to meet one week later at Lang's when from there we would have dinner at the Cathay Terrace on Reservoir Avenue, another of the city of Cranston's landmarks, which I could also see from my bathroom window. I remember how long a wait it was for that following Friday as the hours felt like days and the days like weeks. Each minute felt like actually only sixty seconds however. I was dating an "older" woman and could not wait to experience all that comes from being in a relationship with someone so "worldly". In 1972, the song writer and story teller Harry Chapin recorded the song* **"Taxi"** *which tells the story of a disgruntled taxi cab driver whose fare he has just picked up happens to be that of a former lover. One of the lyrics reads: "We learned the proud love in the back of a Dodge; the lesson hadn't gone too far". Well for us it was in the back of a 1969 Plymouth Fury convertible that my Dad had given to me for a graduation present and our lessons continued in other locations. It was very difficult for me to focus on anything other than Mary and on one particular date while I was trying to do two things at once while driving, I "brushed" a small dog with my car. Behind us laid a frightened little thing. Mary being the kind soul decided for us to see if we could care for the injured puppy. While I turned and backed up, I uttered; "the poor thing probably thinks I am coming back to finish him off"! Don't worry there was a happy ending: Mary picked up the dog and brought it to the house where the owner lived. The dog survived and we continued but now with both hands on the wheel! Never being in love before did not prepare me for the hurt it caused once it was over and on July 12ᵗʰ Mary was headed for Italy for 45 days to return one week before her senior year of college. I was now "working" for my dad as a carpenter's apprentice employed by the Ferland Corporation, in the home improvement division. My eight hour work day while Mary was away, was to day dream that included following the message left by the musical group; The Drifter's 1962 song;* **"Up on the Roof"** *where I literally resided during lunch break. As the countdown continued to Mary's return I thought of two old adages: "out of sight, out of mind" and "absence makes the heart grow fonder"; And although I hoped for the latter, it was not to be, for upon my first love's return she informed me that things were different and so were her feelings for me. What was not different was that Mary at five foot eight was almost three inches taller than I was and that was the main reason for our time together to end. Although, totally crushed I surprised myself at how I handled the loss of Mary and decided to move ahead by leaving Rhode Island for Hot Springs, Arkansas because I could not bear living in the same state as she.*

Left to Right: Soon to be physic: Sister Paula

Baby Sister: Teresa and future; "Gridiron Gumshoe"

Joey; "Ace" Cacchiotti   circa 1959

"Joe Cash"

circa   1960

From here; it is downstairs; to the first floor

To visit "Gramps" and a "Taste"

Of "Homemade Wine" Circa 1958

My 5th grade teacher; Miss Kennedy

(Yes; that was her name)

And sister; Paula 1963

1968: Ninth Grade Picture Taken: **George J. West Junior High School**

Sitting front row with hands clenched: 1st small boy from left: Me:
wondering even today; what it would have been to like to kiss young girl
standing with profile: third row from row of boys sitting; second girl from
right wearing headband: Elaine Balasco.

Even a small lad of four feet eleven inches in stature can receive sympathy
Athletic Certificate in basketball which I did in my ninth grade at my
junior high school: George J. West Junior High in 1968

George J. West Junior High School

ATHLETIC CERTIFICATE

This is to certify that _Joseph Cicchiotti_ has participated in sufficient
athletic contests to be awarded the varsity emblem of the school.

Basketball

_1968_

Principal

Coach

My High School senior picture taken in 1970:

How could Mary Testoni break my heart?

Home Improvement Division's manager;

"Joe Cash"

of the Ferland Corporation: 1972

Angelo "Pic" Piccone and wife; Vivian

At my parent's 30th wedding anniversary

At the Chateau DeVille in Warwick, R.I. 1977

"Pic" always came through when I needed a "job".

Chapter Eight: Hot Springs, Arkansas, Holiday Inn and the "Immaculate Reception".

When I did come down from the roof and decided to go forward without Mary, I befriended brothers' Dave and Ted, who were visiting relatives in Rhode Island. Both lived in Hot Springs, Arkansas and wanted to see what the north was all about. Of the two, I hung out with the younger brother Dave who I **thought** was my age. In early September, still feeling like a lost soul, Dave informed me that he wanted to go back home without Ted who wanted to stay until the holidays. After giving it much thought, 20 seconds later I decided to go with him. I had turned 18 one month earlier and felt this would be what I needed to forget Mary. On Sunday, September 12th, 1971 the two of us headed south on interstate 95 towards the city that is about 80 miles northeast of Hope, Arkansas the birthplace of our 42 President; Bill Clinton. Now that I was of legal age, I could do what I wanted; so I informed my parents of my trek via a letter I mailed on the day before explaining my plans and how I cannot bear to live in the same state as Mary. "Boy, what an asshole. I could have just driven twelve miles to Massachusetts"! I called my mom from West Virginia on Monday to let her know where I was so she wouldn't worry. "Boy what an asshole"; I should have called her Sunday from Massachusetts"!

The farther we traveled from Rhode Island and the closer we got to our destination, I began to learn valuable lessons that would assist me in the "well rounded" individual I would become later in life: If you asked; "I would like coffee regular", you get it black and another just as important; when ordering a cheeseburger specify how many condiments if any you would like or it comes with lettuce, tomato and mayo always. I was afraid to ask for a hot dog.

After speaking with my mom with the callousness of youth, I assured her I would be home for the weekend because I would be bowling in East Providence in the I.B.A and another: to be home Sunday for the opening of the NFL Season. We arrived in Hot Springs on Tuesday after two days of driving, as I continued to pick up valuable lessons along the way that would further enhance my knowledge as again; "a well rounded individual". Dave's friends were cordial and caring and could consume copious amount of alcohol. Later that afternoon, about six of us drove to the "crick". In a scene from **"Huckleberry Finn":** five of us into the water swinging from a tree holding onto a deflated tire. I didn't because I had a fear of the water: I think it's called drowning. When the others weren't reading **"Tom Sawyer"**, they were drinking the 16 ounces cans of Schlitz malt liquor, which is still the *beverage of choice for Art Donovan; the Baltimore Colts defensive lineman who played with Hall of Fame teammates; John Unitas, Raymond Berry, Lenny Moore, Jim Parker, and Gino Marchetti in the golden decade of Pro Football. Just recently my friend Ed , "the one beer to have" Schaffer, who works for the Miller Brewing Company picked up a case of Schlitz for me that I sent to Artie. There is no such thing as an "Indian Summer" in Hot Springs, Arkansas. It's just hot and by my sixth beer I decided to take a nap right where I was. My new friends decided to let me sleep, while they washed my convertible in the "crick". I found out later they decided to take a ride with the now cleaned vehicle. I awoke hours later alone. Actually I wasn't because I was infested with bugs, ants, and some nasty looking insects that I still believe were not from this planet. It was then I decided that the profession of entomology was not for me.*

*One of my new drinking buddies Lee Miller had a sister named Patsy, who liked "guys from the north". I asked; "how many "guys from the north" have you known"? She replied "one including you". But she was pretty. The guys really treated me great: I mean they even let me sit in the front seat whenever Lee drove my car as close to the breakdown lane as possible. Whatever you do; **do not** get a flat tire in Hot Springs, Arkansas. My long trek earlier driving companion Dave was not to be seen after Tuesday. He was visiting his younger friends so I asked: "How old is David"? Well; let's just stay I transported a minor across nine states prior. On Friday morning after three days of becoming one of the "boys" that included an initiation of ordering a cheeseburger, I decided it was time to head back north. I showered and told Patsy; "I'm going home". "Back to the hotel" she asked. "No home". With that; dressed only in pink panties, she started to cry, hugged me and begged me not to leave. It was a tough decision to make but I broke away and never came back, leaving behind Hot Springs, Arkansas, Patsy and those pink panties.*

When I returned from my "vacation" in the nation's 25th state, I decided to look for employment other than that of a carpenter's apprentice. My dad's friend "Pic" had another "job" working for the state and was able to find me work as a bell hop at the Holiday Inn in downtown Providence, Rhode Island. I worked five days a week; Monday through Friday and averaged over $250.00. I began work at three P.M. and clocked out at eleven. That shift introduced me to some of the most recognized people in the entertainment world: Carly Simon, Andy Williams, Tom Jones, and groups; Yes; "The Associations", The Grass Roots and others. I even fetched vitamins for Tiny "Tiptoe through the Tulips" Tim but there was nothing tiny about the man

*born Hebert Khuary who stood over six feet tall and at times weighed more
than 250 pounds. After returning with his order he was most thankful: "Here's
five dollars for you, mister Ace". Friday was my most lucrative day: The Jane
Dale Models who would exhibit in the lounge area hoping to create interest for
the male clientele had me take their lingerie and other items to their dressing
room where they displayed the new goods always asking me if I liked what they
were wearing. It always took me a long time to decide. The Inn Keeper John
Lepore wanted me to stay out of their rooms and at times would actually knock
asking; "Is Ace in there"? I never was: Bless those Jane Dale Models. Lepore
also forbade me to enter the lounge area especially on Friday Nights when the
place was "jumping", even though Rhode Island was one of the 29 States
that had dropped the legal age of drinking to 18. Just as I abided his wishes
concerning the Jane Dale Models; I respected that request as well. As if it was
meant just for me, New Year's Eve fell on a Friday in 1971 and the Holiday
Inn was having an extravaganza to bring in the New Year. I checked in two
women, carried their luggage to their room, received a tip and went about my
business waiting for the innkeeper to leave for the night. Around ten o'clock
Heather and her friend passed through the lobby and asked what time I got
off? I let her know; "In an hour". "Why don't you join us in the lounge for a
drink later"? With Lepore within ear shot I regrettable had to decline based on
the rules of the hotel. Once it was "all clear" I joined Heather and her friend
to "bring in 1972". Hours later with her friend asleep in the next bed, we
celebrated the New Year with fireworks.*

*Six months after my first day of employment, my friend Bobby Stravato became
employed by the hotel and too worked as a bell hop during the graveyard shift.
Another of the many rules of the Holiday Inn: Employees were to refrain from
visiting the hotel once their shift had ended. Once again I decided to respect
the hotel's policy and on numerous occasions "dropped in" on my friend.
My employment ended when I flat out defied the night manager: "You can't
fire me". "You're just the night manager". One week late; once again, I was
working as a carpenter's apprentice for my Dad employed by the Ferland
Corporation in the Home Improvement Division.*

*The NFL Season of 1972 would produce ten 1,000 yard rushers: The
most ever in NFL History at that time. The NFC's Larry Brown with the
Washington Redskins, the Green Bay Packers' John Brockington, New York
Giants' Ron Johnson, and the Dallas Cowboys' Calvin Hill. In the AFC:
The Buffalo Bills' O.J. Simpson who led the NFL in rushing with 1,251
yards, the first team to have two 1,000 yard runners in the same season;*

the Miami Dolphins' Larry Csonka and Eugene "Mercury "Morris. Mike Garrett became the only man to rush for a thousand yards in both the American Football League and National Football League when he gained 1,031with the San Diego Chargers in 1972 and earlier 1,087 with the Kansas City Chiefs in 1967; the Oakland Raiders' Marv Hubbard and the Pittsburgh Steelers' Franco Harris. The latter two would be involved in one of the most memorable games in NFL History on Saturday December 23rd at Pittsburgh's Three River Stadium in the first round of the AFC Playoffs. For only the third time since 1933, the Steelers' were involved in post season play: The first: A 21 – 0 loss to the Philadelphia Eagles on December 21st, 1947 to decide the Eastern Division winner; second; in the "Playoff Bowl" following the 1962 season playing against the Detroit Lions and now 25 years later. In a fiercely fought contest, the Raiders took the lead when backup quarterback Ken Stabler ran down the left sidelines for a 30 yard touchdown giving Oakland a 7 – 6 lead with one minute and 13 seconds remaining. Pittsburgh faced a fourth and ten from their own forty with 22 seconds left in the game when quarterback Terry Bradshaw eluded the Raiders' pass rush and fired down field in the direction of halfback John "Frenchy" Fuqua. Both he and the Raiders' Jack Tatum collided and the ball caromed back towards Harris who "caught" it inches off the ground* and proceeded to run the remaining distance for the incredible

---

* *Interesting Note: One week later, NFL Films produced their* **"Game of the Week"** *and not surprisingly it featured the Raiders /Steelers' playoff contest. At the point when the Steelers faced the fourth and ten, NFL Films' top cameraman Jay Gerber picked up the play from the snap and followed it as best he could when both Tatum and Fuqua collided; the ball ricocheted back so fast that Gerber could not follow it until Harris ran back into the frame. From the end zone using a long lens, NFL Films' cameraman Ernie Ernest covered the play in its entirety as well keeping focus on Bradshaw, losing sight of the ball until a split second before Harris made the "catch". However, the shot never really is clear whether or not the ball touches the ground. Two decades later, Harris reveals to the veteran cameraman; Ernst; the truth about the catch. However, he is sworn to secrecy even to this day. Also the* **"Game of the Week"** *feature is one of the two only times that both top and long lens shots of the play are shown from beginning to end or as Films' reference; "head to tail". The other was* **This Week in Pro Football #15.** *Since that time the shot is edited from the top and "picked" up with the ball being "caught" by Harris. Many historical moments are remembered by "where you were when so and so happened".*

touchdown. The stadium erupted and controversial occurred: If Tatum did not touch the ball the "catch" would have been ruled illegal. A similar play occurred at Super Bowl V regarding the Colts' John Mackey. Mackey's was ruled complete as now was the Steelers' running back's catch. Later, it would be known as the "Immaculate Reception". The Miami Dolphins would defeat Pittsburgh one week later 21 – 17 in the AFC Championship and on January 14th, 1973 the Washington Redskins 14 – 7 becoming the only team in NFL History to finish a season undefeated at 17 – 0.

I was at the Rhode Island Mall in Warwick with a friend of my sister Paula and her husband Steve: Debbie and I on many occasions would spend time together and on this particular day we did doing Xmas shopping when we passed by the Television area of Sears and Roebuck. It was there on numerous screens in all shapes and sizes that we witnessed what would arguably be known as the greatest play in NFL History. We commented on the number of people that spilled out onto the field in celebration. For us; we contemplated where and how we would celebrate that night that actually was no different from any other night. Xmas had come early for the Steelers and for Debbie and me as well.

Chapter Nine: "Ann and Hope" Tony "Dag" and "The Championship Chase".

I wasn't much of a carpenter: My only finished craft was the tool box I built for myself that was large enough to carry everyone else's tools as well. My dad thought it was quite humorous and always thought it was worth bringing up in conversation wherever he was: I told him the priest wasn't interested. Realizing now that my "tools of the trade" did not include a hammer and saw, I sought employment elsewhere. Once again "Pic" came through: I became a "section head" in the summer furniture department at Ann and Hope; a family owned business with four stores in the Rhode Island and Massachusetts areas. It was during my tenure with A & H that I continued to grow as a person. I had already mastered the fine art of beer consumption but now would be able to drink a great deal more at different company's functions; our summer outings and Xmas parties. Each July, A & H would schedule our gathering at some picnic grounds that they secured for a price. It was an opportunity for the employees and employers to get better acquainted and I did: with the supervisor of the music department: Micki Gardner was a woman in her mid forties who was just as intelligent as she was attractive. She "ran" that department as if she owned it and was always on "top of her game". While attending my first summer outing, I was introduced to steamers not to be confused with steamed clams. This Rhode Island only delicacy was similar to the latter except that this clam had a tail with skin that when eaten would and I stress should be removed. (Thirty five years later, my son Joey while visiting me in south Jersey informed me that the tail was actually the clam's reproductive organ which was a third of the total mass of the clam itself that no doubt made it quite popular with female clams). However, surrounded by all that comes with a summer picnic and with who in today's vernacular is referred to as a "cougar" I consumed the whole clam. Thank God Micki stopped me from eating the shell as well. Miss Gardner also accompanied me at other functions including our inaugural employees versus employers basketball challenge and although the employees lost; my sorrow quickly subsided thanks to her lending of an ear and other parts of her anatomy. I guess when I finally realized that Micki and I had a "relationship" was during the Christmas season of 1974. While everyone was merry and enjoying the most wonderful time of the year we too enjoyed all that was the season. On the eve of what over three billion believe is the most celebrated birthday, Micki invited me to her house for a party which I readily accepted. She informed me that it was a small gathering and we would toast at midnight. Her details however were inaccurate and the small gathering *was made up of two. It still is to this day my favorite of all Xmas gifts I ever received. While working for the company, I met other wonderful people including Dick Morrison, a sales rep for the razor blade company Schick. My African American friend was six years my senior and introduced me to some of the finest establishments in Boston's combat zone; a renowned area for x rated adult entertainment. I loved Boston! Richard, as I always called him also "took care" of me financially as if I was his date. I may have been naïve but he was a great guy to hang out with and even took me to see the movie; "***The Longest Yard***" starring Burt Reynolds and Eddie Albert. Former NFL Players' Ray Nitschke of the Packers and Joe Kapp of the Vikings also had roles as prison guards; but the man who left the biggest impression was the seven foot two inch actor Richard Kiel who would gained notoriety as Roger Moore's nemesis as the assassin "Jaws" in two James Bond Films; "***The Spy Who Loved Me***" and "***Moonraker***". However, the first time I saw the former cemetery plot salesman was in the 1959 **Twilight Zone** episode; "**To Serve Man**". An alien race known as "Kanamits" landed on earth and offer to rid the planet of poverty, disease, war and famine. One Kanamit played by Kiel purposely leaves a book in the hands of actor Lloyd Bochner. The title is deciphered as the title of the episode. When the Kanamits "delivered" on all their promises, the world embraces the alien visitors and begins to travel in space and time to the planet of the Kanamits as would tourists vacationing on other islands. When it is time for Mr. Chambers (Bochner) to board the spaceship his assistant frantically tries to stop him screaming; "The book **"To Serve Man"** It's, it's a cook book"!*

Of all the people I met at Ann and Hope none would mean as much to me as Tony Dagnanica. Tony "Dag" was one of the four vice presidents of the Warwick store and immediately took a liking to me. Maybe because I was a paisa no' or maybe because I relished life as he but for whatever the reason, we just became great friends. Tony "Dag" played in the company's golf league as did I and we would encounter our 19th hole at a small neighborhood bar not too far from the Midville Golf Course in Warwick, Rhode Island. Every Tuesday night during our 18 week season we feasted on pickled eggs and pigs' feet; which were usually after an hour of getting acquainted with the different selections of beer which numbered only three. My friend also made our appearances at the V.F. W. Post; nights to remember with the all you can eat pasta and chicken in garlic and wine sauce. One of my most vivid recollections of one of those nights at the Post was the assumption that the large platter of Macaroni was for him - and him only. While the others at the table waited

patiently for the next platter we amused ourselves by watching my paisa no'
bury his plate with red pepper flakes while beads of sweat began to appear
on his forehead. There has always been a special place in my heart for Tony
"Dag": He was a wonderful friend and someone who continues to make me
smile even though he died succumbing to cancer on my birthday; August 7th,
1981; at the same age as I write this chapter today: 56.

1974 was also the year that the Miami Dolphins would attempt to become
the first NFL Team to win three consecutive Super Bowls* having defeated the
Washington Redskins and Minnesota Vikings in Super Bowls VII and VIII
respectively. Head coach Don Shula's Dolphins' team traveled to Oakland to
face the Raiders in the first round of the AFC playoffs on Saturday December
21st in what would become one of the most thrilling contests in NFL post season
history. In a seesaw battle, Oakland trailed 26- 21 when Raiders' quarterback
Ken Stabler led his team to the winning touchdown inches before his knee
touched the turf at the Oakland Coliseum by completing a desperate six yard
touchdown pass to halfback Clarence Davis. The stadium erupted and as
NBC replayed the final seconds, color analyst Al DeRogatis, a former defensive
lineman for the New York Giants made the following statement with all the
conviction of a first year weatherman: "Frankly Curt [Gowdy] this has to be
frankly, maybe the greatest game ever played"! The play would be referred to
as; **"The Sea of Hands Catch"** *given that title by NFL Films.*

It was also that season that NFL Films produced a different year end show
leading up to the Super Bowl. Today the company continues to deliver with
their "Road to the Super Bowl". Prior to 1974 Films would simply state the
year as "NFL "70", "71", "72" and so on. Steve Sabol spoke with NBC
producer Don Ohlmeyer who suggested that Sabol name the year end show;
"The Championship Chase". *The piece was different from the*
previous year end shows. **"T C C",** *focused on all 26 teams from training*
camp to the Conference Championship Games and along the way some of the
best writing by Sabol was delivered in John Facenda's narrations. My favorite
was the introductory segment on the Oakland Raiders: With their Raiders'
theme serving as the music backdrop, Facenda began;

"The autumn wind is a pirate,

Blustering in from sea,

With a rollicking song, he sweeps along,

Gridiron Gumshoe

Swaggering boisterously".

"His face is weathered beaten,

He wears a hooded sash,

With a silver hat upon his head,

And a thick bristly mustache".

"He growls as he roams the country,

A villain big and bold,

And the leaves all shake and quiver and quake,

As he robs them of their gold".

"The autumn wind is a Raider,

Pillaging just for fun,

He'll knock you around and upside down,

And laugh when he's conquered and won"!

The show continues with playoff games and the conference championships and once again Facenda delivers Sabol's creative thoughts:

"They began in summer,

The legion of the sun.

Now as warriors of winter,

The chase is almost done".

"On these wings of victory ride emotions of a year,

Of work and sweat, guts, glory and fear".

Following 45 seconds of impressionable cinematography and Sam Spence's music score, Facenda takes us to the climatic end of one of NFL Films' best ever productions:

"Two teams have gained champions' fame,

Two teams of men both skilled and game".

"Men who have battled as brothers,

In combat through thick and thin".

"And now they confront each other,

For a prize only won can win'!

With that we see the Minnesota Vikings and Pittsburgh Steelers jubilant and celebrating their victories as a shot of the Lombardi Trophy slowly spins and freezes with the title of the show.

While writing **"Grid Iron Gumshoe"**, *I continued to speak with Sabol and at times electronically when I asked about the above production: "Hey Boss, who wrote "The autumn wind is a Pirate"? At warp speed, his return;* **I WROTE IT!** *He did and would again many others.*

Editor's note: Three Professional Football Teams have won three or more consecutive Pro Football Titles: The Green Bay Packers in years 1929, 1930 and 1931, and again in seasons 1965, 1966 and 1967 and the Cleveland Browns won their championships in all four years of the All America Football Conference from 1946 to 1949.

Chapter Ten: "The NFL Today", "Black Sunday" *and* "Joe and the Magic Bean":

By the early 1970's Professional Football had replaced Major League Baseball as America's number one sport. Each Sunday was a major event as hundreds of thousands of football fans flocked to stadiums to see NFL games as John Facenda let it be known: "The game comes alive": "A two and a half hour carnival of color for the ears and the eyes". (See Chapter Seven).

Pro Football was also perfect for television: Cameras were positioned at different locations throughout the stadium so viewers could see different angles of previous plays right in their own living rooms and never miss a critical moment. The NFL was entertaining and prior to the season of 1975, **CBS** *produced for all intents and purposes the first pre – game show:* **"The NFL Today"** *the upcoming games prior to kickoff for any serious length of time leading into the Sunday match ups.* **"The NFL Today"** *was 24 minutes of content of highlights of previous games and in depth looks at some of the surrounding stories. Its' opening theme; fanfare;* **"Horizontal Hold"** *was a piece produced by the London based music company* **DeWolfe.** *The production was visceral with its first two beats on the Kettle drum followed by predominately brass throughout. With each bombastic pause, the hosts' names would be seen across the screen: The show was anchored by Brent Musburger, the onetime writer for the now defunct Chicago American newspaper. His other two co hosts were Irv Cross, the former defensive back for the Philadelphia Eagles, Los Angeles Rams and the former sales rep for the Campbell Soup Company and Phyllis George who was crowned Miss America in 1971.*

Each Sunday Musburger would open with his classic: "You're looking live at sold out (stadium)" and the show would begin. Jack Whitaker would end with some editorial but it were the features with the former Miss America that I waited for with high anticipation. NFL Films working with **CBS** *would produce the two and a half to five minute pieces with George hosting the segment. Films' producer Louis Schmidt would direct and coordinate all aspects of the feature. The "easy on the eyes" young lady was getting "her feet wet" but Schmidt and others made her transition into Pro Football a successful one. In one of her most famous interviews: The Cowboys' quarterback Roger Staubach who had led Dallas to two Super Bowl wins in the seventies was irritated by the media's perception of a "squeaky clean, live by the good book Catholic". When George asked the 1963 Heisman trophy winner, what his take was on* *what others saw him as, the Naval Academy graduate responded; "Look, I like sex as much as anyone else, I just happen to do it with one woman"!*

In 1998, Films began a series titled **"Lost Treasures of NFL Films"**. *It was a look back at its humble beginnings and in particular footage that had never been seen outside the two buildings occupied by the company since 1962.* **"Lost Treasures of NFL Films"** *would add to its numerous collections of television awards. In 2000, Films was producing* **"Lost Treasures of the Network Television Stars"** *of those that worked with the company including the former first Lady of Kentucky: George. While I was in my office, Louis (as Phyllis always called him) Schmidt introduced me to her. It was the first time I had ever seen her in person. After the proverbial greeting(s) she and Louis went back to the producer's office. I meanwhile wiped the sweat off of my hands and discreetly followed her lurking behind with the theme of* **"Mission Impossible"** *in my head. The men's room was at a 75 degree angle from Schmidt's office and I entered to "clean up". Once I left and I did wash my hands because I was an employee of the company, I "innocently" bumped into her and with the heart palpitations of a young boy said; "Phyllis, I used to love watching* **"The NFL Today"** *and especially your features. "Oh and one more thing, you still got it"! With that said, returned; "Oh Ace thank you, you made my day", followed by a kiss and a hug. "Wow; Miss America kissed me"! It would not be the last time I reverted to a school boy in her presence:*

In the spring of 2007, I was approached by Jim Turek who at the time was working with the Kentucky Sports' Hall of Fame. On June 15th of that year the organization would introduce their newest inductees. Turek asked if I could put together a two and a half minute highlight for each being added to the class, which would include; Philadelphia Eagles' linebacker Frank Lemaster, former Louisville Alum and Denver Broncos' linebacker Tom Jackson, Cleveland Browns' head coach Romeo Crennel and the former Miss Texas, Miss America and the former first Lady of Kentucky. After agreeing; I produced the segments and would introduce each at that Friday Night Dinner. I wanted to produce something very special for Phyllis George and incorporated her crowning of Miss America and her days on **"The NFL Today"** *set. I wrote a very endearing piece and needed music to enhance the segment. I decided on NFL Films' music producer Dave Robidoux's* **"A Hero Remembered"** *which he wrote and directed in 1998. I finished editing at 12:45 A.M. that Friday morning, went to bed at 1:15 A.M. At 2:30 with only one hour and fifteen minutes of sleep, I awoke, showered and began the 11 hour trek to Lexington, Kentucky. With an hour and a half to spare I ran three miles at* *the hotel gym and then delivered. Prior to introducing Phyllis I recalled: to the 1,000 in attendance the story of my first meeting with the former first lady of Kentucky receiving applause and another hug and kiss from her. Once her two and a half minute segment was over she began to thank everyone including that young school boy who didn't wash his face for two days but did once again his hands because after all, he was an employee of NFL Films.*

In 1975, the National Football League celebrated its' 56th season and the World Football League its' second. One year earlier, the WFL made good on the promise of a new league and cities across America recruited NFL stars but on October 23rd, 1975, the New League; 30 million in debt folded and the NFL once again was the only Pro Football Game in town. The WFL survived its' first year due mostly in part to NFL Players who were not happy with the Collective Bargaining agreement and went on strike prior to the season. Seasoned veterans now looked for another source of income and signed with the new league in other cities; Birmingham, Memphis, Jacksonville, and Shreveport. But once the NFL Players returned albeit still without a contract, attendance dwindled in the WFL and the inevitable happened. It would not be the last time a new league challenged the NFL*

Now that the NFL reigned supreme I could once again enjoy Pro Football Weekends. NFL Films was now producing **"This is the NFL"** *and* **CBS** *with* **"The NFL Today"** *made this 22 year old a fanatic in every sense of the word.* **CBS's** *number one broadcast team was Pat Summerall and Tom Brookshier and listening to them announce the game one could feel as if the two were in your living room enjoying the game along side. You knew when a key matchup took place at 4:00 P.M. both were going to create as much excitement in the booth as the players did on the field.*

Working at NFL Films for nearly twenty year gave me the opportunity to learn everything about the history of Pro Football, the History of NFL Films and just anything else pertaining to the great game: In early spring of 1977, Paramount Pictures released the Movie; **"Black Sunday":** *A demented Vietnam veteran played by Bruce Dern became a member of the terrorist organization known as* **"Black September".** *This group is determined to kill thousands at America's most watched Sporting event; the Super Bowl*

---

* Editors' note: In 1984 the United States Football League made its debut but after only three seasons the league was no more and hundreds of those players became part of the NFL including Herschel Walker and Reggie White.

*which would take place at the Orange Bowl in Miami, Florida in January. The plan is to hijack the **Good Year Blimp** and with a specially designed dart gun shoot thousands at the Stadium. Major Kobakov, who is played by Robert Shaw of the movie **"Jaws"** fame, had overheard the group planning the attack when he earlier had met Dahlia, played by Martha Keller.*

***FBI** agent Corley (Fritz Weaver) and Kabakov discuss where and when the attack may take place. When Corley suggests "The Super Bowl" major Kobakov replies one of the two most famous lines from the movie: "Super Bowl, what is Super Bowl"? The other is when Miami Dolphins' owner Joe Robbie exclaims; "Canceling the Super Bowl is like canceling Christmas"! The Super Bowl does take place and it is actual footage from Super Bowl X, which took place on January 18th, 1976. The attack seems to be going according to plan so much so that the Blimp can be seen ominously entering the stadium while thousands run for their lives including CBS's number one broadcast team of Summerall and Brookshier. However, Kobakov (Shaw) saves the day by killing both Lander (Dern) and Dahlia (Keller). As for the Blimp armed with the special dart gun; well it explodes harmlessly over the Atlantic Ocean with some of the most obvious special effects. During the climax of the movie, the blimp provides the viewer with aerial footage. However, the view of the blimp itself is from the game played on November 23rd, 1975 between the Baltimore Colts and Miami Dolphins at the Orange Bowl. The actual footage shown from the game as mentioned earlier was from Super Bowl X but was from one camera man: NFL Films' Steve Sabol and that footage due to contractual rights was never used in any post production by Films. Brookshier and I became good friends and through the years I would send him highlights of his football and television broadcasting career. It was later at one of our rendezvous that he informed me that both he and Pat shot their scenes alone in the booth. The history of Pro Football is intriguing but to know the real story behind a story as was the case in the latter has always been most rewarding.*

*By the mid 1970's NFL Films became synonymous with the game of Pro Football. Millions became fans of the gridiron classics because of Ed Sabol and his son's incredible vision. It was at the time ground breaking; that one entity could create an interest with such anticipation from an event that already had occurred. Following the Packers 33 – 14 win over the Raiders in Super Bowl II, Films produced the contest's highlight film that was titled **"One More Moment for the Master"** which was narrated by William Woodson with the same fervor as a John Facenda narration. Sam Spence produced the music with passion as usual and the piece reached its climax with the Packers' head coach lifted up on* *the shoulders of his players, being carried away, the conquering hero: Woodson's narration: "At 6:06 eastern standard time, Vince Lombardi was carried off the football field for the last time. He was carried not to just the locker room but to a few steps closer to the Hall of Fame". With that the title appears again and with the music of the western piece;* **"Open Prairie"** *carries all of us as well as Lombardi to a wonderful place. It was features like that, that "hooked" me and as mentioned before millions of others. But NFL Films and in particular Ed's son could create humor out of a most physical contest as well as creating visceral moments: In 1969, the company produced its first tongue and cheek look at the game with the* **"Football Follies":** *(See Chapter III) a collection of fumbles, bumbles, mistakes and miscues. Players received the half hour look at the humorous side of Pro Football with surprisingly acceptance. Films continues to produce follies to this day and had used both Vincent Price and Jonathan Winters in some of those specials but it was the five minute production of* **"Joe and the Magic Bean"** *that earned young Sabol his first of many awards. In the middle 70's Steve created a fairy tale about a magic bean (football) that all dared to throw but only one could as if he was magical: Joe Namath guaranteed he could and would throw it better than anyone but the big bad men of the NFL would teach young Joe a lesson: They had someone older and wiser; (John Unitas), who had been throwing the bean for years and could do it better. 90% of the footage shown was from Super Bowl III and in the end, Joe threw it better and with one of the most famous shots from NFL Films; Joe is headed to the locker room with his right hand held high signaling "number one". The narrator ends with; "The End". The narration was read by Sterling Holloway, whose voice had been heard for many years for Disney characters including Winnie the Pooh. However, my recollection of the reluctant soldier in the movie;* **"A Walk in the Sun"** *was his role as a television repair man in the 1964 Twilight Zone Episode;* **"What's in the Box"?** *Actress Joan Blondell and William Demarest is a married couple who have their television repaired by Holloway. However, the television now is able to transmit 30 seconds into the future and Demarest sees himself killing his wife (Blondell) by landing a right hand squarely on her jaw as she proceeds to crash through the fourth floor window and pummels to her death to the pavement below. As the police escort her husband away, Holloway appears and asks; "Everything okay with television set sir" and turns to the camera. When NFL Films relocated to one NFL Plaza in Mt. Laurel, New Jersey, in 2001 my son would visit me and hang out in the new building and would always want to watch* **"Joe and the Magic Bean".** *When I asked why he liked it so much he said "because I know the guy who wrote the poem". Add one more from the Cacchiotti family as fans of NFL Films.*

Chapter Eleven: Costume Jewelry, "Two for Rocky" and "In this Corner".

*By the spring of 1977, I was no longer working at Ann and Hope and my income came from selling costume jewelry, which I would "buy" from my Dad. At one time, Rhode Island was the jewelry capital of the world. Jewelry manufacturers were many and would produce an overflow of goods so that they could sell the overruns for cash. My dad was the shrewdest man I ever knew. He always stated; "Selling is easy, buying is hard". Anyone can sell a product if there is demand but if there is not, buying becomes all important and no one could buy better than "Joe Cash". A familiar transaction: I would go with my dad to a manufacturer that was looking to unload some overrun of goods. My dad would have three thousand dollars cash in his pocket and **that's** how much he was going to spend and not a penny more. Once he looked at the jewelry he would ask the owner, "How much for the lot"? Many times the response was three times what my dad wanted to spend and my dad would apologize to the owner for "taking up his time". When the owner would ask what my dad wanted to spend, he would say: "I have $3,000.00 in my pocket and I want to put it in your pocket". Of course the used car salesman would negotiate and my dad would reply with the same response. Eventually my dad took the three thousand dollars out of his pocket and put it in the owner's pocket. I was able to purchase many goods from "Joe Cash" without taking anything out of my pocket. With the merchandise at a gross cost of nil I was able to sell. "See selling is easy, buying is hard"! I would sell costume jewelry to universally known cities such as Fitchburgh, Auburn, Maynard, and Chelmsford, Massachusetts. I very seldom traveled alone and had my high school friend Richard Merlino accompany me on my "business" trips. Many times we would leave in the morning so we could finish our run(s) early and be back in time for some leisure activities which always included many vices. We felt once business had been taken care of we owed it to ourselves to now celebrate. We did often usually resulting in a negative profit but what the heck: I knew how to buy jewelry! We also socialized whenever we could: Friday Night during the Disco era was a time for letting loose. TGIF was without question the day(s) of our lives. We would psyche ourselves up by looking forward to what the night would bring by purchasing beer and other beverages to prime ourselves for what would be a night of drinking. Our other partner in crime was Louie Esposito, whose sister Sandra was someone Richard and I always wanted to include in our excursions. However, her brother decided it wasn't a good idea. Richard and I could never understand why.*

Gridiron Gumshoe

*Friday was met with such anticipation that the other six days of the week really didn't exist except for those days when I needed to "buy" jewelry from my dad. We lived for those nights and would take Richard's Oldsmobile Cutlass 442 Monte Carlo wherever we went. However, Richard had a problem differencing between civilian driving and Formula One racing. It was a regular occurrence for Louie and me to fight over; "I'll sit in the back"! Many times the humorous sight of two men sitting in the back seat together while another man drove could be seen by other motorists. One particular Friday night my high school buddy decided to see how many times he could go through a traffic light once it had turned red. I don't mean through the yellow caution on the fly. I mean bring the vehicle to a dead stop, survey the surroundings and with both Louis and I pleading "**No**" would take off in search for another. He even drove through an intersection obeying the rules of the road when the light had turned green but had to stop, back up, wait for the light to turn red and then "gun it". A total of 32 street infractions were committed that night breaking his **own** world record by four which he had established one week earlier. Another time: Richard drove the three of us from Providence to Fenway Park in Boston, to see the Red Sox play. The trip usually would take a good hour and a half but Richard broke his own world record by thirty four minutes which included a stop for a "beer and a dog" prior to finding our seats. Neither Louie or I actually saw the destination routes; 95 or 93 North on our way: I just focused my attention on Louie's rosary beads.*

*In December of 1976, the movie "**Rocky**" was released in Theatres: A journeyman boxer from Philadelphia played by Sylvester Stallone (who also wrote the script) gets a chance to fight for the Heavyweight Title against Champion Apollo Creed, played by former NFL Player; Carl Weathers, who appeared in eight games for the Oakland Raiders in 1970 and 1971. Against insurmountable odds, Rocky Balboa goes the distance of 15 rounds before losing a controversial split decision against the Champion. Does anyone see a sequel? The movie is not the first kind of that type of sports genre but it is inspiring, giving hope to the underdog and when you take into consideration the uplifting music score; "**Rocky**" is a success. Incidentally, the music was composed by Johnston, Rhode Island's Bill Conti. Stallone later would say; "I knew we had a hit with Bill because he was Italian". The movie won three academy awards including best picture.*

*Today; it is an everyday occurrence to see a movie more than one time. With "**On Demand**" many DVD releases are available the same day as a video release. Now at the touch of your remote in your private screening room at your* *own leisure you can enjoy a movie. Back then, however to see a movie more than once or for that matter 19 times you were forced to drive to the destination. Gregg Pappas and I both rabid New York Giants' fans would have a Saturday Night ritual during the duration of time the movie* **"Rocky"** *was playing: We would see a movie and finish our night with dinner at the restaurant; Papa Brillo's where we feasted on steamers, two large carafes of Chianti and "Chicken Milano con fungi". I think we order the chicken dish just because we liked the way the title of our main entry rolled off the tongue; "Chicken Milano con foongee". Every Saturday Night we drove to the Showcase movie complex on route 6 in Seekonk, Massachusetts and decided on any other movie than* **"Rocky"** *for our movie experience that night. Just when we would decide on* **"Kingdom of the Spiders"** *with William "Captain Kirk" Shatner, Tiffany former Playboy centerfold Bolling and one time Los Angeles Rams' Woody Strode, we would get to the ticket booth and in perfect synchronicity the two of us would blurt out "Two for Rocky"! The movie* **"Jaws"** *came in a close second with 18 movie appearances.*

I was caught up in "Rocky mania" and decided to give my hand(s) a chance at pugilism in the winter of 1977. I began to train in my garage where I hooked up heavy and speed bags; and three hours a day the sounds of "Ace Cash" throwing double jabs, straight right hands and crushing left hooks could be heard by my mom as she went about her daily household chores. At dinner I rested, much to the delight of my next door neighbor; Mr. Russo, those that worked at the nearby car wash and of course Mrs. Cacchiotti. I also would jump rope to the sounds of disco in that same garage until I physically couldn't continue and plus it was time for dinner. My "official" sight of training was in an armory in Fall River, Ma. Under the guidance of Bill Moser, a former boxer who at five feet four inches fought the only way he knew how: "small". I was down to a hard 140 pounds, standing at five foot eight inches and wanted to fight "tall". Because Bill was a smaller fighter he would bend at the waist and try to get underneath the jab(s) of his taller opponent where he could do damage. The problem was I wanted to fight straight up throwing out my left hand keeping my opponent away and I could use **that** *to* **my** *advantage. Bill had me fight "small": So there I was stalking; like one of those crabs who could only move to the side and with that bigger claw throw whenever I got close. The very first night while incorporating this new "style" I looked like I was one of those giant crustaceans from the 1957 horror flick;* **"Attack of the Crab Monsters"**, *which is a sci-fi classic: A research team on a lonely item is stalked by giant crabs who after eating the brains of their victims begin* *to talk like them. Yep, that was me trying to fight "small". I had difficulty getting home that first night because I couldn't remember how to walk naturally. Also, remember the movie;* **"Alias Jesse James"** *starring Bob Hope as Milford Farnsworth; a life insurance salesman who sells an insurance policy of $100,000.00 unknowingly to the notorious outlaw and then somehow has to retrieve the policy? Well Farnsworth has to learn how to shoot a gun and is advised how James leans to the right when the wind blows from the west and how James will lean to the left when the wind blows from the east before he fires. Bob Hope is hysterical as he tries to emulate such movements before the "showdown". Well when I came home that first night after learning how to fight "small", I could have been Bob Hope's stand in. I decided then to look for a new manager and went to the Petronelli Brothers' Vito and Goode in Brockton, Massachusetts, where the late former heavyweight champion Rocky Marciano trained. At the time middleweight number one contender Marvin Hagler was the Petronelli's' "top guy". Hagler had just come back from Philadelphia with a decision win over Willie "The Worm" Monroe. He now had avenged the only two losses in his career after beating Bobby "Boogaloo" Watts earlier. The soon to be middleweight champion of the world was in the process of adding "Marvelous" to his name and was selling tee shirts that read "Marvelous" Marvin Hagler for a dollar and wanted to know* **"How many** *did I want"? Hagler was chiseled and with his bald cranium was very intimidating. But I was a boxer, no make that a fighter and would not be intimidated and bought only a dozen.*

The "sport" of boxing taught me many lessons that I continued to use throughout my life: Mentally I was never more focused. Physically I became a fanatic with the arduous task of working out and to this day no one has more of a "stick-to-itiveness" than me. But to go into the ring takes a very special individual: The training is brutal: I would awake a five A.M. Monday through Friday and run five miles from my home, down Reservoir avenue, right on Park Ave, straight through Gansett Avenue, to Cranston Street, right on Niantic Avenue, passed Lang's Bowlarama and back to Reservoir to my home at 129 Legion Way. Five times a week I was in the garage and three nights a week at Petronelli's gym where I learned how to get beat up in sparring. Even when you "practiced" you took a beating. Do you know why fighters wrap their hands and cover them with leather gloves? Well, I used to think it was for protection for their opponents so when getting hit would "soften" the blow. Well in actuality it is to protect the fighter's hands so he won't break a wrist or a knuckle as he delivers a punch that will rearrange any part of your anatomy.

I remember a "friend" of mine at the gym wanted to spar with me. He had just received new 12 ounce leather gloves and wanted to break them in on me; literally. I of course, am the one side of mano y mano: Well, if I have the choice between being thrown from a second floor window to the pavement below or sparring against new 12 ounce leather gloves worn by my "friend": You get the idea!

I had been sparring for many rounds but could never really find it in me to deliver what was known as "the killer instinct". There were times when I could see my sparring partner hurt after taking a couple of shots from me but I just could not "take him out" and that is why I decided that my first official fight - would be my last: On Thursday May 12th, 1977 I was scheduled to fight at Jack Witschi's Sports' Arena on Route One in North Attleboro, Massachusetts, a complex most remembered for wrestling matches as far back as 1934 and through the years names like Killer Kowalski, Gorgeous George, Argentina Rocca and Pedro Morales graced the "squared circle". Other attractions: Circuses, three on three matches in the mud, a man wrestling an alligator and a woman fighting a 300 pound bear. Two years later on September 20th, 1979, Witschi's burnt to the ground leaving behind more than charred wood but everlasting memories as was the case for me on that spring night in May, 1977.

When you think of two fighters entering the ring against each other, you would think that both know each other's strengths and weaknesses but that is not the case at the lowest level of the "sport" which I was partaking in. I was schedule to fight someone that I had met earlier at the armory in Fall River. The boxers schedule to fight on the card lined up in single file; waiting to get weighed. Right behind me in line was an African American young man who must have stood six feet three but was thin. I am thinking; "this guy musts want to fight "tall". I weighed in at 134 pounds, a true lightweight and my new "friend" 147. "Whew". Meanwhile my scheduled opponent must have visited McDonald's on the way over to Jack Witschi's and "tipped" the scales at 149. Moser, who still felt as if he began my "career", scrambled for me to fight someone else: "Hey this guy weighed in at 135" (and with a record of ten wins and no losses which came to my attention following our fight). "You will fight him". Bill introduces me to my new opponent; "Hello, this is my fighter Ace Cash and you are"? "Is Killer your real name"? We were schedule to fight fourth. The most afraid I have ever been in my life took place when I walked down the aisle with the spotlight solely on me as I wondered would the Romans "thumb down" me. Once I entered the ring I was not able to see the over 1,500 that came to witness the execution. Yet, I could focus on individuals and could see my dad, his friend; "Pic", my uncle John, Richard Merlino, Larry Gibson, Bobby Stravato, Jeff Wilson, many female friends from Lang's Bowlarama and some guy dressed in a black hooded robe holding a sickle. I certainly looked confident: I wore white satin trunks with red stripes down both left and right sides and my white shoes matched with three red stripes across each instep. I was five foot eight with a waist of 29 and one half inches. I was in shape. After all I ran five miles five days a week, sparred numerous rounds, could hit both speed and heavy bags as if I owned my own (which I did) and trained at the same gym as former Heavyweight Champion Marciano, former middleweight Champion; Paul Pender, light heavyweight champion; Willie Pastrano and the soon to be middleweight Champion of the World; "Marvelous" Marvin Hagler. As my opponent and I did the proverbial stare down: He: as if I called his mom a bad name and me; saying "Hi" to Richard Merlino, my first "official" fight got underway: Remembering my training; I "threw" out a left jab, which was countered by a right hand that knocked me back into the ropes. I am not sure if I was in the fetal position in the corner but I knew his punch count was adding up. I'm thinking; "When is the round going to end"? Finally after the longest 20 seconds of my life I responded with a left to the body and a straight right which landed flush on his left shoulder. My opponent obviously was in some type of duress and tried to shake off the effects from the punch but by now the one handed fighter was in no condition to continue. Of course with that "Killer instinct" I did not finish him off much to the chagrin of Rich Merlino who was screaming; "KILL HIM"! I didn't but was awarded a technical knockout in a grand total of 58 seconds which was 14 seconds quicker than Ken Norton stopped Duane Bobick earlier that year on March 2nd. I was undefeated, a celebrity, and with a great future in the "sport", decided to retire on top. I gave away my gloves that night to my "friend" who now had two pairs of ounces weighed bricks but kept my trunks and those cool shoes and with the urging of my friends attended Lang's in my suit of armor: No more grapefruit juice on the rocks, "How about a vodka tonic"? No more boiled chicken with a salad and no dressing; "How about a cheeseburger and of course with lettuce, tomato and mayonnaise"? And no more abstaining from sex; "What can I get for twenty dollars, please?"

To play any sport at any level takes an incredible amount of sacrifice to excel but no one will convince me otherwise that fighters are not cut from a different *cloth: I have the greatest admiration for those that "square off" against each other knowing he or she will never be the same following the encounter. I was never the same. Even now when I look at the trunks and the shoes I wore that night in May of 1977, I ask myself; "Do you think I could get two dollars each for those "Marvelous" Marvin Tee shirts"?*

Chapter Twelve: "The Hackensack Hackers", "Miracle of the Meadowlands" and "Mighty Men and Magic Moments".

As I mentioned in Chapter two: I had been a New York Giants' fan since 1963, the last of three consecutive years the team had won the eastern division title and although the Giants never captured an NFL Championship during that time, the team did set club records for most points with 448 and touchdowns scored with 39. Quarterback Y.A, Tittle threw for 36 touchdowns breaking the league mark of 33 which he had set one year earlier. However, the team only had two winning seasons prior to the 1978 campaign: With a chance to make the playoffs in the year of the merger, the Giants needed to win their last game of the regular season in 1970 against the Los Angeles Rams at Yankee Stadium and lost 31 – 3. In 1972, the Giants ended their season with a convincing 23 – 3 win over the playoff bound Dallas Cowboys to finish at 8 and 6. In the process, Giants' quarterback Norm Snead was the NFC's leading passer. Although Gregg and I were as loyal as fans could be with our "Big Blue" club we knew the team wasn't that good and referred to the team from the Jersey Meadowlands as "The Hackensack Hackers" because of the town's close proximity to Giants' Stadium. However, in 1978 the Giants sported a 5 and 3 mark half way through the season (the league had added two games to the regular season). Was this the year Giants' fans could rejoice in a post season appearance? But as was the case with the previous "Hackensack Hackers" all hopes for a post season appearance were lost when the Giants dropped their next three contests, including a hard to swallow 16 – 13 loss to the Washington Redskins in overtime on that "Damn Mark Moseley's 35 yard field goal". But just when Giants' fans thought it couldn't get any worse it actually did one week later against Dick Vermeil's Philadelphia Eagles: The Eagles had defeated the Giants in eight of nine previous encounters and were in the midst of a 9 and 7 season that would be enough for the team to reach post season play for the first time since the 1966 season*. That November 19th encounter would be for Giants' fans; "A day that would live in infamy"! The Giants led 17 – 12 with less than two minutes left in the game after Otis McKinney's only interception of the season came after a Ron Jaworski deflected

---

* *The Eagles lost to the Baltimore Colts 20 – 14 one week after the 1966 NFL Championship in the "Runner up Bowl" which was played between the two second place finishers of each division in Miami. Following the 1969 season the game was no more.*

pass. The next series of events would change incredibly Giants' fortunes; for the best. Stay tuned and I will explain: With the CBS credits rolling, the unthinkable happened: Giants' quarterback Joe Pisarcik and fullback Larry Csonka could not execute a simple hand off and Eagles' defensive back Herman Edwards scooped up the fumbled ball and returned it 26 yards for the "I can't believe what just happened" touchdown. While all this is transpiring I am on the phone with my soon to be first wife Debbie Mallozzi when I barely could be heard saying "No". "I have to go". That Sunday Night, Gregg and I decided to go to Papa Brillo where Debbie and her girlfriend Patty would meet us. My girlfriend didn't see the game and really couldn't understand what the big deal was; "it's only a game"! With that; Gregg and I following dinner re enacted the most infamous play in the New York Football Giants' history in the parking lot of the restaurant. We might have looked rather comical because we showed the play from three different angles. The play would always be referred to as **"The Miracle of the Meadowlands"** *and years later would be included in some of NFL Films' productions:* **"The 100 Greatest Football Follies", "Worst Coaching Decisions"** *and* **"The 100 Greatest Touchdowns".** *The day after the loss the Giants fired their offensive coordinator Bob Gibson and following the season; their head coach John McVay and general manager Andy Robustelli. The reason why there was such uproar: Why didn't the Giants' quarterback just take a knee and run out the clock? Well after Pisarcik took a knee on first down he was roughed up by the Eagles as he knelt down. McVay didn't want to see his QB take some unnecessary punishment and decided to run Csonka, who hadn't fumbled all year. Through the years; NFL Films replayed the game and in particular the last series in some features but in actuality; Films misses a crucial play: Yes, Pisarcik took a knee which made it second down and eleven. But the Giants did run Csonka off tackle and the big fullback gains ten. The play worked and* **that** *is why the Giants ran it again. The viewer is under the impression that following Pisarcik's kneeling, Csonka fumbled on the very next play and that is not accurate but it makes a better story; not to include the run of ten yards on second down. Also, whenever NFL Films included the* **"Miracle of the Meadowlands"** *in some of its productions, an African American Woman can be seen with her mouth open in amazement following the debacle play. Well that woman first appeared in Memorial Stadium in the 1975 game played between the Colts and the Miami Dolphins but it was such a great reaction that she found herself at many stadiums in many future NFL Films' productions.*

Gridiron Gumshoe

During the 1990's Ken Sheil; a producer for Films did an in depth look on how that one play from November 19ᵗʰ, 1978 turned the Giants' fortunes from negative to positive: After the team let go of their general manager and head coach, the Giants hired George Young as their new GM and Ray Perkins as their new man in charge. Perkins led the Giants to their first playoff appearance in 18 years in 1981. Their first draft choice for 1979 was quarterback Phil Simms. Giants' fans were less than enthused when Commissioner Pete Rozelle announced his name but Simms would become the team's all time leading passer in many categories and in 1981 arguably the greatest linebacker to ever play Pro Football became a member of the "Big Blue Wrecking Crew" when Lawrence Taylor wore the red, white and blue jersey number 56 for 13 seasons. In 1983, Young selected Bill Parcells as the new head coach for the Giants and although his 1ˢᵗ year was a disaster at 3 wins 12 losses and one tie he took the club to five playoff appearances in seven years that included NFL Championships at Super Bowls XXI and XXV. Incredibly on what was the New York Giants' darkest day in November of 1978; emerged at the end of the season: okay here it comes; "A bright light at the end of the tunnel". "Well what did you expect working for Films for twenty years: Anything less than a metaphor"?

The NFL season of 1978 also had its' share of new rules and changes: The regular season increased from 14 to 16 games. It was now legal for a forward pass to be caught from one offensive player to another and defensive backs were not allowed to "bump" any receiver(s) after five yards from the line of scrimmage. That rule was indirectly known as the "Mel Blount Rule" in reference to the Pittsburgh Steelers' very physical defensive back. NFL Films would do its best to educate fans by explaining in their yearend review titled **"Mighty Men and Magic Moments".** *The 48 minute highlight feature is without question one of the most entertaining and informative productions reviewing the season of 1978. Films spent an awful lot of time with the wiring of head coaches and we get to see and hear many of what happens on the sidelines during the actual time; three hour contest: Kansas City head coach Marv Levy can be heard; "You know I went to school with that official" and then berating that same official with "Hey you over officious jerk"! We also hear: O.A."Bum" Phillips the head coach of the Houston Oilers scolding a line judge: "Hey that's three holding penalties against one team in a quarter in a half" and with a slight reaction from the official; Bum replies; "That ain't funny". And from Seattle Seahawks' Jack Patera; "Don't you think you officials should turn this thing around a little and call it even on penalties"?*

Again another; "Oh shut up"! It is amazing to watch and realize how NFL Films was able to acquire all this footage throughout the season and create a recap in just 48 minutes. Of course there are the great plays and the great stories that made that season so memorable, including a rather lengthy segment on the Philadelphia Eagles and their third year head coach Dick Vermeil. Films followed the team closely and had Vermeil wired on three different occasions. I can in all honesty say I hated the Eagles mainly because they always beat the Giants and I didn't want to watch the Eagles' head coach cry. Plus, I hated their cream cheese! At the end of the segment which had also included the November 19th game against the Giants, Philadelphia needed a win in their season finale to reach the playoffs for the first time since their 1960 NFL Championship. They are at home playing against my favorite team. Vermeil is wired and although Philadelphia has the game in hand the Eagles' head coach can't relax until linebacker Frank Lemaster intercepts a Pisarcik pass and returns it nine yards for a touchdown. The Eagles win; 20 – 3 and make the playoffs. NFL Films had access to the Eagles' locker room at Veterans Stadium and we can see Jaworski yelling; "Were winners" and Vermeil crying on the shoulders of Eagles' owner Leonard Toes: "This was for you"!

I remember watching the show with mixed emotions. The production was top notch and you get to see all the great plays that made the season exciting including the 35 – 31 victory by the Pittsburgh Steelers over the Dallas Cowboys at Super Bowl XIII but I wanted the Giants to make the playoffs and yet for Philadelphia Eagles' fans it was quite moving especially if you liked their cream cheese.

Chapter Thirteen: "Roots", "John Facenda is on the phone" and "I do" (for the first time).

I met my first wife; Debbie Mallozzi in the summer of 1978 at a discotheque in Franklin, Ma. The five foot one inch dirty blonde haired 21 year old caught me staring at her and since I was so discreet I decided to strike up a conversation with her. She worked for an insurance agency, taught jazz and ballroom dancing. Debbie would also perform at both in some productions. Immediately I thought what she must have looked like in one of those jazz outfits: The kind that always seems to accentuate a tight gluteus max. But what really "won me over" was that we shared a couple of seven ounce Miller High Life draft beers in my car that Saturday Night. That did it for me: She could hang and plus I couldn't wait to see her in one of those outfits. We dated for two years. The very first NFL game we watched on television together was Saturday night's August 12ᵗʰ 1978 exhibition (later to be called pre – season) game between the New England Patriots and Oakland Raiders; the night Darryl Stingley's professional football career was cut short by a vicious hit delivered by the Raiders' Jack Tatum, which left the Patriots' receiver paralyzed until his death at the age of 55 in 2007.

*Most of my time was now being taken up by my future wife and my "job" at selling costume jewelry: In 1979, Ed "Fast Eddie" Skovron and I decided to advertise in Atlanta, Chicago and Dallas for people who could sell our goods in those major cities. One person who responded was Harvey Alcorn, who had created a unique jewelry item in sterling silver which is actually 92.5% of pure silver. The piece looked like a tree trunk with a thin chain of 18 inches to complete the necklace. Harvey called it **"Roots"** and wanted to know could we manufacture it? Eddie and I flew to Dallas and met our new "partner" and we enjoyed our two day stay in **"Big D"** visiting some night time establishments. Anything and everything is bigger in Texas; especially the women and I mean that in the most flattering way. When we came back to Rhode Island we decided to manufacture the new item working with my brother in law Steve Torregrossa who married my sister Paula, but not in sterling silver but in white metal and we also took it upon ourselves to see if we could add the logo of the 28 NFL teams to the piece itself. The first was the Dallas Cowboys' logo. I wrote a 50 word synopsis on the Cowboys' history so as to speak the team's **"Roots"** completing the piece but we now faced that "damn copyright crap" with NFL Properties: "Regretfully we were denied" and what* *could have been was in actuality: no chance of happening. It would not be the last time that the league office would "put the kibosh" on some of my ideas.*

*My office was located on 412 Broadway in Providence a main drag that connected downtown Providence to an area known as Olynville, which was a much smaller version of the capital city but without the hotels, restaurants and arts. Actually it wasn't anything like the capital city. One day when I was busy watching television still pouting over my encounter with NFL Properties; I heard a voice I recognized: It was NFL Films' John Facenda "pitching" life insurance for some company. I took down the number, called it and after some private eye work called three different numbers and left a message for "the voice of God". My message: "Mr. Facenda; my name is Ace Cacchiotti. I own the company Ace Creations and am in the process of contacting the NFL with my new jewelry item. I will be looking for a spokesperson for the product. At your leisure please contact at me at 401 421 4208". I mean; 401 555 4208. "Thank you". Although I was already denied by the league I thought "What the hell, imagine if he calls back"! One week later in my office being just as busy as I was that week prior, I was on the phone with Dan Rinaldi; who only came to work at his leisure, when I hear a beep indicating someone else is calling. "Hold on Dan". "This is Ace" and on the other line I hear; "Ace Cacchiotti, John Facenda returning your call". "Hold on Mr. Facenda". "Dan, John Facenda is on the line I'll call you back"! "Thank you Mr. Facenda and I went into my business mode explaining my connection with the league and the **"Roots"** jewelry piece. We ended with to keep in touch and then "Oh one more thing sir; "I am in awe of your voice and blah blah NFL Films, blah, blah, blah (this was before the yada, yada, yada) since I was a small boy blah, blah, blah" and with that we said goodbye. It was the only time I ever spoke with him: John Facenda died September 26th, 1984, which was four years before I became an intern in 1988 with the company.*

By now Debbie and I had set the date to be married that would take place on October 26th, 1980; a Sunday during football season. (Whatever happened to a June wedding)? As the date neared I continued to sell my goods on the road with Dan as my co pilot although not one time did ever he drive. Dan became a confidant and someone who has had a major impact in my life. Dan knew more about me than I knew basically because I would forget after a night of drinking with him. As a matter of fact on the morning of my wedding day we were "working" at the office: Dan convinced me that marriage was a good thing and for posterity we recorded our conversation that Sunday morning. Recently, I listened to that tape and at no time did I hear my best man say

64

Gridiron Gumshoe

I should get married but all the arrangements had been made and Debbie and I were married at St. Ann's Catholic Church in Cranston. I remembered the priest asking "Do you take" and turning to my best man; gave me the nod. With that; "I do". I did and my new bride and I became husband and wife and two days later we spent our honeymoon in North Conway, New Hampshire, where I spent most of the week on my stomach with the worst case of hemorrhoids in a room at the ski lodge where the two newlyweds did not even know how to ski! Oh, and one more thing: The Giants lost to the Denver Broncos that Sunday 14 – 9.

Chapter Fourteen: Thursday Nights, "My good friend Earl Holliman" and "The History of Pro Football".

At 27 years of age, I was married to a wonderful young woman, had a business that began to prosper and continued to keep in contact with all my childhood friends. Since 1977, my buddies from the old neighborhood would get together and play basketball at Our Lady of Providence located on 21 Regent Avenue about a mile away from downtown Providence. Dave, Kevin and Dan Rinaldi, Jeff Alexander, Vinnie Escoli, Mark Del Deo and his buddy Steve who we called "Apple" for reasons no one knew, Pete Crisostomi, me and some other guys whom we would recruit from a nearby basketball court ran up and down that hardwood floor trading baskets for two straight hours. Those Thursday Night contests were very competitive and Dan and I who always played on the same team needed an "edge" prior to the games: We would finish work at 4:30 P.M. and head to our favorite bar consuming two Michelob beers, two shots of some brown stuff and two dozen wing dings. Once we had the "edge" we needed, we arrived on time to play ball. During warm-ups we would look at each other and in sync; "I'm still drunk". It didn't matter because even in a stupor we knew we could still play based on our abilities to know where each other was at all times. Example: Whenever the ball was turned over I would run to retrieve it and Dan would be breaking away towards the other basket when I would lead him beautifully for an uncontested layup. After four years of playing you would think by now the other team would get wise but we believed they thought we were still feeling the effects of our "edge". Thursday Night basketball was one of my favorite time(s) in my life but just one of many most memorable with Dan:

In April of 1981, Dan and I loaded up about $8,000.00 worth of wholesale jewelry and headed south to Atlanta with stops in New York City, Philadelphia, and Silver Springs, Maryland before reaching Georgia's capital. Whenever we went on the road, I paid all expenses and would pay Dan whatever I felt. On this trip which would take seven days, I promised Dan; one thousand dollars. After a stay over in Fredericksburg, Virginia we arrived at the Hilton Hotel in downtown Atlanta 10 hours later. Once there we noticed three huge trailers with cables and wires and what seemed to be motion picture cameras. I knew I started to make a name for myself but all this for our arrival? In actuality, Orion Pictures were producing the movie **"Sharkey's Machine"** *starring Burt Reynolds, who also directed. Tom Sharkey*

Gridiron Gumshoe

(Reynolds) is a vice cop who puts together a group of gung ho associates to bring down an Atlanta crime lord (Vittorio Gassman). Other actors: Brian Keith, Henry Silva, Charles Durning, Rachel Ward, Earl Holliman and Bernie Casey, the former NFL wide receiver for the San Francisco 49ers and Los Angeles Rams. Not only would the hotel serve as a backdrop in many scenes of the movie but many of the actors would be residing at the hotel during the production. Once Dan and I checked in I began to make arrangements to sell the rest of the jewelry to Ken Alphin who owned Alphin Wholesale Jewelry on 419 Bankhead Highway in Atlanta not far from the hotel. Dan informs me he is going down to the hotel gym to work out. Once I have secured my business with Ken, I head down to the gym area where I see Dan working out holding a conversation with the actor Brian Keith who is "curling" about 110 pounds in each hand. Keith was a big man who towered over both Dan and me. After our session, Dan and I decided to see Atlanta at night. Southern belles are many. The next day we "dumped" the "load" for $5,700.00: "We're rich"! During our stay we got to see some production of the movie and individually some of its "stars": While in the elevator traveling up to my room a man wearing sun glasses got on at the fifth floor and is headed to the "Space Lounge" when he says "Space Lounge"; "That is where you go to get high". Just as I am about to get off at the eleventh floor, I turn and yell; "Hey you're Henry Silva" You were in the **"Outer Limits"** *in the episode* **"The Mice"** *(gee was that the best I could come up with?) "Yes I am". I responded with "Okay Goodbye". Another time I recognize Bernie Casey; again in the elevator and asked "Do you miss football"? "Hell no"! "Okay Goodbye". My conversations with my new "friends" were at best succinct unlike my main man Dan, who had a buddy named Earl Holliman. The night before we were to leave Atlanta, I went down to the gym to work out when I see Dan in one of those steam boxes where all you can see is the occupant's head and he is introducing me to the man who co starred with Angie Dickerson in the television series* **"Police Woman"**. *All I can see is Earl's head from another one of those steam boxes and after the proverbial introductions, Dan who had not asked for any of the $1,000.00 he has coming asks for money because he wants to go out that night. I playfully deny him where and when without missing a beat he responds with "No problem, I'll ask my good friend Earl!"*

Following the NFL season of 1981, NFL Films produced **"History of Pro Football"**, *a 90 minute special which covered the game's inception from 1920 to now what was its' 62ⁿᵈ season. Some of NFL Films most iconic shots are used in the production. Two of my favorites: The Green Bay*

Packers' Bart Starr running towards us in slow motion with helmet in hand being introduced and the Dallas Cowboys' Roger Staubach in a similar angle but tighter with helmet on; again right towards us. Throughout the features many are interviewed including the former defensive tackle from the Baltimore Colts' Art Donovan, who spins many a yarn at his country club bar near Baltimore. "Artie" tells the story how teammates' Gino Marchetti and Don Joyce "faced off" in a Maryland fried chicken eating contest to see which could eat the most chicken. Well in his most colorful story telling he begins: "Well here comes the food and Joyce starts to eat the mash potatoes, peas and we say for Christ sakes just eat the chicken"! "Gino eats 27, pieces but Joyce eats 37, or 38 and wins the bet". "With that Joyce says I'm full, I can't eat another bite; I need to wash it down"! "There is a big pitcher of iced tea and we say; There you go champ, eat it, I mean drink it all we don't care if he blows up we won the bet". "With that he pulls out a pack of saccharin the artificial sweetener and pours it into the pitcher: He was watching his calories"! Another colorful character from the golden age of Pro Football was Bob St. Clair, who played 11 seasons with the 49ers at offensive tackle. St. Clair who stood at six feet nine did and actually still does eat raw meat. It seems his grandmother used to feed him raw liver as a child and he grew accustomed to the taste. In the **"Fabulous Fifties"** *segment he tells the story how he was sitting down at the cafeteria at the 49ers' training camp with a small pile of dove hearts when this big rookie comes over to the table where he is and asks what was he was going to do with the hearts? St. Clair looks up and responds; "I am going to eat them". The rookie asks; "You mean in some sauce"? "Sauce", replies the veteran: "No; they're good just like this" and puts one in his mouth. St. Clair again: "He turned white as a ghost and I thought he was going to faint right there"! I had such a close encounter with the 1990 Hall of Fame Inductee in 1998 at Canton, Ohio. Following the Saturday that Tommy McDonald, Anthony Munoz, Dwight Stephenson, Mike Singletary and Paul Krause were inducted into the Pro Football Hall of Fame, St. Clair, his daughter Lynn, my wife Susan and I had dinner together. When it came time to order I knew what to expect but the poor waitress didn't: Bob asked for a flank steak and when our waitress wanted to know how he wanted it cooked, he replied; "Have them take it out of the refrigerator and put it on a plate under the lamp and bring it to me". Our waitress thought Bob meant rare but he was persistent. As funny as that was it is not the punch line to this story: My wife Susan does not eat meat and is allergic to all fish and nuts as well, so when she orders she has to be very specific. Susan ordered ravioli while*

Gridiron Gumshoe

Bob's daughter and I ordered some type of chicken fully cooked. When our food arrived all eyes are on the slab of meat on Bob's plate. It was there and then my wife conveyed to our waitress once again her allergic reaction to fish and if right on cue our waitress asked: "You want to know if there is any fish in the Lobster Ravioli"?

Chapter Fifteen: Thanksgiving (the truth), Atlanta (number two), and the "A.C.E. System".

Americans are under the assumption that we celebrate Thanksgiving on every **fourth Thursday** *in the month of November because it has something to do with Pilgrims landing at Plymouth Rock, Massachusetts in 1620. Well, that's partially true: The "official" first Thanksgiving was in 1621 when the Wampanoag Indians shared a harvest meal with the Plymouth Colonists giving thanks to the harvest and in general to all: But why on a Thursday? I mean Canada celebrates their holiday on the second Monday of October. Well, here is the truth: Some of the colonists believed that by reading tea leaves known as "tasseography" one could see the future and one colonist in particular saw that on a particular Thanksgiving Day, Thursday, November 29th, 1934 the Chicago Bears defeated the Detroit Lions 19 - 16 in front of 26,000 fans at the University of Detroit Stadium. That same colonist saw a family huddled around a box that emitted sounds from that game and realized that Professional Football was being played on that day. So without changing any event in the past that we all know could alter the events of the future, the colonists decided to continue to celebrate Thanksgiving Day on the fourth Thursday of November so that families could listen to the Professional Football game that day and thus become a family tradition. Incredibly, one other colonist, while performing that same art of tea leaf reading saw another NFL game being watched with images also on a box on November 22nd, 1956 between the Green Bay Packers and Detroit Lions, which also happened to be on a Thursday. From there it was a no brainer: Americans would celebrate Thanksgiving Day on the fourth Thursday of November every year so that families could huddle around either radios or televisions so that they could hear and view Professional Football. That's my story and I am sticking to it. Thanksgiving has always been my favorite holiday. I looked so forward to all that is the holiday: The gathering(s) of families, the wonderful anticipation of gorging oneself on traditional foods and of course Pro Football. Following a fifty seven day strike by the players' union the NFL resumed play on Sunday, November 21st, 1982. Four days later on Thanksgiving Day, the Giants played the Lions at Pontiac Stadium. In a defensive struggle the game entered the fourth quarter with the scored tied at 6 when the Lions threatened to take the lead at 11:52 remaining when Giants' linebacker Lawrence Taylor intercepted a pass thrown by Detroit's Gary Danielson at the three and raced 97 yards down the sidelines before sliding into home safely giving New York its first victory of the season. While number 56 is performing his coast to coast jaunt, I am running with him* *holding my feast; leaving behind a trail of mashed potatoes, cranberry sauce and a big drum stick. Once I had fixed my second "unofficial" helping of turkey, I settled in for the second game between Cleveland at Dallas.*

The Giants finished the regular season at four wins and five losses but were not one of the 16 teams to be invited to the playoffs based on some confusing tie breaking results although they shared the same record as the Detroit Lions, the same team they defeated on Thanksgiving day. The 1982 season ended on January 30th 1983 when the Washington Redskins defeated the Miami Dolphins 27 – 17 as the game's most valuable player; John Riggins rushed for 166 yards including a 43 yard game breaking touchdown in the fourth quarter in his team's victory.

Although I wanted the Dolphins to win, I wasn't really disappointed because I was in the process of coordinating another trip to Atlanta, Georgia where I had been financially successful two years earlier when Dan and I had visited the city. It would be two months before I would head south again but this time with my "I am here to have a good time" friend Richard Merlino. However, our stay in Atlanta would be strictly on a vacation basis because our main business was scheduled for Montgomery, Alabama where we would make the transaction of "goods" with a new client from Biloxi, Mississippi. In early April, we headed to Alabama's state capital and decided that both would share the driving with some basic rules: Neither could exceed the speed limit by more than the sound of speed and when we would encounter a traffic light that has turned red no individual records could be attempted that day. (See chapter eleven).We stopped in Richmond, Virginia for an overnight stay, stayed out of jail and continued on our journey; however not without a humorous moment: I had awakened first and showered when I turned to Richard who was "resting" in the other bed. "Are you going to shower"? Richard replies; "I am just going to brush my teeth" and gets out of bed throwing the blankets on the floor where I see he is fully dressed and incredibly he had slept with his shoes on so we could get a quick start on the next day's proceedings. Once again I had confirmation for a five day stay at the Atlanta Hilton downtown where my Schick Razor blade friend Richard Morrison secured a fee through his company at half price for us. Once in the city we visited the highly respectable "Gentlemen's club"; "Cheaters". We were able to fraternize with a couple of those employed at the establishment and Richard would not need me for any type of transportation or for that matter residence because his new acquaintance gave him two keys: One to her 1982 280 GTX and another to her apartment. The next morning I picked Richard up and the two of us headed to Montgomery for what would hopefully become a very lucrative transaction. It was - and 161 miles later we were back at our hotel and back to our favorite place with a great deal of money that by the night's end had noticeable dwindled. We made many new friends! I too had one special friend: Diane. Karen informed me she had been working at the club for two years and planned to "retire" soon as she had enough money for "the two of us". Not for me and her; she and her daughter! This story I had heard before. Being a frequent visitor to other Rhode Island establishments such as the "Foxy Lady" and the "Peppermint Lounge" I could only think this whole scenario would make an intriguing movie. It did many times including 1996's **"Striptease"** *starring Demi Moore as Diane or Karen. Actually in the film her name was Erin Grant. Once our "business" was finished, Richard and I headed home. On the way we stopped at a roadside establishment on wheels proclaiming "The Best Ribs in the South". "Rich, let's stop and pick some up for Dan". Two days later we returned with the ribs that had never been refrigerated. Dan couldn't have been happier.*

On October 31st, 1983, one of the NFL's founding fathers passed away at the age of 88: George Halas was a player, head coach, philanthropist, owner and the iconic long time leader of the Chicago Bears. Professional Football had lost a great man and two weeks later NFL Films paid tribute to "Papa Bear" with a look back at the history of the Chicago Bears in their weekly Pro Magazine series, which included numerous black and white footage; footage as far back as 1904. Other highlights: Harold "Red" Grange running, the NFL's first 1,000 yard rusher; Beattie Feathers and surprisingly good film quality from the 1940 Championship game won by the Bears 73 − 0 over the Washington Redskins. This was not the first time NFL Films had used black and white footage in some of their productions: As I mentioned previously, **"Big Game America"** *and* **"The History of Pro Football"** *included footage in their* **"Fabulous Fifties"** *segment and in 1980 Films' production:* **"Best Ever"** *looking back at the greatest who ever played Pro Football. But considering NFL Films' first ever game shot was in 1962 and in color; how did the company acquire such nostalgia? In 1980, NFL Films purchased the Tel Ra library for the amount of $30,000.00. 95% of the company's film stock was black and white and what was color was actually from two teams that had their own cinematographer; the Detroit Lions and New York Giants. In the spring of 1992; my fourth year with Films, I approached Steve and asked what was the "story" with all that black and white footage from Tel Ra? He informed me that it was only used periodically whenever the company* *did a nostalgia piece, i.e.* **"History of Pro Football".** *In his own words: "Well Ace, we've never really had anyone who could make any sense of what is in there (vault) and you are more than welcome to make any heads or tails of it". With Steve's blessing, I began to embark on a personal trek to log every single piece of black and white negative film stock which was introduced in a weekly series; Pro Football Highlights that "ran" from 1949 to 1964. By utilizing old media guides, I was able to name the players responsible for what was being displayed on the gridiron. Of course I added my own colorful characterizations along the way. For instance: "The Browns' Jim Brown takes the handoff from quarterback Tommy O'Connell, breaks through the first line of defense gets into the secondary and is off. The Syracuse graduate who in later years would star in the two riveting movie gems;* **"Riot"** *and* **"Tick, Tick, Tick"** *goes all the way as Rams' defensive backs Will Sherman and Corky Taylor can only catch a glimpse at the future Hall of Famer's backside". Because I typed at the speed of a sun dial, Diane Meo assumed the duties of incorporating my synopsis in a program designed by our "computer guy" Dave Franza. With this new tool we were now able to save an incredibly amount of research time looking for certain players. Now we could type in Frank Gifford's name and an extensive readout would appear for number 16. I also included other categories: Great catches, great runs, in climate weather and follies, which we used in 1994 when Dave Plaut and I worked on the* **"100 Greatest Follies"** *in NFL History. For two and a half years I logged that series working nights and weekends until I finished what would be appropriately named the* **"Advanced Cinematic Encyclopedia".** *The acronym: The* **A.C.E** *system. It was one of the many time-consuming projects I would immerse myself in during my stay with the company. It is something I was very proud of and is still used by the company and whenever I see any black and white footage used by ESPN, HBO, SHOWTIME, and the NFL NETWORK, I look to see if my name is listed in the credits. I am still looking.*

Chapter Sixteen: Divorce (number one), A new business (again) and "You are Walter Payton".

By the summer of 1984, I began to experience "happy feet", a lot like the Giants' Eli Manning had when he replaced starting quarterback Kurt Warner in week ten of the 2004 season. Pressure was getting to me and I had to move and escape the pocket of marriage. (Did I actual say that?). I can honestly say I was the reason for our separating. I just felt that I had not reached my potential, which is just another way of saying I wanted to see more women without the guilt of being married. Debbie was perfect: A beautiful young woman, a career in dancing and a wonderful partner who wanted to be married. On the other hand - I was a jerk. I embraced Friday nights with Richard Merlino so much more than I embraced my wife and finally we decided to separate. As soon as I realized that a divorce was possible, I "begged" for a second chance and that I would be more attentive to her and her family. For four years I basically called my own shots and Debbie was a wife in name only. I think what really changed my mind about leaving was when I attended one of her jazz recitals and she wore one of those revealing outfits and I thought "Oh my God, I may never see that gluteus max again". So after convincing her I would "change" she agreed and we decided to "stick it out". But in actuality I was very much like the character Wendell "Sonny" Lawson played by the actor Burt Reynolds in the movie **"The End".** *It seems Lawson has a rare disease and has only six months to live. He attempts suicide on many different occasions and is comically not successful. At the film's end he attempts to drown himself in the ocean but finds out that he does not have the disease any longer and has an epiphany and realizes he has a lot to live for. As he is struggling to make his way back to shore, he promises God that he would change his ways and be a good person if God would grant him the strength to swim back to shore. As he gets closer, he then amends a few promises that are really not life changing to the degree they were when he was farther out at sea. Now that he realizes he is going to make it back alive he now is his old self again. Well, that was me: I promised Debbie things were going to be different and for the better but once she agreed I reverted to my old self: On September 2nd the Giants opened the regular season at home against the Philadelphia Eagles, the same Sunday Debbie had asked me to join her at her parents' house for a cookout. What faced me was a monumental decision: The Giants' starting quarterback was Phil Simms who had not seen for all intents and purposes any length of regular season duty since 1981. Now under second year head coach*

Gridiron Gumshoe

Bill Parcells, many felt (Giants' fans) the team may be a considerable playoff contender. I really wanted to watch the game but if I didn't I may jeopardize my future with the former Miss Mallozzi. I told Debbie the importance of the game and she understood. She did understand but did not like the fact that I was that Wendell "Sonny" Lawson character. Simms had his best day as a pro completing 23 of 30 passes for 409 yards throwing for four touchdowns as New York defeated Philadelphia 28 – 27. Maybe the Giants are for real! They were and reached post season play with a nine and seven record, defeating the Rams in the wild card game before losing 21 – 10 to the eventual Super Bowl Champions' 49ers, as was the realization that I had "blown" it with my first wife. Once again I opted for a Sunday watching Pro Football with my friend Gregg Pappas instead of spending time with my wife and her family. It was the first and last time my wife ever requested my presence at one of her gatherings. Yes; I was an asshole! Debbie realized that I would never change and we divorced officially in the spring of 1985 but I was "free" and thriving in my new business which was manufacturing costume jewelry by way of casting lead and other "precious" metals - Well, the metal lead anyway.

Previously, I had attempted to produce white metal into a jewelry piece which looked liked a base of a tree with its roots and failed in my soliciting it to the NFL because of some "copyright crap".

Although I had been turned down by the National Football League in 1980, I would again get an opportunity to manufacture costume jewelry: My dad had purchased casting equipment he bought in a "closeout" and wanted me to cast jewelry for him as well as now for me. Now I had an outlet to sell to on a regular basis. Just think: Whenever I needed to go on the road and sell jewelry I would get it for free from my dad and whenever I manufactured cast items I would sell it to my dad for a profit. Now that's good business sense. The problem was Dan nor I knew anything about casting using any type of metal but since we had this opportunity we decided to make the best of it. The average temperature for lead to melt is at 800 degrees Fahrenheit but we were afraid to turn the heat up and would set the gage at 400 degrees which meant the metal never melted and we would waste many a day not understanding why. So I hired my friend Pete Crisostomi who had no jewelry experience to work with us and between us three decide to raise the temperature to 500 degrees. Then incredibly, my brother in law Steve told us it would melt at 800 degrees after spending three weeks in the casting business. One of the most comical sights was when we attempted to put a new bar of lead into the pot, when the temperature did not reach its peak. The pot would "pop" metal out

75

and we would "duck" for cover. Pete decided to hide behind a desk and then use a pole to push the brick in. It was then and only then we felt comfortable. Once we had conquered our fears I decided to change the name of business to Ace Casting and Sales, which was my fourth different business name change in four years. I changed my business name almost as much as the former NFL Player Alvin Maxson changed teams - who incredibly played for the Pittsburgh Steelers, Tampa Bay Buccaneers, Houston Oilers and New York Giants; all four teams in 1978!

*Now that I had mastered the art of casting, I was now responsible for all aspects of the jewelry industry; manufacturing, finishing, selling and delivering. The latter was my favorite: Dan and I would travel together to deliver the goods to our clients and would always make it our number one priority to celebrate after each sale. A book with those anecdotes may surface in another literary gem but for now I share this: After selling $380.00 worth of junk in Palmer, Massachusetts, the two of us headed east on route 20 back to Rhode Island, when we stopped into this massage pallor with the intention(s) of getting **only and only** a massage. The woman who greeted us must have worked for the owner because she was not one of those beautiful women who work at the spas I had seen in **"Club"** and **"Hustler"** magazines. We were escorted to the steam room where we both entered our individual steamed boxes. I asked would any other women be available of requests for other towels; "If we needed them?" One minute later, we were handed two towels by two other women who definitely had to have had been employed by Barnum and Bailey. Each must have "tipped" the scales at the Chicago Bears' William the "refrigerator" Perry's weight. By this time I had seen as much of the circus that I wanted and bluntly asked "are there any women that work here"? "What do you think we are"? I replied; "I mean women"! Dan and I quickly departed, finishing our journey at **"Cheaters"** in Auburn, Ma. Another one of our most memorable treks occurred when we left for New York City to deliver about three thousand dollars of finished casted goods to Mrs. Chin whose store was located in the Chinese district between 34th and 35th street on the east side. Dan and I would leave Rhode Island at 3:30 A.M. to get a head start before traffic became heavy on the Cross Bronx expressway. It would have been faster if we had traveled the FDR Drive but I always opted for the former because it was the way my Dad would take me into the "Big Apple" while he ate grapes with his Mario Andretti helmet on. We then would stop for breakfast before meeting Mrs. Chin. Our culinary delights were usually made up of the proverbial: eggs, bacon, toast, juice and coffee. However, one day we decided to diverge: "I'll*

have two eggs over easy with sausage, wheat toast, orange juice and coffee".
Dan: "I'll have three eggs scrambled, pancakes, ham, toast, tomato juice and
coffee. With that our waiter turns around to the cook and orders; "Two number
twos". I look at Dan and say; "Either one of us is not getting what we ordered
or that guy back there is the smartest mother f---ker who ever lived"!

In the fall of 1985, Ace Casting and Sales was actually making some money
as Dan and I continued to deliver goods once again in well known New
England cities; as Leicester, Maynard, Bellingham and Chelmsford, Ma. The
Giants were in the midst of their second straight playoff appearance sporting
one of the league's best defensive teams that season and Phil Simms would set
an NFL record for most passing yards in consecutive games with 432 against
the Cowboys on October 6th and 513 against the Cincinnati Bengals one week
later. My all time favorite player would also be selected to the Pro Bowl that
season and was named the game's Most Valuable Player by throwing for three
touchdowns in the second half as the NFC defeated the AFC. That 1985
season however, belonged to the Chicago Bears who crushed the New England
Patriots 46 – 10 in New Orleans at Super Bowl XX. The "windy city"
franchise was made up of a colorful collection of characters and produced a
rap video prior to their win at the Super Bowl, exuding much confidence along
the way that year. The Bears and the NFL's all time leading rusher; Walter
Payton who after eleven seasons with the Bears could now include an NFL
Championship to his already impressive resume. At Five foot ten 200 pounds,
"Sweetness" as he was called was not a large back as backs go but what he
lacked in size he more than made up for it in determination. (If there ever was
a line more used by NFL Films, I don't know of any). Incredible the Bears'
running back and I would cross paths on May 2nd 1986:

Richard Merlino and I would be traveling to Atlanta that weekend to sell more
junk. Once we arrived at the downtown Hilton we were pleasantly surprised
to be informed that the Boston Celtics were staying at the hotel and on that
Friday we went down to the restaurant for breakfast and saw some of the
Celtics' players that included Larry Bird, Danny Ainge and Robert Parrish.
Boston was in town for their playoff contests against the Atlanta Hawks. I
wanted to give the big three; Bird, Parrish, and Kevin Mchale their space and
I advised Richard to do the same. My friend abided and later while I am in
the hotel lobby he shows me three signatures from Larry Bird, Robert Parrish,
and Kevin McHale. He wasn't able to get Danny Ainge's because "he was
an asshole". Somehow I think the Celtics' guard meant that for Richard. I
went back to the restaurant and got Scott Wedman's autograph; but did ask

the waitress where Bird was eating and before she could clean the table I stole a napkin. Later, that afternoon, I notice someone that looked familiar and I unassumingly advance towards the Avis Rental Car booth to catch a closer glimpse of the five foot ten 200 pound black male; "You know you look a lot like Walter Payton". And with a voice that sounded like the King of Pop; Michael Jackson replied; "Yes I am". I replied; "I'm a Giants' fan and I can't wait for them to meet you again in the post season this year"! The gracious Payton gave me his autograph and wished me good luck. I would meet him again in Canton, Ohio when I handed him a copy of a two and a half minute highlight piece I produced for him during his induction in 1993. One of the classiest men to have ever played Pro Football would die six years later at the age of 45, after battling the rare liver disease sclerosing cholangitis. Many cried: As for the napkin: It came in handy.

One of my "jobs" at Ann &Hope
Department Store was to reach as high
as I could for mouthwash.

Another job: to look for sympathy.

My Schick Safety Razor Buddy:

Dick Morrison with our waitress
at the *Beef and* Bistro in Boston; 1974
from there it was to see the movie
"*The Longest Yard*" starring Burt Reynolds

From Left to Right:

Sisters' Paula and Teresa,

Niece Rachel (Paula's daughter)

and wife #1 Debbie

My Parents:

Mom and Dad

Carolina and Joseph Cacchiotti

How's this segue:

My parents instilled in me;

That it was better to give than receive

And I did in 1977 as the saddest looking

Santa Claus ever!

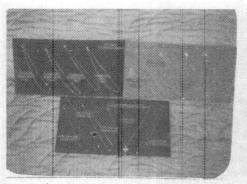

My "high fashion" chain necklaces line

Circa 1980

Trying to sell my "high fashion" chain

Atlanta sales rep Harold trying to sell

"high fashion" chain

More junk

The man behind the "Roots" necklace:

Harvey Alcorn and me but were prevented:

Due to NFL "Copy right crap"! Circa 1980

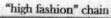

This group "ran away and hid"

Taking 1st by 11 games

From left to right:

Mickey, Mike, Dave

Tim and Ace

1983

Another sports' "activity":

Was to throw the ball "around"

Before a N.Y. Giants' game followed

With "Hot Buttered" popcorn

Actually; (with no butter)

And "Big Steak". Circa 1989

Interesting note: In snapshot of

Gregg throwing; I took picture and of

Me catching; Gregg threw football, then

Proceeded to pick up camera and

"Nailed" an NFL Films type shot

Of me just in time

Making reception!

Chapter Seventeen: Sawyer School, "Goldie Fox" and "A Giant Stride to Pasadena".

*In August of 1986, I celebrated my birthday by spending time at the Red Roof Inn on Fellowship Road, Mt. Laurel, New Jersey preparing to travel to Philadelphia to sell jewelry. I was feeling that I hadn't really accomplished much in my first 33 years except for winning the spelling bee in the fourth grade (my final word was c-o-u-n-t-r-y; country). I decided to call my m-o-m and expressed my concern with being a; "l-o-s-e-r". My mom as moms do tried to cheer me up and reiterated; "You did win that spelling bee in the fourth grade"! I told her I needed a career change which is pretty difficult when you have no career to change from and told her I wanted to get involved in sports. My mom suggested I seek out my friend Gregg Pappas who suggested I look into the **Sawyer School** for Radio and Television Broadcasting in Rhode Island and when I returned home I enrolled for the upcoming semesters. Located in Pawtucket, ten miles north of Providence, Sawyer School was not renowned but did have its own television and radio facilities that could be used to produce many audio and video resumes. I would use both throughout my tenure there. I was particularly interested in the radio aspect of the industry and got my first "break" three months later when a position presented itself at the radio station **WSNE F.M.** also located in Pawtucket. The position as the morning producer for the Jones and Joan show became available and the station informed the school that a replacement was now needed. As luck would have it I filled the position. I would get to the studio at 3:30 a.m. just in time to record the morning feed of what had happened the night before for both world and local news. Other duties included being able to insert 8 track cartridges into individual decks so that commercials and promos could be heard over the airways, leaving to pick up the morning edition of the Providence Journal, which included a stop at Dunkin Donuts and most importantly doting on both on air personalities. The last I did better than anyone else. I think we still call it "kissing asses". It was also at the Radio station I met Dave DiLorenzo, who was the overnight deejay. David had one of those Gary Owens' voices from the television variety show; **"Laugh In".** Dave was also a standup comic and appeared at many comedy shows throughout New England. My Italian buddy could also do impersonations; his best: Rodney Dangerfield. A line he still uses today goes as follows; "I tell ya, I get no respect, the other day I was watering my grass, my hose gave me an enema"! From 1997 – 1999 he did the voice over for the pieces I produced for those inducted into the Pro Football Hall of Fame and for other personal projects including Deacon Jones, Mel Blount,*

Willie Lanier, and the late Gene Upshaw. We would stay friends for over 20 years until a "misunderstanding".

The more things change, the more they stay the same: Although I was pursuing a new career, I continued to keep all my old habits which included visiting the night clubs that featured exotic dancers. I had been a "regular" at the Foxy Lady for a good ten years and continued to do my best work at the establishment while I studied for upcoming exams. On one particular visit while Kevin Rinaldi and I were playing pool, one of the dancers approached us and asked if she could join us in a game. "Goldie Fox" as her name implied played until it was her time to once again grace the stage. When it was time for my friend and me to leave, I could not find my car keys. Eventually I did; when my new exotic dancer friend handed me my now found lost item. "You owe me" I kidded and she replied "How can I make it up to you"? Well she did for the entire 1986 NFL season. It was also a most memorable year for Big Blue: The Giants had reached post season play in consecutive years prior to that season for the first time since the team played for the NFL Title on three straight occasions; 1961, 62, and 63. However, New York had not won an NFL Championship since 1956 when they defeated the Chicago Bears 47 to 7 at Yankee Stadium. This Giants' team of 1986 had been one of the pre season favorites to take home the Lombardi Trophy. The Giants lost their season opener to the Dallas Cowboys on Monday Night 31 – 28 on newly acquired Herschel Walker's ten yard touchdown run. The Giants would return home to face Dan Fouts and the high flying offense of the San Diego Chargers who put up 50 points in their win over the Dolphins in week one. Two days before the matchup, Gregg and I were having dinner at the Steak Loft in Milford, Ct. after a "business" trip in the "Big Apple" earlier that day when we overheard a group behind us bashing the Giants and what the Chargers were going to do to our favorite team. My voiced raised a few octaves and taking a line from Super Bowl III; "I'll tell you right now the Giants shut down Fouts, I guarantee it"! Well five interceptions later, New York had their first win of the season; 20 – 7 that Sunday which also continued the ritual of middle linebacker Harry Carson dunking head coach Bill Parcells with a bucket of Gatorade after each victory that year. Only once; in week seven against Seattle did the head coach stay dry since that opening loss to Dallas: Maybe because they played in an indoor stadium; the Kingdom. Another ritual also took place during that Giants' championship trek: Each Sunday I would drive to 106 Mowhawk Drive, in Seekonk, Massachusetts to watch the game with Gregg at his house. Before my arrival, I would stop at a music store to pick up two audio tapes so that

Gregg and I could record our reaction(s) to the game. My buddy would pick up two video tapes so that we could record for posterity. Once I arrived we would then drive to the supermarket and pick out two porterhouse steaks for our meat contribution(s) to our two man tail gating party. Many times the steaks in the beef selection didn't meet the grade (no pun intended). We became friendly with the butcher who would then return with two 2 inch thick slabs of Choice A beef. Our day continued with throwing the football around in my buddy's back yard, returning for some hot buttered popcorn which had no butter at all. Once the game began we proceeded to record both the video and audio portions of the day's events. At halftime: A big salad and those steaks from the grill. Gregg was a master griller and I a master eater. From others' perspective it must have been quite humorous to watch two grown men live and die during those games. Superstition was the norm: Whenever the Giants were on offense, my friend would slip on a Phil Simms' helmet and when on defense a bird cage with the Giants' logo. Some of our best and most used lines: "Too many"; referring to kickoffs for the opponent; "Giant D"; obvious. "We're not happy"; returning from commercial with the Giants trailing and "It's long enough" following a successful extra point and as if the Giants' quarterback could actually here us after an interception; "Phiiiiiiillllllllll"! How many times have you heard "It's only a game"! Well it isn't. When your team wins you are ecstatic because you know you can relish in that victory for a good week but with a loss the week becomes nine days with six mulling over an L in the right sided column. That is why so many times both Gregg and I could be heard pleading; "I want a good week"! Well we had many a good week that season. Unlike today when all NFL games are available for viewing with direct TV, back in 1986 in order to watch a Giants' game from Rhode Island, one would have to travel to Connecticut to catch the team whenever the Patriots were playing opposite at the same time. In week four; Gregg and I rented a room at the Holiday Inn in Old Lyme, Ct. to watch the Giants face the Saints. New Orleans had built what many thought was an insurmountable 17 – 0 lead. With the audio recorder accompanying us on our journey; "We came all the way here, just to lose and we came all the way back just to lose"! Both expressions were nil when Simms hit Zeke Mowatt with the winning touchdown in a come from behind 20 – 17 win. The Giants continued to win and in week fourteen traveled to RFK Stadium to face the Washington Redskins for 1st place in the NFC's eastern division. Once again the day consisted of tossing the ball to each other, albeit just once because December in the north east can make outside activities quite difficult, trying to speak with a mouthful of hot buttered popcorn, a big salad and red meat from the grill. It was also the day I blurted out a line that would have made the "Master of the Malaprop" Norm Crosby quite proud: In the second quarter, the Redskins' Jay Schroeder was being rushed while he rolled to his right. It is obvious that only doom can come to the quarterback so he throws the ball back to the middle of the backfield with no receiver in sight. No call is made and I scream; "What was that? You can't do that! Throw a flag, that's preventional flagging"! Despite my new addition to Webster's, Gregg and I felt pretty good about home field advantage throughout following the Giants' 24 – 14 victory. The Giants would continue to win and as long as Gregg and I did not sway from our normal routine(s) a Super Bowl Trophy was realistic. On January 25, 1987 while the Broncos and Giants met in Pasadena, New England was buried in a blanket of snow. We did throw the ball once to each other, had hot buttered, but no steaks on the grill. Our routine was compromised and another reason to feel negative about Big Blue's chances; was the addition of two uninvited guest to the Pappas' home; "Goldie Fox" and her very physical and intimate "friend" Susan. What could I do, we only had enough popcorn for Gregg and I! By now Rebecca Wienzimmer (I don't why she used "Goldie fox" as her stage name) and I had become very friendly and we continued to be such especially when the Giants trailed late in the second quarter. Late in that period, defensive end George Martin sacked Broncos' quarterback John Elway in the end zone resulting in a safety as New York trailed 10 – 9 at halftime. The Giants would score 30 points in the second half as Phil Simms had the performance of his life throwing for 268 yards and three touchdowns on 22 of 25 as New York captured Super Bowl XXI; 39 – 20. Rebecca, Susan, Gregg and I decided to celebrate together by going out for drinks later that night continuing a celebration that began earlier in the day despite having only enough popcorn for two.

*Following the Giants win at Pasadena, I decided to put together an hour highlight film chronicling their most productive season by utilizing NFL Films' highlights and the video recordings of the Network Games that Gregg and I "without the express written consent of the National Football League" taped. Utilizing video equipment at **Sawyer School** and the audio at **WSNE**, we produced the highlight in the early NFL Films' tradition: Music was "instrumental to the mood" and would carry the production throughout. Gregg and I in our best Pat Summerall and Tom Brookshier' looks was the talent and would voice over each segment. However, production was tedious and time consuming. Whenever I would try to incorporate any voice over I would have to time narration accordingly on the fly with the music playing in the back ground. Example; "In week fourteen the Giants traveled to RFK to face* *the Redskins". The music I used was from Volume three, on vinyl "Return of the Victors". Whenever there was a break in the music Gregg would speak and 26 seconds later, I would cue him again. Once the music and narration was together I would drive back to Sawyer School and see if I could match the audio to video. Never was I able to see both at the same time.* **"A Giant Stride to Pasadena"** *was finished in three months with the total time being 56 minutes. Feeling confident I sent a copy to NFL Films hoping Steve Sabol would view it. I don't know if he ever did but Kennie Smith sent me back the tape with a thoughtful letter expressing her regret that the company wasn't hiring at the time but wished me the best in my pursuit of a sports' career. It would not be the last time I would speak to Mrs. Smith. Ironically, I also sent a copy to Phil Simms and again to this day I don't know if he ever viewed the "production" but in 1994 he would ask of me a favor concerning the latter. But for now, I needed to graduate and did so with a four point average with the help of the future second Mrs. Cacchiotti.*

Chapter Eighteen: "A Rose by any other name" and "Who is this guy Ace"?

In a South Park episode; the cartoon created by on the cutting edge producers' Trey Parker and Matt Stone parodies the character Jared from the Subway sandwich commercials. It seems this man weighed over 400 pounds but by eating nothing but Subway sandwiches he "got down" to a svelte 180. Now feeling confident in his new iconic look he tells the children of South Park, Colorado that he wasn't able to lose all that weight by him: He had help, he had aids. However, it was misconstrued and the community thought he had the terrible disease, which was one of the two stories within the story. The other: the children decided to approach City Wok and for a fee of a million dollars would eat nothing but "shitty wok chicken". Finally, the community realizes that Jarrod had assistance and he was a fraud which led to the realization that eating nothing but "shitty wok cuisine" would not make Cartman, Stan, Kyle, and Kenny rich. The message(s): Everyone needs aids and "Shitty Wok" still cooks with MSG.

*In the spring of 1987 and in my third semester at **Sawyer School**, I began a relationship with Rose Lepre. Although of Italian decent, a feature of hers may have seemed more Lebanese; (Rhino plastic surgery would later change that characteristic). My second future wife was very assertive and could be very dominating which is really a wonderful quality when presented in a very intimate setting in a room next to the bathroom but at other times could be difficult. However, because of her ethnic background I became "into her". Rose was very helpful my last two semesters: I could not type worth a lick and incredible my assignments were finished on time with no corrections needed. As spring turned to summer and summer turned to fall, it was no secret that I would graduate with a four point average; head of the class. Now with a degree in actuality nothing, I continued to sell costume jewelry and as my late friend Bob Stravato had once quoted "had no direction in life"; I had to make a decision: Would I; "Fill my Daddy's shoes and make a living out of playing pool" (a line from Rod Stewart's **"Maggie May"**) or would I pursue a career with NFL Films? I opted for the latter and in August of 1988, I decided to coordinate the selling of jewelry with a face to face meeting with anyone at the reception desk at 330 Fellowship Road, Mt. Laurel, N.J. As I began my 271 mile trek south or for those that live overseas 436 km to the company that gave us "The frozen tundra of Lambeau Field"(in reality; John Facenda never said that, that was an ESPN's Chris Berman original), I* *thought of what it would be like to meet Ed and his son Steve Sabol. I followed NFL Films since 1964 and now I may have a chance to work for them. Once I stopped dreaming, I began to have reservations: My dad told me a story of this guy who was driving along a dirt road in the middle of nowhere when he gets a flat tire. When he looks in his trunk he has no jack. He's screwed! He now has to walk until he sees some sign of civilization. As he continues, negative thoughts began to surface; "What am I doing out here"? "I'll never find anyone"! As he continues to walk he sees a house up on a hill but again he is pessimistic; "With my luck no one will be home"! As he gets closer to the house; "I'll bet its some hillbilly family that has no contact with the real world and will probably kill me and feed me to the animals"! He reaches the front door and when he is greeted with a; "May I help you", he replies; "Keep your damn jack"! Well those thoughts were with me all the way and when I pulled into the parking lot and entered the building I had already made up my mind; NFL Films can keep their damn jack"! All negative thoughts were erased as soon as Denise Hurst began to tell me about an internship program that was headed by Denine Moser. One week later, I met with Denine and she explained how the internship program worked: Students would receive credit for their time at Films which would add to their final grade at whatever school he or she was attending. This was perfect for me except I wasn't in school and lived 271 miles north from the company and for those that live overseas 436 km. (I just wanted to see if you were paying attention). Denine's biggest concern was the geographical distance between Films and me. "No problem, I will put myself up in a hotel for three nights and work four days". I was scheduled to begin my internship in week two of the 1988 season. "Wow, I am an intern at NFL Films" and didn't even need their damn jack"!*

My excitement turned to anxiety my first week so much so that I had broken out in a rash that covered both hands. Not to bring attention to what was now an eye sore I decided to wear gloves. No one will notice and do I really need to use my hands working at NFL Films? I left Rhode Island at 7:00 a.m. Tuesday, and arrived at Films at noon just in time for lunch. Denine greeted me and for some reason kept staring at my hands which I could not understand considering I was wearing gloves.

The very first time we hear the legendary voice of John Facenda was when he narrated **"The Called it Pro Football"** *which was produced in early 1967. Through the years Films documented the very 1ˢᵗ words that were spoken by Facenda: "It starts with a whistle and ends with a gun". That may have been what his first line of script was but what we actually hear for* *the very first time was; "It was a game, a handful of spectators came to see, 22 nameless men grappling in the mud, they called it Pro Football". Well I remember my first introduction to Steve Sabol and what I said; "See I was so nervous to meet you I broke out in a rash"! My first assignment was to cut and splice film using a print from a negative original which we called low con. I still don't know what that stands for. See, I knew I wouldn't be using my hands. I was shaking and the gloves didn't help much either. Eight minutes late; I made my first splice; (it wouldn't be my last). Now that I had officially had my indoctrination, the sky was the limit. Each day I would introduce myself to anyone who would listen; "Hi my name is Ace Cacchiotti, I live in Rhode Island but I will be working here four days during the week, if there is anything you would like me to do, I will be available". During my internship I worked primarily in the Media Services' Department which was responsible for all research requests within and outside the building. Media Services would charge a research fee to Network affiliates for the use of NFL Films' footage. The Supervisor of the department was Don Thompson. Bill Driber and Scott Scharf were the two main researchers. I began a relationship with all three with all different results. Don was very anal and ran the department accordingly. He felt that the ¾ inch tapes was his private stock and if other producers needed to use them for research purposes, they would have to sign an agreement that it would be returned. That written request usually was followed by a strip search. Bill had been with the company for two years and was Don's personal "go to guy". Whenever Don needed anything done he would "go to that guy". Scott did his job but had aspirations of becoming more valuable on location as an audio engineer. Later; he needed to aspire no longer. By this time I began to make a name for myself so much so that Steve was quoted as asking;"Who's this guy Ace"?I didn't understand why so many were taken back by "this nut" who would drive five hours, spend three nights in a hotel and work for free. Each Thursday the company would meet in the Ed Sabol Theatre and critique and discuss the shows that were produced by the company during that week. The two major productions were HBO's* **"Inside the NFL"** *and Steve's favorite:* **"This is the NFL".** *Prior to the 11:00 a.m. meeting on this particular Thursday, Steve called me into his office and told me he was going to introduce me to everyone in the theatre. He did and to steal a line from* **"A tale of two Cities",** *"It was the best of times it was the worst of times"! I became known as Steve's "Golden Child" and although I wasn't naïve I thought I had now been accepted. I wouldn't be for quite some time.*

Chapter Nineteen: "I broke the Light"; "You're nothing but a stock boy" and "Dream Season".

The NFL season of 1988 would be remembered for many things: The Houston Oilers 38 – 35 thrilling victory over the Los Angeles Raiders in week two when the Oilers' Allen Pinkett ran it in from six yards out with 31 seconds remaining, Morton Anderson's 49 yard field goal as time expired giving the New Orleans Saints a 20 – 17 win over the Dallas Cowboys on Monday Night Football October third and of course the San Francisco 49ers' 20 – 16 Super Bowl Championship win when Joe Montana connected with John Taylor for the winning touchdown to defeat the Cincinnati Bengals but for my friend Gregg and I it would be remembered for the game played between the New York Giants and the Philadelphia Eagles on November 20th at Giants Stadium: I was on my way to NFL Films from Rhode Island when I made a stop in Staten Island, New York to sell jewelry to my friend; Jeff Steltzer. I had been listening to the game on the radio and arrived at his house just as Reggie White delivered what I thought was a late hit on Giants' quarterback Phil Simms, knocking him out of the game with a separated shoulder. The Giants however; led late in the fourth quarter until the Eagles' wide receiver Cris Carter recovered a fumble in the end zone to send the game into the fifth quarter. Meanwhile at 106 Mohawk Drive in Seekonk, Ma. Gregg was recording the broadcast video and his personal audio as well when the Eagles' Luis Zendejas lined up for a 31 yard field goal, which if successful would have given Philadelphia the victory. It was blocked! The ball was recovered behind the line of scrimmage by the Eagles' Clyde Simmons who taking a line from Chris Berman; "rumbled, bumbled and stumbled"; 31 yards for the winning score. Well I was obviously beside myself but back home Gregg had lost it and recorded the following; "This is it". "It could be the whole season right here". "Blocked"! "It's blocked"! "Aw nooooo"! "We blocked the f---kin field goal and he runs it in for a touchdown"! "We block the f---kin field goal and he runs it in for a touchdown"! "Expletive, expletive", and crash followed by a pause and: "I broke the light, I broke the light"! I would find out later my Giants' buddy had thrown a pillow up in the air and it "broke the light". Once I arrived back home, I took his audio and the network broadcast tape with me to NFL Films and put together an edited version just before Zendajas' kick to the incredible ending and presented it to Steve Sabol and years later; both Bill Parcells and Phil Simms. All three remembered that 1988 season as the year the Giants finished out of the playoffs and also for the year Gregg Pappas "broke the light"!

During the week following "I broke the light" episode, I ran into Steve at the reception area on the video entrance. As the NFL Films' president approached me he asked if anyone had contacted me regarding employment with the company. I had not and as if he couldn't wait to tell me; "Ace I always said if anyone walked through my door that I believed could help us I would hire him". Although the company policy was to release and hire following the season I felt I now had secured a position with NFL Films. Believing and wanting to believe whatever my psychic sister Paula would say, she "saw" me employed on the first of February to which I responded with; "the company usually hires in March". Two days after the 49ers had won their third Super Bowl, I received a phone call from the head of the media department; Don Thompson asking how soon I could get "down here". "Tomorrow" at warped speed I replied. "Well, you got a job". That phone call came the last day in January.

A memo was released later that week announcing my employment with the company. I would be working in **Media Services** *with Thompson, Billy Driber, and Scott Scharf. Scott and I became roommates in Blackwood, N.J. I liked Scott: We came to realize that we had much in common: He liked all the four major Philadelphia Professional teams; the 76ers, the Phillies, the Eagles and the Flyers. I hated all the four major Philadelphia Professional teams. Throughout the hockey season, Scott would live and die each Flyers' game as we on many occasions would settle in with Chinese food, Beer and vodka. Now that I had a new buddy, I could hold conversations discussing life at NFL Films with him. However, those discussions came only between periods or I would get the "look". Once during the second and third period intermission Scott told me that Steve was very interested in how I was doing and was "Ace happy working with the company"? I was and was about to tell him why when the linesman dropped the puck to begin the last 20 minutes of play. My roommate came to a tragic end twenty one years later deciding to end his life at the much too soon age of fifty. I was lucky to have known him.*

My first three weeks at Films were made up mostly of tape research for the affiliates across the country who had obtained a license to air NFL Films' footage; and for me to listen to every single piece of music used by the company in their productions. One weekend after returning from Rhode Island, I took the record player from my parents' house and brought it with me to Films so that I could record every vinyl record song and create my own music library including those original scratches on to cassette. Each night I would place the needle down on vinyl and listen to myriad songs such as **"Return of the Victors", "Classic Battle", "Championship Chase"** *and one of my all time favorites;* **"Latin Fire".** *It would have been much easier to record in the music department but then I would not have been able to record all the other sounds that surrounded me. You see I recorded to a tape recorder that did not have any outlets so it was what you hear is what you get even if someone walked by media services and sneezed.*

*February 24ᵗʰ 1989, Friday afternoon: I walked by Steve's office for the sixth time that day, which I always made it a point to reach at least that number. (Once it was a baker's dozen). Finally I hear; "Ace come in here". "Take a look at this". It was an idea he had proposed to the Entertainment and Sports Programming Network where the 20 most celebrated teams in NFL History would play against each other via NFL Films' footage and with assistance from the computer company XOR. Steve had produced a pilot for ESPN where the 1966 Green Bay Packers faced off against the 1984 San Francisco 49ers. By using archival footage from games played between each other from 1964 to 1987 it would actually appear that when Packers' quarterback Bart Starr walked to the line of scrimmage and stared straight ahead he was looking at the 49ers' linebacker Jack Reynolds. Steve had researched numerous films to create that illusion. I thought it was a great idea and would have also thought it was a bad idea if Steve had said so but Steve thought the former and I concurred: "What do you need from me"? What came next was the beginning of when I truly believed he really **believed** in me: "Ace, I think you're a sleeper and that there is a lot more of you than you are letting people to believe". "I need someone that can assist me in this major project, who will immerse himself in his work and I think that someone is you". "What do you think; would you like to work on the* **"Dream Season"** *with me"? Quickly I thought back to the movie* **"Rocky"** *when boxing promoter; George Jergens asks heavyweight club fighter Rocky Balboa if he would like to fight the Heavyweight Champion of the World; Apollo Creed? Balboa responds with "no" and adds "It wouldn't be much of a fight". "Ya see I'm a ham an egger and Creed; well he's the best"! The promoter tells Rocky; "It's the chance of a lifetime, you can't pass it up"! Well, here was an opportunity to work with Steve Sabol on what would become my first chance to take charge and grab on to something and not let go. Here was a chance to work with a man I admired all my life and he asked me! I couldn't pass it up! Now I don't really remember if I thought of the scene from the Rocky movie but it was a great opportunity. Steve was right: I did immerse* *myself in the* **"Dream Season"** *but all would not be (ready for this?) dreamy. I would not have the well wishes from some of my co workers.*

I never gave it a second thought that others would not welcome my good fortune: I mean aren't we team players just like those that play in the National Football League? (Scratch that). I don't think I was being naïve. Don Thompson who was my immediate supervisor actually did not want me to be taken away from the department and made it clear with; "If you work on that Dream Season, I will make it a nightmare for you"! What my "friend" didn't realize was that I don't take kindly to threats and told him "There is not anything you can say or do to stop me or I will tell Steve"! ("Na na na na na na"). (I mean the President of the company had my back, didn't he?) Once it was "all clear", it was time to earn my $16,200.00. I was now relocated to another office with a window; a film station, with split reels, a movie scope, Mylar tape and a flat bed movieola which could view release print film and listen to magnetic audio tape. This was the same type of flat bed the writer and director Spike Lee used when he produced the movie; **"The Girl's Gotta Have It"**. *I began to load up with numerous film cans between the teams that would be participating in the* **"Dream Season".** *Each week would showcase the Marquee game while footage from the other nine games played would be shown in a highlight package at halftime narrated by ESPN's Chris Berman. The co anchors for the main attraction each week were Sabol and the Philadelphia Eagles' radio play by play man Merrill Reese. My job was to find footage compatible with all the games played and for the other producers working with Steve on the show. Bob Smith produced the 1976 Raiders' victory over the 1969 Kansas City Chiefs, Bob Ryan was responsible for the 1986 Giants' win against the 1982 Redskins, Lou Schmidt made sure Joe Namath and the 1968 Jets would fall short to Don Shula's undefeated 1972 Dolphins and Steve had the 1976 Raiders "eek" out a victory over the 1985 Chicago Bears. The first week The 1985 Chicago Bears defeated the 1977 Dallas Cowboys and in week two Vince Lombardi's 1966 Green Bay Packers gave Bill Walsh's 1984 San Francisco 49ers their only loss of the* **"Dream Season"** *which was also produced by Sabol. Other games that we only saw highlights from was the 1963 San Diego Chargers lose to the 1968 Jets and in a rather humorous look we saw Weeb Ewbank coach both 1959 Baltimore Colts and the 1968 New York Jets which prompted Berman to relay a Dave Douglas piece of script; "Weeb; beside himself"!*

Although I had only been with the company a short time, I knew what to look for and it became fun to discover shots that would work. Some games were easily produced such as the 1966 Packers against the 1984 49ers because the uniforms of both teams had not changed in the 25 years of film footage we were looking through. I would look through different camera angles from each game and also from games that were not played between the teams involved: Camera "god" Ernie Ernst who had captured some of the most memorable shots in NFL Films history such as Franco Harris's **"Immaculate Reception"** *and the Raiders' Dave Casper's* **"Ghost to the Post"** *would shoot film at a long lens. Those "tight" shots made it easy to use in production for the* **"Dream Season":** *So we would see a bust size view of Joe Montana walking to take the snap from center Fred Quinlan and the next shot see Ray Nitschke with smoke coming from his ears anticipating that snap. Now obviously both never played against each other but we now have what Steve was trying to accomplish in the "illusion", that they are. Because we only see from the waist up those two shots could have come from any game. Earlier, I made reference to two sayings Ed Sabol believed in: "Pay attention to detail and Finish like a Pro". While working on the show which would air during the 1989 NFL season, I did what the founder of NFL Films always stressed: The 1978 Steelers were led by Hall of Fame quarterback Terry Bradshaw. During the Louisiana's Tech alum's career he had many injuries to his wrist and on numerous occasions a soft cast was seen on either wrist. I couldn't have Bradshaw walk to the line of scrimmage with that cast and then cut to a top shot with him delivering a perfect strike without it from another game even if this "illusion" might have worked. During the Steelers run towards Super Bowl IX, the superstitious Steelers' QB sported a beard. Again he has it and on the next play miraculously he's endorsing Schick Safety Razor. I had to "pay attention to detail". If the Packers are hosting the 49ers in Green Bay and we cut to the crowd and obviously the game had been played in December from previous years between the two teams, I can't cut to another fan's reaction wearing short sleeves. After awhile it became second nature to create the right "look". Many times we were lucky in some of our choices: the 1976 Raiders played against 1986 Giants. The Giants' Phil Simms wore number 11 and in a game played in 1973 between both Raiders and Giants, Randy Johnson the Giants' QB wore number 11. Prior to a play we see Simms tight over center and we cut to the Raiders' Jack Tatum. On the next play here comes the safety blitz and number 32 drops number 11 from that game played in 1973. To create this "look" a great deal of research was needed and I spent seven days and nights and when you includes weekends that makes nine days a week to produce it.(math was not my favorite subject growing up). I guess the word is obsessed but there was someone else who worked at 330 Fellowship Road that* *was just as crazy as I was: Six offices down from my room late at night a light remained. Steve was again burning the midnight oil. "Shit", I can't leave before the boss"! So even when I wanted to leave I couldn't. There would be no way I was heading back to the apartment before the boss left. After awhile both he and I knew what the other was thinking and it became a quiet competition. Later we both confessed what each other already knew.*

Many times I said; "Next to my dad, Steve Sabol was the nicest and most generous man I had ever met". After a late night edit session working on week two of the show, the next day Steve introduces me to his soon to be ex wife Lisa and gives me a leather key ring in the shape of a football that has the name NFL Films on one side and Ace on the other. He also hands me an envelope; "Ace, you have been doing a great job". Not knowing what to expect I waited until I got back to my office before I looked to see the content of what was inside: Five one hundred dollar bills. This was when Ben Franklin still had a little head. It would not be the last time that "Sudden Death" showed his gratitude - financially.

I continued to relish all aspects in the production but can honestly say I sided with the girls in the film department with their frustration with the producers who did not rewind the film to the beginning once they were finished looking through. Some film cans have as much as two thousand feet of footage and to continually have to rewind usually took about three minutes. Now that might now seem like much but looking through 30 cans per day well: However, there was a positive side to the effort if you wanted to stand in for Popeye (forearm). Finally, at one of our Thursday morning critique meetings, Betty Kaplan who worked with Nancy Weigle, Laura Gellathin and Kathy Monzo in the films research department expressed her frustration with the producers and was told; "It takes too long to rewind". Being a veteran of three months, I felt I had the right to express my feelings; "Hey, no one looks through more film than I do and yet I rewind"! Someone heard a pin drop and I think the producers wanted to stick me with it. After the "cut the tension with a knife" meeting dispersed I was confronted by producer and camera man Bob Smith who had captured the iconic ground back of the end zone catch of the 49ers' Dwight Clark in the 1981 NFC Championship Game between San Francisco and Dallas when he "let me have it"; "Who do you think you are telling us to rewind, you're nothing but a f---kin stock boy"! He then took his six foot three 215 pound frame and removed it from my face and proceeded to leave. Shaken but not stirred, I handled it well and ran to Jay Gerber; the vice president of all production and physically expressed how upset I was. My immediate father gave me a glass of milk and told me to go to my room which I did and continued to rewind. Incredibly, the confrontation between Bob and me was big news at NFL Films. Bob Smith had been with the company since the mid seventies and was well respected and yet I seemed a "threat" because I was Steve's "boy". People actually took sides. It really was unfortunate because Bob and I did not speak until three years later even though I tried but my hello(s) became a distant cry into the night (well, actually into the afternoon).

In week five of the **"Dream Season"** *the 1968 New York Jets played the 1972 Miami Dolphins. The Dolphins had things pretty much under control when Joe Namath started to "click" and brought the Jets within a field goal to tie the game at 24. Lou Schmidt who produced the segment used a tight shot of placekicker Jim Turner who proceeds to drive his right foot forward. From there we see from a top angle the ball in the air and it hits the cross bar. No good! Dolphins win! The actual top shot was kicked by the Jets' Bobby Howfield in a game played in 1972 but it seemed Turner was unsuccessful. The very next day Steve calls me into his office and tells me he just got off the phone with Jim Turner who read him the riot act complaining he never missed a big field goal in his life! See; it's not just a game even when it's not just a game. Later that same Monday; I received a phone call from the wife of Norm Evans; Bobbe, who is very hurt and disappointed. When the starting lineups were shown, Schmidt had Wayne Moore start at the position of offensive left tackle instead of her husband Norm. The reason why she was so upset was that the Evans' family had invited friends to their home for the viewing of the fictional matchup between the Jets and Dolphins. Bobbe was heartbroken that it was Moore and not Evans announced on the screen as the starter. To make matters worse on the very first Dolphins' snap we see number 73 which is Evans. What had happened was an oversight in Schmidt's opening line up. Now somehow I have to appease Norm's wife and I did: On August 19th of that year Wayne Moore had passed away at the young age of 44. I told Bobbe we thought it would be a nice touch if we announced him as the starter although throughout the game we only see **her husband** delivering blocks. Well it worked. The kicker: Ten years later while my wife Susan and I attended the annual NFL Retired Players convention in Maui, Hawaii, I pulled Norm aside and told him the story of when his wife called NFL Films and that it was I she spoke with. I then sat down with Bobbe and as if no time had passed she still expressed to me how hurt and disappointed she was that day!*

How did we decide which teams would defeat which teams: The computer company XOR, which I believe resided at 330 Fellowship Road printed out the results extrapolating with the stored information of those twenty teams involved. It even decided on the statistics each week and for the entire season. To validate the company's involvement those stats were made available each week. Again I found myself wearing another hat as each week I came up with those fictitious numbers but hey; they loved the exposure.

The **"Dream Season"** *Playoffs had the 1972 Dolphins defeating the 1976 Raiders which prompted the manager of the general partners' Al Davis to call Steve and complain and the 1984 49ers lose when Joe Montana's last second pass was intercepted by the 1978 Pittsburgh Steelers' Jack Ham. If you look closely, you could swear the 49ers' quarterback resembles Scott Bull who played for San Francisco from 1976 to 1978 and wore the number 19. So how does he have the number 16 on his back? A process then known as roto - scope was relatively new. Digitally a field had to be changed by drawing with pains taking accuracy. There are two fields per frame; with 30 frames per second. So if a shot takes 10 seconds to complete an individual roto - scope process would need 600 individual procedures to change the number 19 to 16. Steve's future live in girl friend and future wife Penny Ashman common wife Penny Ashman created the "look".*

The **"Dream Bowl"** *was the biggest event on the planet and NFL Films produced it to be just that. With pageantry it was a gala event albeit with our best tongue in cheek. As air force jets flew over Three Rivers Stadium, the smoke was so great that it engulfed our studio booth and we see all of the broadcast team gasping for air but like true professionals we were able to continue. With just seconds remaining Franco Harris scored the winning touchdown as the 1978 Steelers became* **"Dream Bowl"** *Champions; 21 to 20 over the previously undefeated 1972 Miami Dolphins. The next day Steve expected and did receive a phone call from a disbelieving Don Shula who had a valid question: "How can a team that went undefeated in a season lose to another team that lost twice; I don't know what kind of computer you used"! Three years later at the 1992 Hall of Fame induction weekend, after Raymond Berry introduced me to the Dolphins' head coach and told him what I did for a living; with an incredulous look Shula asked;" How can a team lose a game that never lost a game during the entire season lose to a team that lost twice; I don't know what kind of computer you used"! Since I was a team player and stood by my boss's conviction I explained; "I thought the same thing coach but Steve thought, I mean the computer thought differently".*

Gridiron Gumshoe

When the group finished the last edit session for the project, I went back to my office and wrote to what Steve would refer to as the first of many "love letters" to him. It simple stated; "Hey Boss; Thank you for allowing me to partake in what was a "dream". As I began to leave Steve stopped by and in the doorway; "Ace I got your letter and with a noticeable pause of a few seconds; thanks" and walked away. It was now over and I would return to media services knowing I had worked on something special but not forgetting the constant reminder of my peers that I was "nothing but a f---king stock boy"!

These Presents Certify that

JOSEPH CACCHIOTTI, JR.

Is a member of the
National Honor Society

Alpha Beta Kappa

INCORPORATED

by election of the Chapter at the

SAWYER SCHOOL

Witness our signatures and the official seal of the Society.

David A. Torkmiller
PRESIDENT

SECRETARY

Considering I couldn't type worth a lick and needed "aids"

From my future second wife; Rose, somehow I graduated.

60 Foxglove Drive
Cranston, RI 02920
September 10, 1987

Mr. Steve Sabol
Producer
NFL Films
330 Fellowship Road
Mt. Laurel, NJ 08054

Dear Mr. Sabol:

I am a recent graduate of the Sawyer School of Radio and
Television Broadcasting. I have spent 22 weeks on a video
production of the New York Giants 1986 football season. I was
personally responsible for the writing, video and audio editing,
and overall supervision of this production.

Enclosed is a 15 minute demonstration tape which includes
excerpts from this video. Please take into consideration that
during this production, the equipment available was not as
refined as the high-tech equipment used today.

I would be pleased to meet with you personally to discuss
possible employment with your company.

                    Sincerely,

                    Joseph Cacchiotti Jr.

Enclosure

On September 10ᵗʰ, 1987

I wrote to Steve Sabol but

It wasn't until early December

That I actually sent the video

Of the 1986 Giants' highlights:

On the next page is my return

Letter from Steve's assistant:

Kennie Smith

● SENDER: Complete items 1 and 2 when additional services are desired, and complete items 3 and 4.
Put your address in the "RETURN TO" space on the reverse side. Failure to do this will prevent this
card from being returned to you. The return receipt fee will provide you the name of the person
delivered to and the date of delivery. For additional fees the following services are available. Consult
postmaster for fees and check box(es) for additional services requested.

1. ☐ Show to whom delivered, date, and addressee's address.   2. ☐ Restricted Delivery.

3. Article Addressed to:	4. Article Number
Steve Sabol Producer NFL Films 330 Fellowship Rd Mt Laurel N.J. 08054	P 629397582

Type of Service:
☐ Registered   ☐ Insured
☒ Certified   ☐ COD
☐ Express Mail

Always obtain signature of addressee or
agent and DATE DELIVERED.

6. Signature — Addressee
X
6. Signature — Agent
X

8. Addressee's Address (ONLY if
requested and fee paid)

7. Date of Delivery

PS Form 3811, Feb. 1986   DOMESTIC RETURN RECEIPT

STEVE SABOL
PRESIDENT

December 16, 1987

Mr. Joseph Cacchiotti, Jr.
60 Foxglove Drive
Cranstom, RI 02920

Dear Joe,

Enclosed you will find your "labor of love" VHS
tape on the Giants. Your efforts have not gone
unnoticed.

While we are not hiring anyone at this time, I can
see that you have put a lot of thought into this
project.

Happy Holidays!

Best,

Kennie C. Smith
Assistant to Steve Sabol

Enc.

/ks

Scott Scharf: My roommate
Who unfortunately would
Leave this world at the
Too soon age of 50 1989

Also from 1989: L to R:
Scott, Billy Driber
Ted Manahan,
Don Thompson
And yours truly

My first edit
My rookie year: again 1989

Chapter Twenty: "The Director of Archives", "This is the NFL" and "Going to the Chapel" (at 330 Fellowship Road).

Although I was not accepted by everyone, there were many from whom I did earn respect: Louis Schmidt, Bob Ryan, Dave Douglas, and John Weiss were four of the producers who worked on the **"Dream Season"** *besides Steve Sabol and Bob Smith. Dave and I worked closely together on the halftime highlights working with Chris Berman. Chris was a real pro who would push himself to the brink; losing his voice on one occasion. It slowed production down but I just think Chris wanted to stay another day so he could hang around. It was no secret that my efforts could be used in many of the future historical pieces the company would produce. One of the longest running syndicated sports' shows on television is* **"NFL Films' Presents"**, *which began under a different title;* **"This is the NFL"**, *that premiered in 1975 with co hosts Tom Brookshier and Harry Kalas; the radio play by play man for the Philadelphia Phillies. The segment initially was a look back at the games played one week earlier and a look ahead to the weekend's upcoming games but two years later HBO's* **"Inside the NFL"** *premiered which would recap and preview and* **TINFL** *became in my opinion the best of all Pro Football shows with its visceral and passionate look at the individuals who played the game. Of all the awards the company has won; it is this show that has captured the most. The show was "Steve's baby" and he wanted it to be accurate so he asked if I could work on the show from now on and supervise all segments for any inaccuracies. I again relished the chance. "Oh one more thing"; if you are going to be responsible for all are archival shows, you're going to need a title". "How about research God"? (That was my first choice). I liked the way that sounded but Steve had one already picked out: "The Director of Archives". With this new title came more responsibility and more resentment from many of the producers who did not like the fact that this "rookie" would oversee their work; checking for mistakes and there were plenty but we do "Pay attention to detail and Finish like a Pro." (Don't we?) I guess we didn't because Denine Moser made it clear to me that team morale was at best terrible and for the good of the team I should play a more direct role indirectly. (What does that mean?) I should be aware of the shows content but do it in a way that doesn't give the impression that I am correcting the producers work. (What does that mean?) Black and white: Assist only when asked! A memo was sent out: Ace Cacchiotti has been given the title of "Director of Archives" and will be* *available for anyone who needs his help in researching any shows where and when archival footage is needed.*

*I was now on my own and no longer a full time researcher in the Media Services department which with no surprise drew the ire of Don Thompson. Don felt his and **only** his department should be responsible for all research and he would be damned if anyone left by scaling the Berlin Wall. But by now that wall "had been torn down" and I was able to put forward my best efforts as my new title would indicate. I worked with many of the producers who also were some of the best film camera men in the world: Phil Tuckett and Bob Angelo who were immune to envy had no problem seeking out my assistance and I jumped at the chance to work with these two professionals. It was Tuckett who in 1992 produced a segment on Jim Thorpe on one of the shows we produced on the rag days of Pro Football and even asked if I could do a New York accent voice over as Arthur Daley, the New York Times' sports writer and the 1956 Pulitzer prize award winner. When he was talking about the Carlisle Indian in the segment, it was my voice that was heard. I could not understand why Tuckett, who had received nine stitches over his forehead covering his first game for Films in 1970 when the Rams and Bills played, would want to use me for a New York accent: I was from Rhode Island. Another producer I had the good fortune to do research for was Bob Ryan, who was the senior producer and had worked for the company since 1964. Bob who was responsible for the name given to the Dallas Cowboys as **"America's Team"** when he produced their 1978 highlight film in 1979 asked me to do research for Dick "Night Train" Lane who played 14 years in the NFL with three different clubs: The Los Angeles Rams, The Chicago Cardinals and the Detroit Lions. As a rookie In 1952, he intercepted 14 passes which is still the most in any year and in just a 12 game season! Everyone likes to get a pat on the back and I welcomed all accolades: When Steve asked Bob how his research was going on "Night Train" Bob replied;"It's under control, I have Ace doing the research". Another wonderful way of recognition was when my name was included on the credits as NFL Films' "Directors of Archives" each week. After awhile it becomes old but as soon as your name does not appear, you realize how special it was to be mentioned. Of the 22 Shows that aired that season, the segment that required the most in depth research was the week we produced **"First and Lasts"**. Producer John Hock, who would later create his own production company and produce two of ESPN's **"30 for 30"** shows was one of our best at "crossing the T's and dotting the I's", was responsible for the show's content and it was no secret that he wanted me to work on the feature.*

Some research needed: Footage on Dick Plasman; the last man to play without a helmet which was in 1943. The last zero to zero game played; again in 1943 between the Lions and Giants and the last successful NFL drop kick for an extra point (The San Francisco 49ers' Joe "Little Toe" Vetrano was successful in a game played against the Cleveland Browns of the All America Football Conference in 1948). The kick by the Bears' Ray "Scooter" McLean was the last point scored in his teams' 37 − 9 win over the New York Giants in the 1941 NFL Championship Game and would come to our attention again 64 seasons later when the Patriots' Doug Flutie dropped kicked the final extra point for his team in the final regular season game played in New England against the Dolphins on New Year's day 2006. As soon as that happened, I was waiting for CBS to make reference to McLean's kick. As time went on there was no mention of it when I received a phone call from Gregg asking me if I knew. "The reason why you haven't heard anything is because the network is scrambling to find out who it was" I said and from there I told him who did and he had told a friend who was watching the game with him that he knew I would know. Finally after more than an hour the Bears' halfback received his long awaited additional 15 minutes of fame that actually took one hour and seventeen minutes.

With all the time I had been spending at NFL Films one would think I had no social life but that was not the case: Rose had made it clear to me that it was her attention to marry. I had my doubts since I had been married before and things "didn't work out" but she assured me it would be the best for both of us if we "tied the knot". Billy Driber who was a proponent for; "Don't get married!" witnessed the signing of the marriage certificate and on June 9th, 1990[h] Rose and I would be officially married. However, since I had committed a sin in the "eyes" of the Catholic Church, I was not able to have a church wedding. Where now could we be joined in matrimony? 5 seconds later we decided to be married by the mayor of Mt. Laurel with the vows being exchanged in the NFL Films' Vault. Gregg was my best man and he and his future wife Chris and the newlyweds celebrated at Bally's Casino in Atlantic City. Steve found our location amusing and many times would introduce our getting married in the vault in his interviews as "Can you believe that"? Later, that year we did a piece on the Giants' head coach Bill Parcells at Films and I heard him say to Steve; "Where's that nut Ace?" "I can't believe he got married in the vault"! As for me I couldn't believe I had gotten married again and in three years I would be no longer.

Chapter Twenty One: "Dream Season Two", "Giants again" and the All America Football Conference.

Just when you thought it was safe to go into the water again, **(Jaws II)** *ESPN and NFL Films decided to produce* **"Dream Season Two".** *However, it would be between just two teams: The 1978 Pittsburgh Steelers and the 1989 San Francisco 49ers. Dave Douglas and John Weiss produced while I once again was responsible for the research. For the upcoming show that would air late during the 1990 season a great deal of liberty was given and definitely taken: The game would be played at each team's home field giving us the freedom of both home and away uniforms and in any type of weather. In other words, we used all footage from the six games played between the two teams from the game played in 1973 to the last game played (at that time) in 1987. The first half of the game would be played at the 49ers' home field of Candlestick Park and the second half at the Steelers' Three Rivers' Stadium. Immediately, I told Steve I had the ending for a Steelers' victory, which was the team the computer at 330 Fellowship Road had winning: In the game played between the two teams at Pittsburgh in week nine of the 1981 season, the 49ers' Joe Montana is intercepted by the Steelers' Mel Blount, who races down the sidelines for a 50 yard touchdown in the third quarter cutting San Francisco's lead in half at 14 – 7. Both Douglas and Weiss had the game with ebbing flows reaching overtime before the Steelers' Hall of Fame defensive back decided the contest. Weiss was responsible for the pregame build up and incorporated some of the NFL's American Bowl games using the global fan base. ESPN'S Charley Steiner did the play by play and Sabol was the color analyst. In reality; it was a comedy routine with Steiner playing the straight man. Again; the biggest game in the Milky Way Galaxy produced a gala spectacular. Over 100,000 balloons were released in an indirect tribute to former commissioner Pete Rozelle who loved balloons. Hundreds of balloons found their way into the broadcast booth where Steve and Charlie were engulfed in helium. The funny man in the two man act took it upon himself to inhale the chemical element with an atomic number of 2 and when he responded to straight man Steiner, Alvin the chipmunk explained what the Steelers needed to do to contain Montana. Later, funny man Sabol exhibited a talent for balloon sculpturing sporting his newly made hat. Also, through the years Steve had displayed a unique and creative way with his words: "A midget's perspective in a crowded elevator is different from others" and "It's as subtle as a turd on a white sheet of paper"! But following halftime right before the start of the* third quarter, the NFL Films' president added another Sabolism to his what had become **his** own; "The world according to Steve" when he said; "What I failed to mention that needs repeating". The 1978 Steelers had once again proved they were the masters of the "Dream Season" and would forever hold the title as "The Greatest Team ever". It would take a decade later to challenge their supremacy.

The 1990 Pro Football season was one of the most exciting in the league's 71 year history and I am not just saying that because I am a Giants' fan (yes I am). Both Giants and 49ers were undefeated in their first ten games and appeared would stay that way when they would meet in a Monday Night Matchup on December 3rd. However, both teams suffered losses a week before the National Televised game: The 49ers lost to the Rams and the Eagles handed Big Blue their first defeat 30 – 13. Although now not undefeated, the game still would decide which team would eventually host the NFC Championship. With the 49ers clinging to a 7 – 3 lead, the Giants' Phil Simms was sacked ending the game which prompted number 11 to get into a heated discussion with the 49ers' Ronnie Lott. There had always been bad blood between the two teams and two years earlier in 1988 with New York needing the 49ers to defeat the Rams in the last game of the season in order for the Giants to make the playoffs, San Francisco went down quietly 38 – 16 after already clinching the NFC west. The Giants' quarterback was quoted; "They died like the dogs they are". I agreed. The two would meet one month and 17 days after that 1990 Monday night contest later in San Francisco for the NFC Championship. But before that would happen the Giants suffered what the majority of New York Giants' fans thought was a major blow for any chance of capturing their second Super Bowl Title: In week fifteen playing against the Buffalo Bills who would later win the AFC Championship by a 51 – 3 destruction of the Los Angeles Raiders, Simms went down with a knee injury that would sidelined him for the remainder of the season and "backup" Jeff Hostetler who had seen limited action in five seasons with the team now was called upon to replace the NFC's leading passer. That Saturday evening after the Giants lost to Buffalo, I received a phone call from Ken Sheil one of the company's producers and the man who had produced the Giants' Highlights since Parcells became head coach in 1983. Ken told me that although I probably was feeling the Giants had no chance without the "Blond Bomber" in fact the team now had a better chance to win with a quarterback who had more mobility. I know my friend meant well but I didn't believe it. "Believe it" stressed Ken. I wanted to.

After allowing just three points in a 31 – 3 (redundant)win over the Bears in the first round of the playoffs, the Giants traveled to Candlestick Park to face; "I hate those 49ers" for the NFC Championship. Just as it was in that week thirteen matchup in early December both defenses took center stage as the game was tied at six at halftime. Meanwhile the intensity was at an all time high so much so that Gregg and I could not maintain our tradition of "big steak" and if not for the "hot buttered" we may have been out of our comfort zone. In the third quarter, Montana threw a quick sideline pass to John Taylor, who broke away and took it all the way for the only touchdown of the day. The play resulted in 61 yards and when the extra point was good the Giants trailed 13 – 6. Giant "D" kept the game close and with the score 13 – 9, Montana on third down rolled to his right and just when he was about to throw downfield got 'buried' by the Giants' Leonard Marshall who drove him into the Candlestick Park turf. On our audio recording of the game, I can be heard; "I hope he never gets up". He does but would not be heard from again that day. NFL Films' camera man Bob Angelo who captured the devastating hit would later say he saw Marshall get knock down, get up and make a bee line towards the 49ers' quarterback so he wanted to be ready for what seemed to be the inevitable. The Giants closed the gap to 13 – 12 but all seemed lost when 49ers' backup quarterback Steve Young converted on third down. All the 49ers had to do was run out the clock and they would be in position to win their third consecutive Super Bowl. But it was not to be: The Giants' Eric Howard hit the 49ers' Roger Craig causing him to fumble that was recovered by the Giants' Lawrence Taylor. Hostetler drove the Giants to the San Francisco 24 giving Giants' placekicker Matt Bahr the opportunity to win it for New York. From 41 yards away it was good and the "Threepeat" was over for the 49ers' as Gregg and I hugged each other rolling around his living room floor like two grown men who had just watched their team defeat the 49ers! One week later the Bills' Scott Norwood would have a chance to win it for the Bills: From 47 yards away his kick was wide and the Giants had won 20 – 19 at Super Bowl XXV as Gregg and I hugged each other and rolled around on his living room floor like two grown men who had just watched their team defeat the Buffalo Bills! (Why change anything now?) Gregg and I had put together an audio cassette that is titled; "Best and Worst of Gregg and Ace". Two phrases that were constant: "He ain't makin' this" referring to a Giants' placekicker and the other; "Nobody misses against us" referring to an opponents' placekicker. But in back to back weeks in January of 1991; He did and He did!

In the spring of 1991 Steve received a phone call from his friend Forrest Gregg; the Hall of Fame offensive lineman who played for two Hall of Fame head coaches; Vince Lombardi with the Packers and Tom Landry with the Cowboys. At the time, Gregg had finished his second season as head coach of his alma mater; Southern Methodist University and was in his second year as the school's athletic director. He informed Steve that he had discovered at the school a good amount of film cans that had what he believed to be footage from the All America Football Conference which was in existence from 1946 to 1949. The league "folded" following the 1949 season and the National Football League added The Baltimore Colts, San Francisco 49ers and the Cleveland Browns to the 31 year old establishment. Steve was interested in the footage and Gregg sent it to him. I told the boss I will log and decipher the best I could by looking through old AAFC programs and I will cross reference with any other resources we had available. Some of those who would go on to have Hall of Fame careers began their Pro Football prowess in the AAFC: Elroy "Crazy Legs" Hirsch with the Chicago Rockets, Len Ford with the Los Angeles Dons and Otto Graham, Marion Motley, Bill Willis, Dante Lavelli, Lou Groza and Frank Gatski with the Cleveland Browns. Even Tom Landry played in that league in 1949 as a member of the New York Yankees. I spent a great deal of time looking through the films so we could produce a feature on **"This is the NFL".** *In 1976, the first printing of* **"The Scrapbook History of Pro Football"** *was published. On page 109, a newspaper clipping reads: Buffalo Bills Rally To Win Playoff, 28 – 17. The Baltimore Colts had led 17 – 7 but the Bills scored 21 unanswered points and came away with the victory. Once the game ended angry Colts' fans stormed the field and began to pummel referee Sam Giangreco and linesman Fay Vincent. Well, I'm thinking; could he be related to the baseball commissioner? We contacted Fay Junior and he told us it is in fact; his dad. So now we have an ending to our feature on the All America Football Conference which was produced by Dave Petralius and we showed footage from that playoff game and even a close up of the Colts' starting quarterback who even had hair: Y.A. Tittle; who was inducted into the Pro Football Hall of Fame in 1971; the place I would become a staple at; during "Pro Football's Greatest Weekend" twenty years later and for eight straight summers.*

Chapter Twenty Two:
"Pro Football's Greatest Weekend", "Satellite News" and "it is cold"!

*In 1990, I produced seven; two and a half minute features on those former players who were inducted into the Pro Football Hall of Fame at Canton, Ohio. Although I did not have the "official" title as producer, I felt then and still do that those pieces were as good as anything anyone had produced at Films. In the time allotted for each, I had to be correct in information and entertaining as well. I always would use the music we used during the early and mid seventies to create that nostalgia "feel". For the piece on Franco Harris, I used **"Round Up"** which begins with a trombone blast and continues to build momentum throughout the two minutes until a "running into a brick wall" ending. By using vintage NFL Films' footage I was able to create a nonstop highlight reel until the camera zooms in and freezes at a close up of Harris during the playing of the National Anthem right at the final note. Many of the pieces I produced for those inducted had that same "feel". I still believe it was the music that made it possible for me to create those everlasting impressions for those during "Pro Football's Greatest Weekend" but I do throw accolades my way concerning what was written for each: The first piece I produced was for the Dolphins' quarterback Bob Griese and one particular film shot has him putting on his eye glasses. The next shot is of him walking to the line of scrimmage which initially is out of but then becomes in focus. Narrator Jeff Kaye: "The man who was renowned for his poised leadership and ingenious play calling; being voted to the NFL Pro Bowl six times, focused his attention on winning". That type of editing does not happen without many hours of research. Every producer at Films was and continues to be that diligent in his research throughout each production.*

In the summer of 1991, after I had produced the highlight pieces for the five that would be inducted, I decided to go to Canton for the weekend ceremonies. Because I wouldn't be actually working for the company during that time, I went on my own "dime" and on Thursday morning July 25ᵗʰ my man Dan and I began the seven hour 16 minute journey west to the city that is the home of the Pro Football Hall of Fame; established in 1963; a shrine to the history of the game and to those that made it the game it is today. For 431 miles or for those that reside overseas; 693 kilometers, we experienced some of the most breathtaking scenery along the way: "Look at that cornfield"! "Wow"! "Look at that cornfield"! "Yeah, look at that other cornfield"! Once we exited from interstate 76 West onto Interstate – 77 South in Akron, we began to see signs for the Pro Football Hall of Fame. Both Dan and I could not contain ourselves; "Thank God, no more cornfields"! After checking in at the Doubletree Suites in North Canton, it was now time to head downtown to the Hilton, where the cocktail gathering would take place that evening. Because I produced the pieces for the inductees, I was given "cart blanche" and we made the most of it as we entered into a room complete with a very impressive buffet, chamber music and 40 of the greatest to ever play the game of Pro Football: "This was being alive and going to heaven"! While I was making it a point to introduce myself to anyone that would listen that included the barmaid, Dan was seated at a table next to a man who introduced himself as John Bankert, who in 1995 would become the Hall's executive director until his death May 9th, 2009 after a long illness. John and I became friends until a "misunderstanding" in 1999 when he felt that I had infringed upon the Hall's right to "dictate" the events during the induction weekend: A story for later. However, now was the time to meet those five new additions to the Hall of Fame: The Kansas City Chiefs' placekicker; Jan Stenerud, the New England Patriots' offensive lineman; John Hannah, the Houston Oilers' powerful running back; Earl Campbell, the Dallas Cowboys' General Manager; Texas "Tex" Schramm and the Chicago Bears' defensive and offensive lineman; Stan Jones. In addition to the buffet, included alcohol and Dan and I made it our business to socialize as much as we needed to with all of our new friends. Since 1964, I had been watching NFL Films preserve the history of the game and now here I was meeting Willie Lanier, Bobby Bell, Art Shell, the NFL Players Executive director; Gene Upshaw and Raymond Berry who would later introduce me to head coach Don Shula who would join that exclusive fraternity in 1997. Although I did not know it at the time but I was establishing relationships with the former players and their families. Those initial relationships are as strong as ever today.

Friday morning was the traditional; "Mayor's breakfast" that began at seven thirty and hundreds attended the proceedings for cantaloupe, juice and coffee but Dan and I decided to sleep in and make lunch our first meal of the day at the Sheraton in North Canton which was where the former NFL Players were designated to stay. The Hall of Fame players were nowhere to be found because they were attending the luncheon at one of the exclusive country clubs. This was the time for those players to be able to sit down with their peers in a room by themselves "spinning great yarns". This room was sacred; the holy ground and no one but those Hall of Fame Players were invited. Following the death in March, 1998 of the Packers' legendary linebacker the gathering was renamed after Ray Nitschke. Even with "cart blanche" I was not able to attend but years later I was able to sit in a room nearby and hear the laughter.

By now it was time for the biggest event of the weekend: In downtown Canton at the Civic Auditorium 5,000 people would attend for the night's activities. Looking like officer material; Dan and I attended in very impressive wear and gathered outside where once again we made it a point to socialize. One of the rather large gentleman attending the pre dinner festivities, with his head and shoulders above the crowd walked by us when I shouted; "Hey Junious", remember last year when you were inducted and they showed your highlight film on Friday Night"? "Well, I wrote that and I have a copy for you"! The seas parted and coming our way was a very anxious African American woman; "You did"? "That was the best of them all". "Thank you"! The wife of the Kansas City Chiefs' all time great defensive lineman "Buck" Buchannan was to become a widow less than a year later on July 16, 1992. We have stayed friends and even now; Georgia and I continue to contemplate the coordinating of an event in her hometown of Kansas City, Missouri. It was time for the thousands to make their way inside for the festivities and for two hours Dan and I became familiar with the mayor of Canton, the queen of Canton, those that produced the most impressive floats in Canton and everyone that lived in Canton but "Now, let's meet the inductees". Two large viewing screens were situated high above the auditorium seating and when the first sound is heard; Goosebumps: Stenerud, Hannah, Campbell, Schramm, and Jones. For 15 minutes all of Canton witnessed my work. I had left impressions for thousands but more importantly for those inducted and for their families. A post party followed at the Sheraton later that night and of course the induction ceremonies on the steps of the Hall of Fame the next day and the traditional Hall of Fame Game but for me it was the Friday Night that made it "Pro Football's Greatest Weekend"!

In September of the 1991 season, Vice President of all production at NFL Films; Jay Gerber called Billy Driber and me into his office: "Gentleman, Don Thompson has decided to leave the company and head west to Hollywood to become a movie producer and that means Billy, you now become head of the Media Services Department and Ace you will assist Billy in all research besides what you do now". This was a godsend because Thompson who wielded a ¾ inch video tape deck like a sword had made life miserable for a lot of people working in his department especially for Billy. Many times the head of media services' minions were forced to do tasks not within the moral realms of the company or else. Many times Billy would face and fight his own conscience to keep his job; "Free at last, free at Last, thank you Jay Gerber, free at last"! The new position also came with a financial reward of seven thousand more a year for me and it couldn't have come at a better time because Rose was pregnant and we would have a new addition to the Cacchiotti household in six months. This new position also directly became my figuratively speaking; ticket to the Super Bowl: Twice a week; The National Football League would provide free of charge to the rest of the world a service called "Satellite News" that would become available on Wednesdays and on Fridays. On Tuesdays of each week during the NFL season; information would be faxed to NFL Films regarding the statistics of the games played that prior weekend. It was our job to relay that information by producing a thirty minute segment using NFL footage that was shot that weekend and once finished would be sent "up to the bird" so that anyone in the free world could use that information for local access. At times I took some liberty and being as opinionated at times relayed the following; "even though you may not agree with antics of the Falcons' defensive back as he disrespects the game, you do have to admit he can flat out play"! What followed was Deion Sanders returning an interception coast to coast. Well, all of our work was screened by the league and on many occasions Billy would get an earful from the league office demanding; "Tell Ace, just to read the script the way it was sent to him initially"! I couldn't help myself. Could you imagine if I still was producing satellite news today: "Following this 73 yard touchdown reception from Donovan McNabb, the second year wide receiver turns with his back facing the end zone at the Jumbo Tron as he watches himself on the big screen before scoring pounding his chest and making it a point to think of Charles Darwin and then proceeds to do what is now the traditional bumping of chests with head coach Andy Reid disrespecting the Giants and all that is good in the game". I know that's a little strong but I never would have said that; would I? On Fridays, Billy would produce a thirty minute segment previewing the upcoming weekend games again using the footage that NFL Films shot that last weekend and never received an earful from the League office.

For the second consecutive time, the Giants failed to reach post season play after a Super Bowl victory and finished at eight and eight. Ray Handley had replaced Parcells as head coach and decided to name Jeff Hostetler as his starting quarterback because he had led the Giants to that NFL Championship. Meanwhile my favorite player remained supportive and in week 13 replaced "Hoss" who had suffered a knee injury. With the scored tied at 14, Simms hit Steven Baker with the game winning touchdown from 30 yards out and New York came away with the win against Tampa Bay. I would include the touchdown as one of the plays reminding all of his character in the piece I produced for him four years later. Although New York finished fourth in their division that year I wasn't too disappointed because I would be going to my first ever Super Bowl. All I could think of was working with NFL Films on Pro Football's biggest stage basking in the surroundings of a warm weather climate. Los Angeles, San Diego, Miami and New Orleans had been the host for previous Super Bowl games and now I would get to enjoy the city of **Minneapolis** and in late January; "Yippee"! I would be leaving for one of the twin cities on the Sunday; one week before the big game and made it my business to buy two pairs of "long Johns" for the trip just in case I wanted to go ice fishing on the Mississippi River but it still was a chance to contribute as a producer for Satellite News. Because we would be working for the National Football League and not NFL Films, Billy and I were designated to stay at the NFL headquarters in the Marriott Downtown, a wonderful hotel with a most impressive sports bar. An indoor basketball area was situated to the right of the main activities in the drinking area(s). Once Billy and I settled in we decided to visit the establishment and "shoot some hoops". It was also the first time I met ESPN's Robin Roberts and immediately was transfixed by this beautiful lady. Does the word crush mean anything? Finally when I stopped staring at the ESPN anchor, Billy and I decided to get down to business when Minnesota wide receiver Anthony Carter, linebacker Carlos Jenkins and four other teammates from the Vikings joined the New York Giants' Ottis Anderson and us in a basketball game of O.U.T. a two letter lesser version of the game H.O.R.S.E. A player calls his shot and if he makes it the person following him in rotation must also make that shot. If he does not then a letter is accessed to the player who wasn't successful. We all "threw" in forty dollars each with the winner taking all; 360 dollars. The patron's in the sports' area began to realize a very competitive event was happening and began to root for their favorites. Whenever Billy and I made a basket to keep our hopes alive, our "fans" of the white persuasion cheered and whenever a basket was made by the NFL Players, the "brothers" responded. Billy stayed in for a long time before he was accessed his final letter and now two remained: Defensive back Audray McMillian and the NFL Films' Director of Archives. Both McMillian and I had two letters and when the Vikings' DB made a left hand shot from the foul line, I had to match or I was o.u.t! With the poise of a Joe Montana: front rim; backboard; front iron and in. The "white guys" cheered and when I had control again I nailed a 20 foot jumper forcing my stiffest competitor a "do or give me the money scenario". He missed and my expense money increased. I gave Billy back his original deposit and an additional $20.00 and we relished victory with our "fans" at the bar. The next morning as I entered the elevator, a giant paw comes crashing down on my right shoulder and I hear: "Who are you going to hustle today Ace"? It was linebacker Carlos Jenkins.

Billy and I began to cover the sights and sounds of the city hosting Super Bowl XXVI. Unlike today when NFL Films would have two individual groups to cover both teams for Satellite News, Billy and I were responsible for covering both teams and wanted to interview the populous on what their views were regarding their city hosting the Big Game. Most of our questions were outside in frigid conditions and yet the locals felt the conditions were not as extreme as the frost bitten employees of NFL Films felt. As I began to attempt to write down some information I experienced writers block but not for the obvious reason but because the ink in my pen froze making it impossible for any chance of posterity. Consensus agreed: "It is cold"!

I mean the entire north of the Mississippi River was frozen but we did stay warm making it a continued practice to "take a bite out of our coffee"! Although we all looked like the character "Nanook of the North" we did enjoy the festivities surrounding Super Bowl XXVI: On Tuesday night the NFL had its traditional Media Party where food and drink were complimentary. As a matter of fact parties were everywhere and following our "work day" Billy and I attempted to make an appearance at each one, including Saturday Night at the city's convention center. Again food and drink was abundant as was the viewing of anyone who was anyone in attendance, including my favorite sports' figure of all time: Muhammad Ali. Although I had a chance to meet the icon; I respected his privacy and missed out on an opportunity to speak with him as I decided to let others push their way into his entourage. It might have been the last opportunity I would have to meet "The Greatest". Finally, after a week of recording the same imbecilic questions from the media, the big game had arrived and I was excited to go as a fan enjoying the hoopla that is a Super Bowl. Like so many of the media, I was transported by bus to the Metrodome, found a concession stand and eventually my seat. The Redskins had their way with the Bills who would lose their second straight Super Bowl; this time by a score of 37 − 24. I was not around for the final two touchdowns by Buffalo as I wanted to beat the crowd to the exits. By leaving early however, I still needed transportation and left the stadium to the elements of a late January Minnesota winter. Each time I hailed a taxi, the driver waved back. It seems the only way they would "pick up a fare", is if I was at a designated taxi stand. I was ignorant of this life saving fact and reached my hotel 30 minutes later with iced water veins and a skin colored blue. As I finally reached my hotel room I thought back to those thirty minutes and how I would have paid anyone the amount of my basketball winnings for a ride!

Chapter Twenty Three: The Early Years.

*I approach this chapter with the intent to write as would an NFL Films'
producer as he reviewed his team's year chronicling the first six games of the
season and then proceeded to surmise why that team was at that record. Well,
I too have chronicled; since my first season as an intern to what would be my
second visit to Canton; but as I look back at those first four and a half years
with the company, I realize I did involve myself in other curricular activities:
With Rose (my second wife) colored glasses and literally wearing gloves I
worked initially as an intern with the opportunity to utilize all the resources
available at Films. I made audio dubs of all my favorite songs; videos of my
favorite highlight films and copies of all information that was privy to the
company and even made it my business to get as familiar as I could with many
of my female co workers. Although I was involved in a relationship with my
future second wife, I still appreciated others that were looking their best each
day and in particular it was the secretary of the company's financial advisor;
Jim O'Brien that caught both my eyes: Diane Meo was a statuesque beauty
who would dress impeccable enhancing all assets. One could not help but be
attracted but what made her so appealing was besides her physical look was a
wonderful and caring personality. Earlier I mentioned; walking past Steve's
office numerous times a day so that he might glance up from his desk and see
me; but I would walk into Diane's office just as many times a day so I could
glance down and see her as I continued to make up some excuse(s) why I
needed to "burrow her pen". Finally, I came clean: "Diane by now you must
know why I continue to walk by your office. You look great today and by the
way; may I burrow your pen"? Although I continued to be discreet I did need
Diane to type hundreds of pages of information through research for Films. In
1992, only two dozen employees had computers and I was one who did not.
I was not familiar with word perfect so all my information was written long
hand and handed over to Diane. Diane could type 130 words per minute. I
could read half that number in the same allotted time. In a major project later;
NFL Films and ESPN decided to rehash some of Films earlier produced
pieces;* **"Search and Destroy"**, **"The Defenders"**, **"Try and Catch
the Wind"**, **"Magicians and Miracle Men"** *and over one hundred of*
"This is the NFL" *and* **"NFL Films Presents"**. *Steve and I would decide
which pieces would fit under what categories. For instance: the Eagles' Tommy
McDonald would be in the category of* **"Magicians and Miracle Men"**;
the Rams' Deacon Jones in **"Search and Destroy"** *and the Redskins'
Charley Taylor in* **"Try and Catch the Wind"**. *The task that lay ahead*

was for me to update and correct all the information from each piece so each producer could now go ahead and rewrite the script. Narrator Jeff Kaye would read the updated version of the piece. I reviewed 162 previously produced pieces; many needed updates and corrections from its original. The list remained with me after Steve told me to hold on to this "Treasure Trove of Knowledge". I did and still have. The new look pieces were scheduled to air during the summer months prior to the NFL season. Steve also asked if I could sit in on many of the edit sessions just to oversee the work being completed which I could not understand: After all just follow the list(s) of corrections that the producer had been made aware of. Surely the directions are easy to follow. Physically I wasn't able to attend all 162 edit sessions but I was able to half that number which happens to be 81 that I didn't get to review. The most noticeable screw up: During the 1980's Films produced a piece on Lance Alworth; the Hall of Fame Wide receiver for the San Diego Chargers and Dallas Cowboys. The former Arkansas razorback became the first American Football League Player to be inducted at Canton. In the piece we see him at the podium and below the screen it reads: January 29, 1978. Well, unless Canton was hit with an unexpected heat wave according to the January date it should have read July 29th, 1978. This was one of the corrections I made for the revision. Incredibly ten years earlier it somehow "slipped" by but now at least it would be corrected. Unfortunately, this was one of the updated versions I did not get to supervise in the final edit but no big deal. When I finally did get to see all 162, there were still over 30 mistakes. I was told later that 90% of the producers never attended his edit session and I think back on those poor Ohio fans that braved the elements at Alworth's induction in late January.

*One of the producers at NFL Films became my "weekend warrior" friend: John Weiss who was one of the producers that worked on the **"Dream Season"** and produced the Pittsburgh Steelers' year end highlights and I celebrated weekends at our respected apartments for a good year and a half before John decided to get married and "ruin everything". Following Saturday church services he would pick up two cases of Keystone Light Beer and the largest bottle of Smirnoff Vodka he could find and arrive at 97A West Bluebell Lane in Mt. Laurel for the weekend activities. Meanwhile, I had prepared wings, ribs, shrimp and sandwiches that were compiled with anything that began with the letter P. Pepperoni, prosciutto, peppers, porkrhines, provolone and a paste, that was brie cheese but it spread like a paste. We would do a shot of vodka, followed by a bite out of the sandwich and then wash it down with a beer. This became indoctrination for anyone that wanted to visit our place(s)* *on the weekend. My wings and ribs became legendary but I had two culinary favorites: One was a toasted then baked English muffin with American cheese, tomato, and bacon. I would make two dozen and we would finish a dozen between us and save the other dozen for John's Sunday breakfast, which included eight beers – before noon! The other: a pillow sandwich. My mother's mother made hot dogs in the red gravy. This might not sound the most appetizing but trust me; one bite and you will become a fan. The recipe: In a saucepan: four tablespoons of extra virgin oil; heat garlic and onion until each "sweat" and remove leaving the oil; cut up one dozen individual Ballpark Franks; the one's that plump up when you cook them and cook for 10 minutes until brown on each side. Remove dogs; leaving oil in pan and add one eight ounce can of tomato paste; cook for twenty minutes and then add the onions, garlic, dogs and add enough water to cover. Bring it to a boil, then simmer and then cover for 45 minutes. Meanwhile, make sure you have **real Italian bread**; Crusty on the outside and soft in the middle. Cut loaf in half and remove most of the soft bread from the middle. By now you will have two big pieces of bread with a cavity so you can fill with the "Hot Dogs in the Red Gravy". The drink(s) of choice: Keystone Light Beer and Vodka. Oh; the reason why we called it a pillow sandwich was because it usually was the last item on the menu and we would hit the pillow next. It is safe to say that we had to pace ourselves if we were going to indulge in the art of drinking. Whenever either one of us felt we couldn't "hang" he would take the "plunge"; Stick his head in an ice water cooler filled with Keystone Light Beer. Once this was achieved; one was revised. We had many other friends from Films attend out weekend activities but only John and I would "last" until Sunday evening. This we did until John got married and from what I understand he has never again had "Hot Dogs in the Red Gravy" and has never taken "the plunge". I continue to.*

Another somewhat food related story: During the production of the **"Dream Season"** *Steve wanted to take me out for dinner and suggested the original:* **"Bookbinders"** *in Philadelphia. I would follow the "Boss" on interstate 95 until we reached;"Center City". However, for the twenty minutes in route I was concerned for my dinner companion's safety: Steve's Cadillac seemed to be continually drifting to the breakdown lane and just before contact, would "straighten" out. I immediately felt he had "hit the bottle" before we would "hit the bottle". Once we arrived without incident at our destination I asked: "Steve what was going on with you, I was afraid you were going to get into an accident"! Unfazed; he informed me he was writing down a new idea he had* *for an upcoming project. It seemed that the president of the company carried a note pad on his steering wheel and whenever a new thought came to him, he immediately charted it down no matter at what speed he was driving. Again I asked; "Were you aware you almost hit the side wall"? "Oh – that must have been when I dropped my pen and it took me a few seconds to find it. No big deal; -- It's happened before but one time I didn't find my pen"!*

More "food for thought": In week seven of the 1992 season; The New England Patriots who at 0 and 6 faced the Cleveland Browns at Foxboro Stadium. Camera men Billy Driber, Jim Jordan, quality control guru Kevin McLaughlin and I decided to take one of the NFL Films' vans to the game and left Saturday morning. I was excited because I was going to show my colleagues a "good time" in my home state; that meant introducing them to some of the area's traditional food; clam cakes, hot wieners and later some iconic night spots that included **"The Foxy Lady".** *At exit 57 on the Connecticut Turnpike we decided to have lunch at the* **Guilford Tavern***; a familiar stop of mine and what would be the setting for my marriage to my third wife; Susan on July 12th, 1996. Proprietors' Nick and George were hospitable as always and we continued to include our favorite beverages during our stop. Actually, it was a continuation of enjoying our favorite beverages since we first entered the van back at 330 Fellowship Road in Mt. Laurel, New Jersey. I had driven the first 182 miles and was in no condition to continue as I attempted to sit in the driver's sit. Divine intervention: Luckily, I slipped and landed head first into the ice cold cooler of Keystone Light Beer, which was situated between the driver and passenger seats; and although I had taken the "plunge" my friends thought it would be better if anyone else but me drove to the hotel.*

Two hours later we checked in and made plans for the rest of the evening which no doubt included food, drink and **"The Foxy Lady"***. We all got our "second wind" and had dinner at a seafood restaurant;* **Carries** *located in North Providence. It was now time for the introduction of a Rhode Island staple: Clam Cakes. Battered deep fried much like a fritter chock full of clams and with cold beer there is nothing better as was the fish. From there it was onto the viewing of completely naked women except that they weren't completely naked except for the dental floss each "dancer" was wearing. I was the designated driver and for me that meant I still could indulge in alcohol but still be responsible for getting my "spirit de corps" home. I did and the next morning the group entered* **Foxboro Stadium** *for a pivotal matchup between two teams that had won a total of three games. Security believed it was pivotal and treated it the same as Super Bowl XXV, when security was at its highest at the* *time of the United States invasion of Iraq. I did not have the proper credentials and ended up watching the game from the press box, which is where I wanted to be all the time and although it still was only October, the wind chill on the field made it more preferable to be sitting in a room with food, drink and most importantly; a private bathroom; a prerequisite for me wherever I go.*

After falling behind 9 – 0 on three Matt Stover field goals, New England scored the next seventeen points and were on the verge of getting into the win column for the first time in 1992 but when Browns' quarterback Mike Tomczak connected with Scott Galbraith from six yards out, the New England faithful went home on the short end of a 19 – 17 score. Story ends right? No.

It was now time to load up and drive five and a half hours to south Jersey to deliver the film to the company headquarters: But of course we decided to stop for food drink and if lucky scantily clad women. As the group **Meatloaf** *A day documented; "two out of three ain't bad", we watched the Steelers/Chiefs' game on ESPN at the* **Steak Loft** *in Mystic, Connecticut and continued with by now was a familiar theme; f and d. future Hall of Fame player Rod Woodson electrified the ESPN audience when he returned a punt 80 yards in the first quarter. With the score 13 – 3, our "troops" now set out to "finish like a pro". Once again, I took the helm and drove south on 95 in what was beginning to become very eerie: My compares' were fast asleep and I was navigating alone when I decided to get a little more comfortable and attempted to remove my NFL Films' sweatshirt. In mid release I was stuck; with it covering my face, I was not able to see and with quick response; "Can't see, Can't see"! Finally, three mile post markers later, Kevin pulled and extricated the sweatshirt from my eyes. "Whew" thanks. Okay go back to sleep". He did; four hours later we delivered the film with no more incidents - to tell anyway.*

Chapter Twenty Four: It's a boy!
"Hey the big guy bumped me"
and "Thanks Troy".

"Excuse me sir, are you okay"? "Yeah, I'm fine; I always change colors whenever my wife is giving birth to my son". "Oh, one more thing; is there another room that I can use, pass out and hit the floor without disturbing anyone"? On Saturday Night, March 14th, 1992 at 10:37 Eastern Standard Time, my son was born: Joseph (named after my dad); Daniel (named after my main man Rinaldi); Cacchiotti (named after - because that was my last name); "checked in" at six pounds eleven ounces. Once I got up from the floor and cleaned up, I was taken to a room to see Joey get cleaned up, probed and pricked; the last causing him to cry and look at me as if to say; "What the"? I was a father and couldn't wait to include the word pediatrician to my every day vocabulary. Now my parents had a grandson and would probably spoil him as they did their two granddaughters, Rachel and Christina. But for me, I couldn't wait to visit the aisles that shelved Pedialite and other good things for babies. "Maybe Joey would like this football" or a Phil Simms card or maybe an autographed picture of Steve Sabol"? On weekends I would play the song **"There's a kind of hush"** *sung by Peter Noone and Herman Hermits to Joey as he lay in his crib. I was a dad and loved being all that was associated with it. As a matter of fact I completely understood when others would say; "The greatest day of my life was when my child was born"! – Although; when Joe Danelo made that field goal in overtime in week sixteen that 1981 season; Saturday afternoon to defeat the Cowboys 13 – 10; well......*

For the second straight year, Dan and I would attend the ceremonies during the Hall of Fame Induction weekend. That year the four inducted were; Al Davis, the manager and General Partner of the Raiders, Detroit Lions' defensive back; Lem Barney, the Washington Redskins' fullback; John Riggins and the Baltimore Colts' tight end; John Mackey. Once again, I was responsible for the writing, editing and overall production of the pieces that would be shown on Friday; August 1st, at the Civic Auditorium. I was excited for Mackey, who had played from 1963 – 1972 and many felt his induction was long overdue. He was voted the NFL's best tight end in the first fifty years of Pro Football and yet it took 20 years following his retirement to make it to Canton. Barney played 11 seasons with the Lions from 1967 to 1977 and was one of the best at his position. "Riggo" was a powerful runner, who played 14 seasons for the Jets and Redskins from 1971 to 1985, excluding the 1980 season because he was upset over the last second loss to the Cowboys in week 16 the previous year. He was persuaded to come back in 1981 reaching a financial agreement with Washington; "I was broke"! Al Davis: The General Partner of the Raiders. Even today, I still have no idea what that title means. Davis bled silver and black; the colors of his team and believed in the mantras; "Might makes right", "Just win baby", "Pride and Poise" and "Commitment to Excellence". Although born in Brockton, Massachusetts, he grew up in Brooklyn; part of a wealthy family and liked to personify that tough borough image. Often described as a rebel he was a tough negotiator and believed in all out war; especially with the NFL when he was commissioner of the AFL in 1966. Cooler heads prevailed and an agreement to merge with the two leagues became a reality in June of 1966. Davis also went "head to head" with the National Football League regarding his desire to move the Oakland franchise to Los Angeles. One of the most uncomfortable post Super Bowl interviews occurred following the Raiders 27 – 10 win over the Philadelphia Eagles in New Orleans at Super Bowl XV when commissioner Pete Rozelle handed Davis the Vince Lombardi trophy and congratulated him on his team's victory. It may not have been as uncomfortable as the Tom Brookshier "interview" with the Cowboys' Duane Thomas at Super Bowl VI but it was obvious that both parties wished they were someplace else. Steve Sabol and Films always seemed to "go out of their way"(s) to accommodate the Raiders' boss. Whenever a producer was responsible for Oakland's year end highlight piece, the team's Al Locasale would "assist" with the writing. At conclusion of the piece you would have thought the Raiders won the Super Bowl; invented the wheel; the flush toilet (my favorite) and the remote control because LoCasale did have control of what was written and displayed in the 24 minute feature. Also during the seventies, it seemed we always would include the same piece of music in the team's highlights so much so we named it; "The Raiders' Theme". Today; whenever anyone connected to the game of Pro Football hears that theme they know it can only be the Silver and Black. When I began to produce the piece for the four inductees, Steve informed me he was a little concerned: The Davis piece had to be a tribute like no other; something that would make the General Partner a fan of Films again. It seemed Davis was still seething over the 1972 Dolphins defeating his 1976 Raiders in the Conference Championship of the fabricated; **"Dream Season"** *back in 1989. Steve oversaw my script and had a few changes; especially the last line: While I made it an obvious to end with "Ladies and Gentlemen, please welcome to the Pro Football Hall of Fame"----, Steve had me write "A MAN for ALL SEASONS".*

When Dan and I reached the outskirts of North Canton, we began to see billboard signs that read all of Davis's beliefs. The Raiders' "Boss" who always "took care" of his guys had an entourage of 150 with him during "Pro Football's Greatest Weekend" and on Thursday Night, I handed Al a copy of the two and a half minute piece he was going to see the next night at the Civic dinner: "You know Ace, I was wondering; is there any way your company could put together a list of every play that the Raiders have in your library"? Before I could bow down; Dan (tongue in cheek) "You know Al we could do it but for a price". "Hey Ace. The big guy bumped me". One of Davis' 150 pushed my main man out of the way and made it clear to "stay back". I thought it was positive reinforcement in securing good relations with Al and the Raiders.

Saturday morning: Prior to the induction ceremonies all of Canton partook in the brunch which was located in the parking areas of the Hall: Dan and I sat with the Raiders' George Blanda, Dave Casper, Ted Hendricks and "Dr. Death" Skip Thomas. Although all had retired from the game; the "Commitment to Excellence Crew" was committed to having a good time and brought to the table a barrel of beer submerged in; "Ice Bucket Chill of a Wisconsin Winter" temperatures. I mean it was so cold we would have to take turns just to reach in and grab a beer(s) for the six of us for fear of frostbite. In a type of "that's an order voice"; Dan says; "It's your turn Skip"; "No its not"! "Yes it is"! "No it's not"! "Listen, I don't care if you think you're the big bad "Dr. Death"; you don't know what tough is; "I grew up in Federal Hill and yes all Italians are related to the mob, so do yourself a favor and get all of us a beer"! Pause: (Gary Cooper; **"High Noon"**)*; "Okay" and then; laughter. I was so glad the Silver and Black had a sense of humor otherwise we would have been sporting other colors: black and blue.*

Super Bowl XXVII would pit the NFC Champions' Dallas Cowboys against the AFC's Buffalo Bills. The Bills had a chance to make history: No NFL team had ever lost three consecutive Super Bowls having lost to the Giants and Redskins the previous years. The Bills were loaded offensively with the triumvirate; Jim Kelly at quarterback, Thurman Thomas at running back and wide receiver Andre Reed. On defense; the soon to be all time leader in sacks of quarterbacks; Bruce Smith presented a problem for the Cowboys. "The third time's a charm". This had to be the year the AFC would win. As a matter of fact; the last team to win from that conference was the 1983 Raiders at Super Bowl XVIII. The Cowboys displayed a pretty impressive trio of their own: Troy Aikman; the team's leader at QB, Emmitt Smith, The NFL's leading rusher for the second consecutive year (a streak that would reach four) and "go to guy" wide receiver Michael Irvin. All three would add to the number of those enshrined at Canton following retirement. Once again, Billy Driber and I would be working for the league as we continued to bring to the masses the surrounding stories at the Super Bowl for satellite news and once again my crew would have to cover all the press conferences, practice schedules and anything of interest concerning both teams. However, since we were on Pacific Standard Time all the information we would gather had to be edited and sent up to the "bird" at 2:55 P.M. so that the east coast would have the visual footage for the local affiliates just in time for the six o' clock news. That meant my crew had to hustle and react with a "no huddle offense" to "finish like a pro". Now that was the con of the "pros and cons" because that meant we were finished for the day and had to find something to do for the rest of the day to occupy our time. Once Billy finished his narration we did and the pros took precedent. On Tuesday Night the league as they had done in previous Super Bowls, threw a party for all of the Media. The Media who never looked the other way when it came to a free meal relished at the sight of the year's party at Universal Studios. Different flavors from the area were on display and all included need I say - alcohol. Many of my colleagues at Films attended and we couldn't wait to try the local dishes that did I already mention; included alcohol? During our time at the party, Satellite News was responsible for video tapping the event and we had both camera and sound men accompany us while we treated on tofu. At one of the designated areas for alcohol was a very attractive young lady who for all intents and purposes was responsible for my sightseeing to end. I had seen what I wanted and it was right in front of me: Caroline Carrigan was captivating and for the next two hours I listened and looked. She was performing in the Arts and had appeared; albeit in small roles in a couple of movies. We decided to have lunch the next day. With the official licensed NFL vehicle for Super Bowl XXVII serving as our transport we arrived to a "chic" but "line out the door" restaurant. "No problem; I am driving a licensed NFL vehicle". We were able to "cut" the line and enjoy our tofu although we both felt very uncomfortable as the thirty we passed for lunch began acquiring knives. "I hope those blades they're carrying aren't too serrated". Caroline and I would write chapter two of the story three years later when I appeared on ESPN's **"Up Close"** in the summer of 1995".

The "King of Pop" would be performing at halftime of the game and held a press conference Friday in the main ballroom of the Hotel the league was staying. To be honest, I was caught up in the frenzy that was Michael

Jackson; the icon. I couldn't wait for him to show me how to do the "moonwalk"! However, no questions were permitted and no instructions pertaining to his dance moves were also allowed but he did say he was happy to be performing. "Wow. I heard Michael Jackson talk; live"!

I loved working at the Super Bowl: You get to stay at the finest hotel: Eat the best cuisine and meet some of the most discourteous people in the media and get to ask the same inane questions over and over. On Wednesday, we covered the press conferences for both teams. Head coach Marv Levy and quarterback Jim Kelly of the Buffalo Bills would address the crowd first and was subjected to many insightful questions from the media: 'What is your favorite food and what size shoe are you'"? Meanwhile; I was responsible for putting together a scenario from the players asking; "If you had a chance to win the game for your team; how would it play out"? Most of the players were quick to "play along" but on one occasion I was "left out to dry". Earlier in the week, the Cowboys who were not proponents of the shotgun formation hinted that they may experiment with it. I asked Aikman my scenario question that included 'Okay you're in the shotgun and etc. etc. etc." The Cowboys' quarterback quickly let me and everyone in the room know "we wouldn't be in the shotgun". I persisted and let him know; "You know Troy, you are making it awfully difficult to write something"! Aikman: "Okay I'm in the shot gun on third and eight from the Bills 26 with 18 seconds left and I throw the game winning touchdown; okay"? "Thanks Troy". When we returned to drop off the video of the day's events Billy called me and asked "What the --------- happened with Aikman"? I responded with "I don't know what you mean". "There is no footage of him". "The only thing I have is you sweating asking him those stupid questions"! It seems my camera guys thought it was pretty funny that I was "left out to dry" by the Cowboys' future Hall of Famer and kept recording me in the most vulnerable of positions.

Following Dallas's 52 – 17 win over Buffalo, I wrote the Cowboys' head coach Jimmy Johnson a letter; thanking him and his staff for the total access granted to our NFL Films crew and added he performed magnificently on Pro Football's biggest stage. Two weeks later I received; "Thank you Ace, it means a lot coming from a professional like you. You guys do a great job". But no matter how hard I looked I could not find anything in that letter mentioning; "Troy thanks you too".

Chapter Twenty Five:
"The 100 Greatest Touchdowns",
"I live in the nineties....But sleep in the fifties".

In 1993, PolyGram Video; the home entertainment arm of PolyGram records decided to become the video distributor of the National Football League's Film and Video Division; NFL Films. Our new video distributor wanted to "kick off" with a "blockbuster of a video" and decided that Films would produce the **"100 Greatest Touchdowns in NFL History".** *This was an opportunity to "utilize the vault to its fullest capacity" and Steve appointed Bob Ryan and Dave Douglas to write and produce the one and one half hour feature and once again I would be responsible for the historic content. PolyGram and Films began to send our press releases to promote a film that "has never been done before"! Steve also queried over 100 of the top sports' writers in America for their opinion(s) on which touchdowns should "make the grade". Again; I was amazed how many of those sports' writers resided at 330 Fellowship Road. How do we come to determine what is a great touchdown? Is it a last second score that snatches victory from defeat? Yes, but the game must have some significance i.e. John Brodie's two yard touchdown pass to Dick Witcher with less than a minute left to defeat the Vikings in the last game of the regular season and win the NFC's Western Division in 1972. Could it be a great individual effort that defies all logic? Yes; but what if the score comes when a team is comfortably ahead i.e. Bengals' rookie Isaac Curtis who breaks five tackles on his way to a 67 yard touchdown against the Oilers in the third quarter giving his team a 27 − 10 lead; and do you include a score that culminated a great drive under incredible circumstances; i.e. John Elway's five yard touchdown pass to Mark Jackson which tied the score forcing overtime in a game the Broncos would win 23 − 20 over the Browns to send them to Super Bowl XXI? Those 98 yards that Elway circumvented would forever be known as* **"The Drive".** *Those were some of the questions that made the countdown to number one not an easy task − and only the last of the three mentioned made "our" list. Many of the touchdowns that were included were "no brainers": the Giants' Ward Cuff's 92 yard interception return for a touchdown that increased New York's lead to 21 − 0 after the Redskins were driving for a score. The winner of that game would determine who would play Green Bay in the 1938 Championship; (Ward who?); The Dolphins' Charley Leigh's tightrope down the sidelines' effort from 34 yards out against the Colts on November 11th, 1973. (Wasn't that the last touchdown in a 44 − 0 win?); and Colts' quarterback Gregg Landry receiving a lateral on a botched field goal* *attempt against the Browns and running it in from eleven yards out as his team "cut" the Browns lead to 28 – 14 on October 25th, 1981. (The Colts went on to lose 42 – 14 and finished the season at 2 and 14). So; again what was the criteria?*

Dave Douglas was also responsible for the opening and Philadelphia local Jeff Kaye would do the "tease" informing us; "that since 1920, 9,192 games had been played and there had been over 41,000 touchdowns scored". I was able to come up with that number by adding to the 3,000th game played in NFL History that occurred on November 29th, 1964 at Metropolitan Stadium between the Minnesota Vikings and the Los Angeles Rams and by process of elimination the amount of six pointers registered since 1920.This was arduous – and this was before the days of the website; **Pro Football Reference.com**. *The list of touchdowns included follies;* **"The Holy Roller";** *the touchdown scored by the Raiders' Dave Casper who recovered a fumble for the winning score in Oakland's improvisational victory over the Chargers in week two of the 1978 season, great individual efforts; one of Cleveland's Jim Browns' best against the Cowboys in 1963 and the St. Louis Cardinals' Terry Metcalf's 94 yard kickoff return against Cleveland in week three of the 1974 season but the "Top Ten" did fulfill the criteria needed: the Baltimore Colts' Alan Ameche's one yard touchdown run in "Sudden Death" giving the Baltimore Colts a 23 – 17 win over the New York Giants in what has been called;* **"The Greatest Game Ever Played"**, *Bart Starr's quarterback sneak in frigid conditions as Lombardi's Packers drove sixty eight yards to their third consecutive NFL Championship 21 – 17 against Dallas embodying the Packers' legend, Gale Sayers' 85 yard punt return for his sixth touchdown of the day on December 12th, 1965 against the 49ers weaving his way in and out of danger and the number one; "Greatest Touchdown of all time"; Franco Harris's 60 yard touchdown with five seconds left on fourth and ten to give the Pittsburgh Steelers the most amazing of all victories; 13 – 7 against the stunned Oakland Raiders on December 23rd, 1972: The catch would always be known; as* **"The Immaculate Reception"** *and although the Steelers did not win the Super Bowl that year it was a streak of eight consecutive post season appearances for a franchise that had not reached the Playoffs in their 1st 40 years of existence. Producers' Dave Douglas and Bob Ryan paid me the ultimate compliment by recognizing me as the lead producer for the feature; number one when the credits rolled and later; "Big Ed"; "Ace, I just saw; the* **"One Hundred Greatest Touchdowns";** *you did a great job". The production was one of my most proud accomplishments and just the beginning of our* **"One**

Hundred Greatest" *series, that would include;* **"Follies", "Tackles"** *and* **"Sound Bites".**

When Films got the go ahead to produce the **"100 Greatest Touchdowns",** *I buried myself in my work and neglected to work on my marriage and what ensued was inevitable; we would separate with Rose going home to Rhode Island and I would stay in South Jersey. I was still married but it was to my job. If you look up the definition of what a man is; at no time do I epitomize. Is the word "asshole" in the dictionary? Other words that could have described my behavior for abandoning my son should also include the "f" word as in "f---king" jerk, "f---king" dick and "f---king" idiot. Selfish comes to mind as well. Although I was soon to be "one of NFL Films' most eligible bachelors", I could not see "the writing on the wall": On April 22ⁿᵈ, 1994 my marriage to Rose was officially over.*

With only my work to occupy my time, I spent 88% of my day (the other 12% visiting the room with a toilet) in the research for the project; so much so that Steve suggested; "Ace, you have been spending so much time in this building, why don't you move in"? It was a choice that I needed time to weigh both the pros and pros of my boss's offer: "When can I move in"? Ralph Caputo was my "paisa no" at Films. He was physically responsible for the everyday maintenance of the building and was the man behind the actual construction of the company's second location that was completed in 1980. It is amazing how people whose last name ends in a vowel can "get things done". Ralph and I formed our own little company that totaled two employees; whenever we would go out for lunch that always included anything with at least 20% alcohol content; the "Chief Executive Officer" would pick up the check. We would always alternate so that the same employee wasn't responsible for our lavish lunches and that is why "the president" of the company would add the total to the company's expenses. That's only fair but Ralph would conveniently alternate his "title" so he always paid for everything. I decided I wanted to live in the film vault and Ralph was able to come across a cot that I slept in on the second floor between the footage that we had purchased from Tel – Ra in 1980. What first seemed like a novelty act actually became something much more and I was able to really as Steve had said "fulfill my destiny" (sorry Luke Skywalker). The word got out that NFL Films has "some guy living in the building" and curious minds wanted to know who he was: Ray Didinger who at the time was writing for the **Philadelphia Daily News** *contacted me and wanted to hear my story. Ray would be inducted to the Dick McCann writers' wing of the Hall of Fame two years later and would become an employee of NFL Films. We would have* *a running gag between us: "Ray; you were always a good writer but you reached Hall of Fame stature when you wrote the article on me"! On September 22nd, 1993 Didinger's* **"This Guy's for Reel"**; *introduced NFL Films' "Director of Archives" to Football fans across America; many who wanted to read my story. The Ritter Wire Service picked up the article and I became somewhat of a celebrity albeit a curious one. Jim Donaldson from the* **Providence Journal** *also contacted me and I became the lead story in early October of that paper's Sunday Sports' Edition. Many wanted to know; "how can you live there"? I would reply with; "It has all the convenience of home; a shower, a kitchen, a movie theater (the Ed Sabol Theater could hold 75 people and was a great way to impress) and ample parking". I would do my "wash" in the shower and then let my laundry dry outside on the grass situated behind the basketball net where that "ample parking" was situated. Make no mistake: Reality was the furthest from my everyday life as; "I live in the nineties but sleep in the fifties". What seemed like the ultimate life now and should become even better; was in reality - not to be.*

Chapter Twenty Six:
"What; I could have made something of myself"
and "Is that you Valerie"?

While I was engrossed in my research for the **"100 Greatest Touchdowns"**, *I received a call from Bob Roller of the Adcraft Corporation located in Lexington, Kentucky. It seems his group had been in contact with the PGA of America to try and locate an archivist to assist in creating a program where all their archival footage could be retrieved. Of course I wasn't interested until; "Hiring on a consultant basis" caught my interest. After informing Steve that I was now a free agent, we agreed to meet with the representatives of the PGA. Roy Hamlin and a very attractive blond haired woman flew to NFL Films in the summer of 1993 to negotiate for my services. Pete Albert who Steve had hired as a sought of morale leader for Films and I began to listen to the association's offer: For $1,000.00 per day, the PGA would hire me on a consultant basis to view and review their archival footage and at the same time create a "start" of cross references so that "we can make heads and tails of what we have". Pete asked for $1,500.00 and I'm thinking; "Wow, I would have done it for free"! We did agree on the initial offer and Steve informed me; "You get half".*

What did I know about golf? Well, I did know if I was going to meet with the heads of state at the PGA in West Palm Beach, Florida, I had better learn something: I purchased an encyclopedia that listed every single PGA golf tournament ever played, which included the four majors: The British Open, U.S. Open, PGA Championship, and the Masters. Again relocating to my place of sanctuary, I memorized every champion of the majors as far back as Willie Park Senior who won the first official British Open in 1860 in a field that included just eight. Prior to my leaving for Florida, Pete Albert called me into his office and asked was I prepared for my trip? From Park Senior to Greg Norman and four minutes later he called Steve; "Steve, Ace is in my office, get in here, he has something to tell you". Ralph Caputo joined the group and once again I recited the 121 winners of the oldest of the four majors adding that 1871, between the years 1915 – 1919 and 1940 – 1945 the tournament was not played. The three just looked at each other and Steve in amazement; "Jesus Ace; with a memory like that you could have – before he could finish I did for him; "What; made something of myself"!

Arriving on a Monday I met with Hamlin and he introduced me to those that handled the everyday operations at the PGA, including the Vice President of the company. I was a little uncomfortable and felt like I was in a cage as the feature attraction much like Roddy McDowell must have felt in the **Twilight Zone** *Episode:* **"People Are Alike All Over"** *from 1960. McDowell is the lone survivor of a spaceship crash and finds that the occupants of the planet look just like people of earth, including the very sexy Susan Oliver. They befriended him and even built a home for him much like the one he resided in on earth. However, he realizes he can't escape and is imprisoned to be the amusement of the aliens who gawk at him as if he was some circus animal. After we had lunch that curiously included a banana, I was able to convince my abductors that the only way to utilize your archives is to create a program that is readily attainable and that begins by logging. I was able to cross reference quite a large number of archival footage that included the right handed Sam Snead playing left handed. I did my job without incident except for my last night in my "home": I stayed on the grounds of the PGA in what is known as a Villa surrounded by the tranquility. It is one of those; "A nice place to visit but I* **WOULD** *want to live there".*

However, Hamlin told me; "Ace whatever you do; do **not** *leave any container of food open on the kitchen table or for that matter anywhere"! Okay, so now I have to remember; "Don't get any water on them, they hate bright lights and don't feed them after midnight"* (**Gremlins;** *1984). I decided to stay in that Thursday Night and picked up some Chinese food and a bottle of Smirnoff. Settling in to a night of watching baseball, the effects of the Vodka dulled my senses and I couldn't remember what Roy had stressed. Friday morning I began to pack for my flight back to Jersey when I remembered; "Shit"; from the outside patio through the kitchen up to the table and into my Chinese Food were Gremlins; I mean ants; at least a hundred, no thousand, gazillions. I did my best Fred Astaire impersonation and finally survived the infestation - and five hours later found myself in familiar surroundings; once again with no cage; just a vault surrounded by film.*

"God I feel like Albert Brooks when he anchored the Evening News in the movie; **"Broadcast News"**: *I need a new shirt"! When the NFL season of 1993 was underway I was asked to participate in an infomercial "pitching" NFL memorabilia. I would be behind a blue screen that would impose the NFL Films' vault behind me. Bob Papa who today is the New York Giants' radio play by play man and Tom Brookshier would tease the product and "throw" it back to me. I would then give some historical facts including some*

about Joe Namath but being a little intimidated by the camera, I did not load up on the Old Spice deodorant. Finally, after a few takes that included a new shirt we were able to finish. The director; Mike Cimino (no not that Mike Cimino) wanted to know if he could "do something for me". I thought the five hundred dollars was enough but asked; "Does your wife have any girlfriends"? One week later, on Friday Night September 28th, I was scheduled to meet Mike, his wife Gina and her sister at the South Philadelphia four Star Restaurant; "the Saloon" located in South Philadelphia between 7th and Fitzwater Streets. It had been awhile since I left the friendly confines of the vault after my life threatening experience at the PGA grounds so I was anxious although it had nothing to do with the Philadelphia mob war(s) that were making front page news daily. When I arrived (fashionably late – I couldn't find the place), I located my three dinner companions and twenty minutes later, I remembered Mike's sister in law's real name was Valerie Panichelli, not Gina Lollobrigida. For most of the evening I was mesmerized by the 31 year old cascading black haired beauty. Our group "closed the place" and from then on I was under her hypnotic spell (**"She's just a devil woman with evil on her mind"**; *Cliff Richard; 1976 and* **"Shoot that poison arrow through my heart"**; *ABC 1983). Valerie and I would meet every Thursday Night at* **"The Rose Tattoo"** *restaurant on Callowhill Street in the "City of Brotherly Love" and boy was I! I was so caught up in the relationship that I could not think of anything else but her and each week I thought of new ways I could make a fool of myself; and I did on numerous occasions: Valerie's mom asked her daughter if I could make copies of some Italian recipes from a book that had over 750. "Sure, I look forward to spending four hours at the* **"Zerox"** *– and yet I loved chasing her; writing poetry to her; sending her flowers. One particular time; I drew a portrait of her that I had copied from a four by six and faxed it to her place of work. Valerie could dress and I became a regular at Victoria Secret but it was no secret that I was "out of control". Although I was headed for an abrupt end to this "state of bliss", Saturdays were worth everything: I would pick up Valerie at her home on Catherine Street between 8TH and 9th streets; spend some time with her parents' Pat and Theresa, whom I really liked and then spend the rest of our evening at my house; well, where I resided and I would cook for the both of us in the cafeteria. We then shared dinner in the Ed Sabol Conference room and I would show her the picture I drew of Steve's dad Ed – you know the one that "was hidden and tucked away". Valerie would sit at one end of the conference table and me the other; much like Kim Basinger and Michael Keaton in Tim Burton's 1989;* **"Batman".** *Once we called it a night the two of us would* share my cot "sleeping" between the 1950's and 1960's. To compliment Valerie's sexy taste in underwear, she also was very fond of accentuating with a pronounced fragrance. On more than one occasion when Ralph Caputo would enter the film vault on Sunday morning he would pause; sniff and ask; "Is that you Valerie"? It was; until she decided to leave for the Virgin Islands in early March on a "vacation" that included another love. I always waited for a return call and an explanation but from that first meeting looking over my shoulder at the "Saloon", sharing with her day old wilted salad with oil and vinegar to shelling and deveining ten pounds of large shrimp for Xmas Eve, I was in love and if I had to do it all over again – "Well fool me once shame on you"; "Fool me twice; I couldn't wait"!

Chapter Twenty Seven:
"I was lucky; my ribs broke my fall" and "Fleet of Foot with explosive speed".

For the most part; *living in the vault had more pros than cons: I mean, who wouldn't want to spend each day looking through film reliving the serpentine cross country exploits of a Hugh "The King" McElhenny, the bone crushing power running of the great Jim Brown and the ball handling wizardry of Rams' quarterbacks' Bob Waterfield and Norm Van Brocklin. (I sound like Steve Sabol). Sure it was a novelty but "what the hey"; life was good even without Valerie and yet my bliss wasn't shared with all of my peers: Just because I was still sleeping at 6:00 A.M, the rest of the company was not and on many occasions my alarm would sound with a "Good Morning Ace" over the Public Announcement System. I wasn't naïve; I knew that many were not happy with the extra attention I was receiving from the media because of my "new digs" but I just wanted to look at the serpentine cross country exploits of a Hugh --------------". Steve also informed me that many resented the fact that "How come he doesn't pay any rent"? The "Boss" responded with; "If you would like to move in you can but after I do"! I really believed Steve would have loved being a vault dweller and on more than one occasion made the statement hoping "his ashes would be sprinkled there". (I didn't even know he smoked). Another of the pros; was that I had access to Steve's refrigerator, which was always stocked with Finlandia Vodka that I bought him. Although it was a gift from me; each weekend I would make sure that he would need a new bottle on Monday. Another tells tale sign that my co – workers embraced my residence: Whenever anyone from the company received accolades in print, the article would be posted on a wall in the 1950's cafeteria for all to read. It would last the work week if it was posted on Monday or in general for about five days before being taken down for new news. Whenever my articles were posted; I too would have the same number five but for hours until it became part of the day's trash. Finally, Steve decided that I should "move" and find a real home because my living in the vault was in violation of the township's residency laws and that 99% of the employees signed the bill and also that my "home" was getting a "face lift": In 1980 when Ralph Caputo and his crew built the film vault, he probably had no idea and for that matter who could know the amount of film footage Films would be shooting more than a decade later. More room was needed to accommodate all the celluloid and physically each row of film cans had to be moved closer to gain space. Once that was achieved more shelves could be built to handle the influx. On the second level plywood was laid to cover each opening from one new row to the other. You know that old adage; "accidents happen within twenty five miles of the home"? Well; on Tuesday; July 18ᵗʰ, 1994, I was on the second level of my "home" searching for the original film of Tom Dempsey's 63 yard field goal that stunned and defeated the Detroit Lions on November 8ᵗʰ, 1970 and while looking; I was not aware that one of the areas still was without the plywood needed to cover an opening to the floor below. As I continued to look for that record breaking kick, I failed to negotiate properly and stepped on the invisible piece of plywood and "Whack;" against the iron shelf. Luckily; my ribs broke my fall and I was able to hold on muttering the sounds much like those of Sergeant Hulka (Warren Oates) when he fell from the observation post in the movie* **"Stripes"** *starring Bill Murray and Harold Remis. Nancy Weigle and Laura Gellathin; two of my co workers got help and I was able to extract myself from the compromising position. News spread as always when good things happen and while I waited for the ambulance to arrive I tried to make "small talk" with the "Boss". It was small and sounded something like this; "arrugh; ah, ah, arrugh: "Ace, save it for later". Five broken ribs later, I was given Percocet for the pain and responded; "Now I know why people do drugs"! Friday I checked out of the hospital and on the very next day I was back at work writing a letter to those for their kind words while I convalesced. While at work I called Steve at his home and "Big Ed" answered. After a few words with Mr. Sabol, I began my conversation with his son; "You know Steve, I really love working here and I can't thank you and your Dad enough for giving me the opportunity to be part of the greatest company in the world and if you ever need anything from me – well ----------". Finally after listening to forty seconds of slurred speech, Steve interrupts; "Ace did you do a perk"! "Yeah, life is great and I want you to know that I really love working here and ----------------". Monday I posted the thank you letter on the cafeteria wall and by day's end it found its eternal burial ground waiting to be part of some landfill.*

Earlier in June I had the option to produce the pieces for the Hall of Fame Class of 1994: Should I complete the six two and a half minute features or should I wait until I break five ribs and produce after the accident? Luckily, I had foresight and chose the former. (Gee, maybe I should have chosen not to break my ribs). The class included; half back Tony Dorsett of the Dallas Cowboys and Denver Broncos, Head Coach Harold "Bud" Grant of the Minnesota Vikings, Cleveland Browns' running back Leroy Kelly, Jimmy Johnson; the 16 year veteran defensive back of the San Francisco 49ers, tight end Jackie Smith, who played fifteen seasons with the St. Louis Cardinals *and one with the Dallas Cowboys and the Cowboys' defensive lineman; Randy White. I left for Canton early Thursday morning but unlike my first three trips to the Hall; I was alone; unless you include five broken ribs and a half not enough bottle of Percocet. I made the very uncomfortable trip in nine hours and checked into the Double Tree Suites in North Canton and as I had done before with my earlier visits left my door open while I played the six produced pieces for anyone that was within distance. Two that were; were employed by the hotel and made it clear that one of them would be responsible for cleaning my room for the weekend ahead. Although both attractive I had made plans with someone just as attractive; Sharon Nixdorff; whom I had met one year earlier during "Pro Football's Greatest Weekend". Sharon accompanied me for three days, meeting some of the best to ever play the game, including Jackie Smith who was so overjoyed, his initial greeting(s) with anyone always included a hug; "Somebody give him some room"! "Are you okay Ace"? "Yeah Jackie; I'm fine, could we just shake hands from here on"? The next night it was for anyone that could afford the $75.00 ticket to attend the Hall of Fame dinner, which was held once again at the Civic Auditorium in downtown Canton and once again; my pieces were shown signaling the end of the two and a half hour affair which included everyone who lived in Canton. As mentioned earlier; I took some liberties with some of the features; "One of the most elusive runners ever, Dorsett painted a picture of improvisation and his bold strokes left defenders breathless; gasping and grabbing for and at air"! The screen is split in three and we see the Cowboys' running back eluding the opposition within hands' reach. Another line; "Fleet of foot with explosive speed, opponents had a better chance to catch the wind than number 33"! I ended with; "for twelve years he ran to daylight, it's befitting that his journey ends at the footsteps of Canton, Ohio; Ladies and Gentlemen; Tony Dorsett". Following the dinner a post celebration was held at one of the function rooms at the Sheraton, in North Canton. Sharon and I attended as we would all the activities that weekend when I hear; "Hey Ace; "Fleet of foot with explosive speed, opponents had a better chance to catch the wind than number 33"! Paying me one of the highest compliments was the Cowboys' Hall of Fame running back and the next day he included in his speech; "for twelve years I ran to daylight". It was as much a tribute to me as it was for the company and it wouldn't be the last time that an inductee paid tribute to NFL Films: In 1997, Mike Haynes during his induction speech who played for both Patriots and Raiders during his fourteen year career clearly thanked NFL Films for the highlight feature the night before. Saturday night ended with saying goodbye to Sharon and as I entered my hotel room I noticed I had a message: One of the employees of the hotel had made* *it her business to wish me a safe trip back home and was on her way up to my room to see if I needed anything. I mean what could I need; extra towels? "Does the hotel allow you to wear that type of attire while you clean"? My new friend informed me she just got off and was hoping we could go out for a drink. Looking to do a good deed and since she did bring extra towels; I agreed. For those of you that have never broken any ribs and for those of you that have; you can actually tolerate the pain as long as you don't breath and unfortunately I needed to. All I could think of was Ed Sabol's mantra; "Pay attention to detail and finish like a pro"! As uncomfortable as I was I did pay attention to her every detail and although from a passive position I finished like a pro. I have always had the utmost respect and admiration for those athletes that played with pain and in a way, I too became part of that exclusive fraternity my last night during "Pro Football's Greatest Weekend".*

From Left to Right:

Halloween party with Rose

Bob Angelo's home 1991

My son Joey: Excited

To know he will be

Watching Steve Sabol's

Joe and the "Magic Bean"

What an experience:

My son Joey two weeks after being born:

Late March, 1992.

Dallas Cowboys Football Club

February 19, 1993

Jimmy Johnson
Head Coach

Ace Cacchiotti
NFL Films
330 Fellowship Road
Mt. Laurel, New Jersey 08054

Dear Ace:

When good friends who understand the dedication and commitment necessary for a championship season write and express their appreciation, it means so much and makes the victory even sweeter!

This has been an outstanding year in my life and the Super Bowl win a cherished moment.

Many thanks for your friendship and support through the years.

Sincerely yours,

Jimmy Johnson

JJ:bg

Following the Cowboys 52 – 17

Thrashing of the Buffalo Bills,

I wanted to wish head coach

Jimmy Johnson the best.

Ten days after sending him

Congratulations – he responded:

Not only did I feel John Mackey

Was arguably the best to play the

Position of tight end, he was one of

my dearest friends.

OBSTACLES

July 1, 1993

Ace
c/o NFL Films
330 Fellowship Road
Mt. Laurel, NJ 08054

Dear Ace:

I really appreciate you sending the tape to Jill. I viewed it. It's
exceptional!

I owe you dinner.

Your pal,

John Mackey
Chairman

Ace!
You are to film what I am
to Tightends

Thank you.

Matt #88

May 3, 1993

Mr. Roy Hamlin, Jr.
President
AdCraft Assoc., Inc.
6100 Dutchmans Lane
Louisville, KY 40205

Dear Mr. Hamlin:

I would be very interested in working with you in the development
of a new and exciting project. Being able to assist in the
preservation of the past and current history of the PGA is most
exciting. After speaking with Steve Sabol, the President of NFL
Films, we both agree that the opportunity to enrich the great
game of golf by utilizing past and present video throughout the
years would be challenging and most rewarding.

My proposal for development of a P.G.A. Video Library would be
very similar to the one here at NFL Films, Inc.

Example: view each video tape. Establish the tournament, the
year the site, the players involved, no matter if the individual
had been influential in the overall outcome of the tournament.
Thus, being able to go beyond the obvious, when sidebars,
footnotes or anecdotes present themselves. It is a long process
but one that has had its rewards as we have discovered by
utilizing the system here at NFL Films.

I look forward to hearing from you.

Sincerely,

Ace Cacchiotti
Director of Archives

Enclosure

Following this letter to those responsible

For my assisting the PGA in creating

An archives system, I found myself

Battling an infestation of creepy, crawly

Get under my skin ants. Likely; I was able to

Find my way back to the safe confines

Of the NFL Films' Vault.

330 Fellowship Road • Mt. Laurel, NJ 08054 • (609) 778-1600 • FAX: (609) 722-6779

ACE Joe Cash Jr.

My first portrait:

The 14 year veteran:

Defensive Lineman for the

Pittsburgh Steelers; Ernie Stautner

April 1964 at ten years old

My last portrait:
"Big Ed" Sabol who didn't
Like the way I drew his teeth.
Both are well taken care of:
at my home:
April, 1992. 39 years old.

1	
2	TO ACE:
3	
4	
5	
6	JUST SAW
7	
8	
9	100 TD's.
10	
11	
12	You DID A
13	
14	FANTASTIC JOB
15	
16	
17	of RESEARCH
18	
19	
20	
21	
22	ED. SABOL
23	
24	
25	

High Praise from "Big Ed"

MEMORANDUM

TO: Ace Cacchiotti

FROM: Pete Albert

DATE: September 24, 1993

RE: <u>YOUR PRESS!</u>

Dear Ace,

I'm pleased to see that the outstanding work you perform has been recognized by the outside world. You are truly a professional in every sense of the word. If more people had your dedication, enthusiasm, spirit and sense of purpose, this world would definitely be a better place in which to live.

You certainly are the "Keeper of Flames." Keep up the good work!

SPA/csg

Always nice to receive accolades

From your peers after

"The 100 Greatest Touchdowns"

Was produced

Cacchiotti 'ace' of NFL footage

**JIM
DONA...**

There are 41,000 cans of film in the storage vault at NFL Films, 20,000 miles of football footage . . . and one cot.

The cot belongs to "Ace" Cacchiotti, who used to live in Cranston but now lives in the vault.

He works there by day, and usually well into the night, too. And when Cacchiotti finally is ready to close eyes grown blurry from looking at film, he flops on his cot, located up on the second tier, in the section he refers to as "The Fabulous '50s."

"I live in the '90s," he says, " but I sleep in the '50s. It's the greatest thing. I can lie there and

physicist. He knows what ery one of those 41,000 ca film, is familiar with ever those 20,000 miles of foo

"He's a walking compu says Michelle Kline, who i charge of media services i Films. "He's incredible. H

> 'It's the greatest thing. I can lie there and look t
> left, and I can see the film where Del Shofner. W
> he was with the Rams, before he came to the Gi
> makes an incredible, juggling catch. I can look a
> right, and I can see the film of an interview wi
> (former NFL commissioner) Bert Bell. I lie there
> I know, this is where I should be.'
>
> **"ACE" CACCHIOTTI**

look to my left, and I can see the film where Del Shofner, when he was with the Rams, before he came to the Giants, makes an incredible, juggling catch. I can look to my right, and I can see the film of an interview with (former NFL commissioner) Bert Bell. I lie there and I know, this is where I should be."

The story of how Cacchiotti came to be not only the archivist for NFL Films, but also a producer of NFL Films, is like the story of Johnny Unitas' coming off the sandlots of Pittsburgh and becoming a legendary quarterback for the Baltimore Colts.

Calling Cacchiotti an archivist is like saying Albert Einstein was a

He's like one of those 'savi ple. He logs all the footage mind. He knows every pla ever shot."

Whether you want a sh Don Hutson or Jerry Rice Graham or Dan Marino, M Motley or Jimmy Brown, B Butkus or Lawrence Tayl

DONALDSON, Pag

TODAY

■ Seattle Seahawks a
  England Patriots
■ 1 p.m. WWRX-FM
  WARA Radio

TED: Transplanted Rhode Islander Joe 'Ace' Cacchiotti sits on his bad has set up in the storage vault at NFL Films where he works.

The Providence Journal decided to do the lead on my place of residence as Jim
Donaldson let everyone know; "I live in the 90's but sleep in the fifties". 9/19/93

Two; "True" "Keepers of the Flame"

From L. to R:
Photo became a portrait
of Valerie. Valerie at
Phil Simms' Roast in Northern
Jersey. Speaking at the Giants'
Quarterback roast with L.T.
in the background.
From L. to R:
Phil, daughter Diedre, wife Diana
Oldest son Chris, Me, and Joe
From NFL Films' (Missing is
Youngest son Matthew
February, 1994

Chapter Twenty Eight: "75 Seasons; the Story of the National Football League" (unofficially) and "Well you see Mr. Butkus".

In 1994, The National Football League would be celebrating its 75th year anniversary and the league throughout the season would remind its millions of fans worldwide by; "reliving the past in the present". Turner Network Television would air the two hour presentation that was produced by NFL Films. The NFL had a 75th anniversary book produced and during the season each team on at least one occasion would "sport" the uniforms worn by its predecessor(s) so one could "relive" the eye appealing aesthetics of the 1943 Steagles and other teams of past eras. To narrate the TNT special, Films hired the British American actor John Mahoney who played the character Martin "Marty" Crane in the television sitcom; **"Frazier"** *that ran from 1993 – 2004. However, the choice did not sit well with Films' long time narrator Jeff Kaye, who expressed to this archivist that "This was my Super Bowl". I too had a problem: I felt that the NFL was inaccurate in its anniversary year. Professional Football did officially begin 75 seasons ago from 1994; but in its initial year the league was made up of fourteen teams and was called the American Professional Football Association. Its first "official" champion was the Akron Pros with an eight wins, no losses and three ties season. One year later, still under that league name, the APFA had its second champion; the Chicago Staleys who immediately after would become the Bears. In 1922; the APFA became the National Football League and although in 1994 the league did celebrate the 75th anniversary of Professional Football in actuality it was "officially" the 73rd season unofficially. Got it? Who cares? The league didn't and still doesn't. In the year 2019, I will bring attention to the NFL when they celebrate the 100th anniversary of Pro Football or is it the 98th?*

Regardless of whether the league was celebrating its 75th, 73rd or last, I was excited to be working on a major project. Unlike the other nostalgia pieces I had contributed to, I now would research every roll of film from the "Rag Days" to 1987. Along the way; I created research rolls that were appropriately titled; "Ace Research Rolls number; 75 seasons. Although the project had to have perimeters my research did not: Each day I would initially spend an hour in the film vault loading up as many film cans I could fit into my room. I would stop just before I was endanger of creating a fire hazard; although if one was created, I would save the film along with the women and children first. Tom Heddon, Vince Caputo and Dave Robidoux wrote and recorded the visceral audio and Films put our "A Team" on the project; Steve "Doc" Seidman, Chris Barlow, Dave Douglas, Phil Tucket, Lou Schmidt, Greg Kohs, and John Hock who was the lead producer to create a 75 (or 73) history in a two hour documentary. Politically we had to be correct: Many egos were involved and we had to be aware of that as well. The Raiders' Al Davis would have been content with a two hour special on his team but we did produce a segment on the AFL and his team which he coined "The Team for All Decades". Obviously the roots of Pro Football was explained in our "Founding Fathers" segment and the Jackie Robinson of Pro Football segment included Marion Motley and Bill Willis of the Cleveland Browns from the All America Conference and Kenny Washington and Woody Strode of the NFL's Los Angeles Rams. All four broke the "color" barrier in 1946; one year before Robinson did in baseball with the Brooklyn Dodgers. The footage we acquired from the company Tel – Ra in 1980 had given the company an incredible treasure trove of nostalgia in black and white negative, black and white positive and color positive film stock. I am proud to say that every piece of film I produced through my research was of the original quality. Previously; I remembered looking through a research roll that was used for Steve Sabol's **"Big Game America"** that was produced in 1969 when I came across a black player sitting on the bench. Although the Rams were still two years away from their Rams and Horns' logo on the helmet, I knew it had to be the team from Los Angeles and decided that we had a close up of Woody Strode, who would later appear in the movies; including **"Pork Chop Hill"** and **"Spartacus";** the latter which he was nominated for best supporting actor. Everyone assigned to the project had an incredible obligation to be accurate not just for facts and figures but for how each segment had to have a profound effect on the history of the game and that is where problems arose: Should Films produce a longer time segment in regards to the roots, or the war years, the American Football League, dynasties, and the game of today? This was a delicate situation and unfortunately whatever the producers felt; in reality were in a no win situation. Some teams had to be unintentionally slighted because of the length of the feature. One team that was overlooked from this archivist's point of view was the contribution(s) of my favorite team: The New York Giants' Tim Mara purchased the Giants' franchise in 1925 for arguably the amount of $2,500.00. Mara was quoted; "An empty store in Manhattan is worth that much". Reference to the team was at the best miniscule and except for a shot of Lawrence Taylor's "Let's go out there like a bunch of crazed dogs and have some fun" and quarterback Phil Simms with eyes closed during the playing of the National Anthem, the Giants were not really part of the story.

Of course the owner of one of the league's oldest franchises was very upset with Steve and the company: Wellington Mara had a right to be upset but to include all franchises in what was actually a one hour thirty eight minutes and 45 seconds of content was near impossible. He was not the only man to be upset with the documentary:

In late summer of the 75th anniversary; NFL Films, TNT and many representatives from the league gathered in New York City to watch a screening of; **"75 Seasons" the story of the National Football League".** *A list of who's who was present at the affair which included myriad food and drink: (After 28 chapters; does one seem to guess what is an occurring theme with the "Gridiron Gumshoe?") When the segment; Dynasty of the Pittsburgh Steelers appeared; Ray Mansfield the Pittsburgh Steelers' starting center from 1964 – 1976, and who would die two years later in 1996 as the result of a heart attack while hiking at the Grand Canyon; tells the story of a game played in 1969 against the Chicago Bears. The first round pick of the Steelers that year was "Mean Joe Greene" a defensive lineman from North Texas State. While his team was on offense a play ran in his direction while he was on the sidelines. All Pro and one of the best to ever play the game; Bears' linebacker Dick Butkus pursued the play to where the Steelers' rookie is standing. The story continued: While Butkus is having words with the Steelers' bench, Greene spits at one of the "Monsters of the Midway" and number 51 just turned away. Mansfield says "That was the beginning of the end of the Pittsburgh Steelers' problems". Once the presentation was over; many resided to an area for more of F and D. While I was fitting right in, I notice that some of my co workers were in some conversation with that Chicago Bears' linebacker; you know the one Joe Greene spit on. Now I am confronted with him and he reads me the riot act; "Listen I understand you were responsible for that piece of shit lie saying I backed down to Greene"! "Let me tell you something, I have never backed down from anyone and what was I going to do; get thrown out of the game; the only game we won all year; I don't know where you get your information"! I'm thinking; here is the guy that in the feature is quoted as saying how he liked the part in the movie;* **"Hush, Hush, Sweet Charlotte"** *"when the head comes rolling down the stairs and I kind of like to project that image happening on the field and not necessarily to me". In a Michael Jackson octave: "Well, you see Mr. Butkus, it ah really wasn't about you backing down it was about the Steelers' not being pushed around anymore; we thought it would be a good story". With that; any chance of an autograph was not to be but I was relieved that I had the foresight to bring an extra pair of pants.*

Chapter Twenty Nine: "The 100 Greatest Plays in NFL History" (minus) 25, "Jay, do you think they're listening"? and the Greatest Super Bowl Ever!

While I was doing research for **"75 Seasons"; "The Story of the National Football League"**, *Films was contacted by Kelly Cassin who worked for the company Vicaris located near San Francisco. She and her group wanted to put together an interactive video game depicting the 75 greatest plays in NFL History. I thought: "whew what a break; at least it's not 100". I would have not only to list those 75 but support it with video footage so that each could be diagnosed and broken down in its x's and o's. The earliest was Bill Osmanski's 68 yard touchdown run on the Chicago Bears' second play from scrimmage in his team's 73 – 0 trouncing of the Washington Redskins in the 1940 NFL Championship. Others included; the Rams' Tom Fears' 73 yard game winning touchdown reception from Norm Van Brocklin in the 1951 Championship Game, Clarence Davis'* **"Sea of Hands Catch"** *in the Raiders win over the Dolphins in the 1974 AFC Divisional Playoffs and of course; Franco's Harris's* **"Immaculate Reception"** *in 1972 as Pittsburgh stunned Oakland 13 – 7. After coming across all the research for each play and transferring it to a compatible digital outlet, I thought I was finished and could continue my work on* **"75 Seasons":** *"Wrong"! What I failed to realize was that in the agreement with NFL Films, Vicaris wanted me to fly to the west coast and diagram each play; so* **that** *particular feature could be installed in the game. I was very hesitant; I wasn't afraid of flying; I was afraid of crashing. I am not afraid of heights but falling from them I was terrified. I know that statistically you are safer in the air than in your car but how many times have you gotten in and out of your car without an accident: A gazillion plus two billion? Well; how many times do you think those unfortunate souls that have died in a plane crash flew? Get the picture. I have been in five car accidents, the last resembling the number of car rolls at five and still I write. That story is coming. I don't know if anyone could survive five plane crashes even one that rolled over and over: July 19, 1989, Sioux City, Iowa;* **United Airlines flight number 232**. *Well actually 174 passengers and ten crew personal did but what about the 112 that didn't! No; no way was I flying again even if they offered first class: While I was enjoying the view at 33,000 feet with my eyes closed, (a Sabolisim if I ever heard one) my presumptuous new friend told me not to worry; "I have flown over one hundred times and on eight occasions it looked as if the plane was going down". "One time we dropped*

10,000 feet in about five seconds and were headed for a mountain but luckily the pilot was able to gain enough altitude just in time to clear the Rockies"! "Thanks, I feel better" and I promised myself I wouldn't drink. "Excuse me Miss; I'll have what he's drinking"! After reaching my quota of three drinks per hour I wasn't afraid of flying, crashing, falling from heights or Linda Blair talking bad about my mother from the movie; **"The Exorcist".** *As a matter of fact; go ahead land this thing and I dare you to use the landing gear!*

Once I had fulfilled my duty to Vicaris, NFL Films and God and country I continued with other projects that pertained to the league's 75th Anniversary (minus two). One of the representatives from the National Football League was schedule to come to Films and work on a project for the league. Vice President of all productions; Jay Gerber assigned me to meet him at 9:00 A.M. on a Wednesday Morning, which was the day I would usually finish my editing for Satellite News. No one else could replace me so I worked until five A.M. that Wednesday morning, headed home and eventually fell asleep one and a half hours later. Two hours later, I scrambled to meet Dave Hoffman at the designated time. At ten past nine Gerber walks by me and greets me with; "You F----KED ME"! Once again with diplomacy I surprised myself on how well I diffused the situation: "You don't talk to me like that, if you have something to say; let's talk in your f-----king office"! "Sorry, I didn't mean to say office"! Each combatant at the highest decibel level pleaded his case. After five minutes of the loudest sounds ever emitting from anyone's office, I began to lend a deaf ear(no make that both ears) and thought back to the 1974 AFC Divisional Playoff game between the two time defending Super Bowl Champion Miami Dolphins at the Raiders' home field; Oakland Alameda Coliseum. Late in the fourth quarter; Miami's Benny Malone ran to his right and with future Hall of Fame offensive lineman Larry Little leading the way scored from 26 yards out to give his team a 26 – 21 lead. With a little over two minutes remaining in the game, the Raiders' quarterback Ken the "Snake" Stabler drove his team downfield to the Dolphins' six yard line and proceeded to call time out. While discussing what play to call; the Raiders' head coach John Madden began to become very animated. It was at this time that Oakland's field general looked at his head coached and said "You know John, these fans are really getting their monies worth"! In the heat of battle Stabler kept it together and Oakland advanced to the AFC Championship Game. Well; right after I recollected I thought; it's time to end this and said; "Jay do you think they're listening"? Octaves dropped and civility ensued. Both parties went about their business believing the other was right in their accusations (not really)!

Gridiron Gumshoe

The sight for Super Bowl XXIX was Miami, Florida. Miami had hosted the NFL Championship on six different occasions, including back to back years at Super Bowls II and III; the first, last and only times a city was granted two in succession. I was looking forward to the week leading up to the game because my longtime friend Gregg Pappas would be working with us covering the AFC Champions' San Diego Chargers for Satellite News and I would be covering the NFC's San Francisco 49ers. I also had two tickets to the game for "Fast Eddie" Skovron and his son Todd so it was a chance to really impress "my guys". Since this was the "official" diamond anniversary of the league, the heads of state on Park Avenue in New York City wanted to showcase a film presentation of the National Football League during the "Roaring Twenties". I was asked by Susan; whose last name escapes me and for that matter will never be retrieved and who was working with Jim Steeg to put together a two hour history piece depicting play during the decade which would be shown that night at the Commissioner's Party in the inner circle; an area where the owners, and high ranking officials from the league office can sit together in a most pompous fashion looking out at the poor souls who had to wait in lines of 200 for food; albeit definitely worth the wait. By working on the Commissioner's project, I was given two tickets to that area inside the ropes and would be able to display an airs matching those at 450 Park Avenue. However, before I could display "my nose in the air attitude", I had to work on the project, satellite news and research for other producers leaving me very little time to sleep but still enough time to visit sanctuary; the bathroom. One must keep priorities. Waiting to the last minute literally, I finished the Paul Tagliabue project and went to sleep at 4:30 Sunday Morning, slept for three hours and headed to speak at a small Jewish Gathering at nine o'clock compliments of my co worker Jim Barry. Once again doing my best Steve Sabol standup I told the story of how the company's origin began at the 1962 NFL Championship Game under a less familiar name; Blair Motion Pictures, became NFL Films and continues to "create ever lasting impressions" on millions of Pro Football Fans across America and other continents. All information was relayed while corresponding film footage supported my tale. Small applause followed with breakfast consisting of white fish, bagels and lox and a picture taken with some of those that like white fish, bagels and lox. After doing my best to understand the religion in two hours I added "I thought Paul Newman was good in the movie; **"Exodus".** *With that said; I began my own journey to the airport; headed to Miami but not without forgetting to remove my Yamaka.*

Miami was buzzing with excitement in anticipation of hosting its seventh Super Bowl as the city braced for the hundreds of thousands fans that invaded south beach and other tourist attractions. Many of those attractions were of the female persuasion and Gregg and I did our best to focus on the matter at hand, which I can honestly say we lost sight of, in the sights and sounds of Super Bowl week. However, we did live up to our obligations and followed protocol by appearing at all the Super Bowl parties the league had planned for the media and others that were looking for a free meal none bigger than the commissioner's party where the who's who of the Pro Football world gathered at the Miami Convention Center; "Hey Clay beat Liston here on February 25th, 1964". Getting tickets to the commissioner party was a difficult task especially if one had already received two tickets to the Super Bowl Party in the "inner circle" but I was determined to get the Skovrons into the "Big Party".

The Friday afternoon following the commissioner's address to the media answering for the umpteenth time; "Are you going to expand to other countries", Todd and I were lifting weights at the gym in the downtown Marriott; the league's designated headquarters when ESPN analyst Phil Simms joined us and asked if we were going to the commissioner's party. I made it clear to him and to NFL Films' Barry Wolper, who also was working out that I needed one more ticket so that Todd could come but I haven't been able to "get one more". I knew Barry had tickets and pleaded my case and would have done anything he asked for a chance to have my friend attend (well almost anything; not that there is anything wrong with it!). Finally; Barry released the code allowing us to unlock the vault and retrieve the priceless item. The commissioner's party was a chance for thousands to meet former and current NFL players all under one roof and I introduced "my guys" to John Mackey, Mel Blount, Willie Lanier, Simms and others; each gracious enough to have their picture taken with us. Even second year Patriots' quarterback Drew Bledsoe made time to pose with Todd. The food was again as in other commissioner's party excellent although after thirty minutes seated with some of the league's dignitaries in the Commissioner's area, Mackey, Gregg and I decided to leave the unfriendly confines and wait in line for our food just like the other 3,000 people who were "not privileged". I made my rounds and introduced myself again to Bill Walsh who had led the San Francisco 49ers to three Super Bowl Championships and whose Hall of Fame Highlight feature I presented to him six months earlier in Canton, Ohio. 49ers' owner Ed DiBartello Jr. tried to discreetly let it be known he was too busy to be gracious; quickly did a one eighty when the former 49ers' head coach extended his hand to me. Some of the most beautiful women on the planet were everywhere and I tried to locate each within the three hour window that was soon closing. The party had ended but for the four of us there was more to do and we did back at the hotel lounge, taking more pictures with whomever would stand still long enough to capture a "Kodak moment". My moment usually came with my arm around some stunning blonde, brunette, and red haired beauty whose names escaped me then and for that matter now as well. However, one girl's name I do remember was Cindy Katz, who was the producer for ESPN's **"UP Close",** *which was then hosted by Chris Myers who had replaced Roy Firestone. Incredibly, 15 years later I would seek out employment with that same company and be subjected to a great deal of tedious inquiries before I could be "hired" but at the commissioner's party my request: "Hey; I would be a great guest on your show" was all it took and in the summer of 1995 I sat opposite Myers.*

Super Bowl Sunday: While the media were whisked away like cattle via busloads towards the stadium, Gregg and I decided to visit South Beach for our viewing pleasure and once again that stretch along the Atlantic Ocean didn't disappoint. We had no intention of going to the game because; number one we didn't have tickets since I gave my two to Eddie and his son and two; because we didn't have tickets but after our three hour lunch we couldn't find my vehicle never mind the stadium. The next morning; Simms joined us for breakfast and I have never seen anyone before or since enjoy bacon as did Super Bowl XXI's Most Valuable Player. "Where I'm from Ace, we don't have bacon this good". (Phil is from Kentucky where only horses; but no pigs dwell). Most of the crew from NFL Film's flew out that Monday as did Gregg, Eddie and Todd but I didn't leave for Films until Tuesday continuing to read about the 49ers' 49 – 26 win over the Chargers; a total of 75 points in Pro Football's 75th season (minus two) and in a game I never saw because number one: well, you know number one and number two: I fell asleep after "lunch" at South Beach on Sunday.

Chapter Thirty: "Sudden Death" and the "Gridiron Gumshoe".

*"Unitas gives to Ameche; the Colts are the World Champions; Ameche scores"! Those twelve words spoken by radio announcer Bob Sherman signaled the end of the 1958 NFL Championship; a 23 – 17 win for Baltimore over the New York Giants, the first National Football League game to be decided by needing an extra period; overtime or also referred to as; "Sudden Death". "Sudden Death"; a euphemism used in Pro Football jargon and perfect for its abrupt ending as in sudden and for its finality as in death; the end. It has become common in the lexicon of other sports as well: In the sport of hockey during the Stanley Cup Playoffs each team has it all "on the line" when two teams have tied after three periods and are forced to play until someone scores; signaling the end of the game as in "sudden death". The quick striking power of Mike Tyson could end any fight he was involved in and the term was used in the fourth round of the James "Buster" Douglas, Tyson fight on February 14th, 1990 fight as the blow by blow, round by round announcer Bob Sheridan could be heard; "this fight could end at anytime as in "sudden death" by the sheer power of any heavyweight". For me however, "sudden death" will always mean one thing and **one thing only**; the nickname of NFL Films' President Steve Sabol: Born on October 2nd, 1942; the son of Ed Sabol the man responsible for the company known as Blair Motion Pictures from 1962 until the league become the company's employer in 1965 young Sabol was to become one of the most iconic figures in the world of Professional Football. "Never afraid to fail"; he with his Dad introduced to millions the game viewed through the eye of the film camera in a perspective never seen before. Fans had an "Up close and personal view" of opposing lineman at the point of scrimmage butting heads as would figuratively speaking Los Angeles Rams. Fans would enjoy tight long lens focusing on the faces of those playing in sub zero temperatures with icy breath as in the 1967 NFL Championship game between the Dallas Cowboys and Packers at Green Bay's Lambeau field. Steve would say that the football field was a canvas and NFL Films would paint a picture by selecting the perfect shots to produce a masterpiece. (Steve could say it much better than I just did) but each was a thing of beauty. Referenced in an earlier chapter (Chapter Three): his grades at Colorado College were at best that of someone on a "taxi squad" just "hanging around" but his Dad decided to "hire" him working for the new company and the twenty two year old began as a camera man working for the company that forever would leave lasting impressions, indelible images and feelings of the visceral variety. Steve's; **"They Called**

it Pro Football" *that was completed in the spring of 1967 was called the "Greatest football movie I had ever seen" by then commissioner Pete Rozelle and it would be just one of hundred that the "tiny tot from possum trot" would produce. Some I have brought notice to throughout; as* **"Big Game America"** *in* 1968, **"The Championship Chase"** *following the 1974 campaign and* **"Joe and the Magic Bean"** *in 1976 but it was his vision and belief in the "What did we have to lose" attitude that made him special. When he turned fifty in 1992, I asked; "Have you ever had a chance to reflect and really stop and look back on what you have accomplished"? He replied; "Not really Ace, it wasn't a risk, we never were being compared to anyone else so we could take chances and if we failed; so be it". The company also would give a $1,000 bonus to anyone that had the "Greatest Failure" because that individual wasn't afraid to try something different. (I wish I was with the company during those earlier years, I could have bought a house, a car and a toaster oven). When others first learned I was working with the company, I was asked; "Do you know Steve Sabol and do you go to all the games"? "Yes I do and no I don't considering it is humanly impossible". Another question; "What kind of guy is Steve Sabol". "There is no pretense with Steve, what you see on television is what you see in person and next to my dad is the nicest man I have ever known". To say I can speak only for myself would be inaccurate; all that have come into contact with him during their years with the company have stories with the same positive effect that he had on each. Not to tell all but to tell: One of our producers during the year of 1993 and into 1994 was battling some chemical vices and "his game wasn't making the grade". It would have been much easier to "let him go" but Steve gave him six months to rehab, paid for any treatment needed and when he returned; he was once again a producer for the company. Even when I had my confrontation with Jay Gerber when everyone at 330 Fellowship Road could hear, Steve was lenient in his reprimanding of me and he had every right to "let me go" but he always looked at the bigger picture; and I am glad he did. I do believed I was given preferential treatment and believed me I used it: I would leave for Rhode Island at anytime; it could have been Monday, Tuesday or the eighth day of the week; if there was one. It didn't matter as long as I did not let it interfere with my research. Steve had a great line; "Ace, don't let me know what you're doing' but just let me know what you're doing". I usually didn't (or did). On numerous occasions, I would invite many of my fellow workers to my home while married to Susan and would cook, which was always the main reason for attending the Tyson, Holyfield "Bite", the De LaHoya -Vargas confrontation and any other pugilistic matchup. I was always under "the gun" because I wanted everything* to reach the level that my "boss" I felt was accustomed to but that was never the case; Steve as was everyone else at 202 Midway in Riverton, New Jersey would have been happy with a pizza. Steve drank at the time; Filindia Vodka with two olives and would finish two drinks in the same time it would take anyone else to finish a sneeze. Two was his limit and now he could enjoy the rest of the evening. I was invited to cook for Steve along with his lived in girl friend Penny Ashman just two times because "Ace always makes a mess" and although the food was great it was just safer and more convenient to go to Ace's house when the "Boss" can have two drinks at warp speed. It was amazing the number of times I would literally "get goose bumps" whenever Steve called me into his office. I respected the man so and at times was "kidded" about it in a sexual way. (Not that there is anything wrong with it!) (That's twice in two chapters I used that line from **Seinfeld**). When I told Steve how nervous I was whenever he called me in; he replied; "It's a lot like meeting the Pope". "I could handle the Pope"! Steve also was a very good judge of character: In a five and a half month period dating from December 1st, 2009 to May 10th, 2010, I pursued a position at ESPN and found their restrictions hard to swallow. When I told Steve I was pursuing employment with the company; he emailed me: "Ace you were born an original don't die a copy". At the time I couldn't understand why he wouldn't want me to work there. After following all protocol and even being asked when I could start and what type of salary I was looking for I was informed; "It wouldn't be a good fit" after being interviewed by Joan Lynch and Vinnie Maholtra in New York City. John Dahl one of the company's best and most insightful producers let it be known to me; "The interview didn't help" my chances and although he swore it was a business decision, I knew the real reason and so did Steve who knew it long before that meeting in the "Big Apple".

Steven Douglas Sabol is the only man in the industry to receive a television Sports' Emmy award in five different categories; writing, producing, directing, editing and film making. All greatly deserved as in all accolades he has received throughout his career(s). He left everlasting impressions in me as stain in wood. I am proud to call him "friend".

Although it was Steve who titled me; "The Director of Archives" my "Gridiron Gumshoe" moniker was given to me by producer Dave Swain after doing research for one of his projects and coming up with some never before seen "nuggets". When trying to explain what I did and what made me so valuable to the company to others; I would hear: "How difficult could it be; don't *you just go back to the game and look at the film footage"? That would be accurate if that question was asked today because from 1988 to the present, NFL Films has shot each game in negative film stock and that original film is never cut or removed from the game. However, from 1962 – 1987 the company shot each game in positive film stock, which we called o'ekta, short for ektachrome. Whenever, we would need some of that footage from a game to be used in another production, we would physically remove the film(s) that we needed to that new piece. For instance: From the very first game that Blair Motion Pictures filmed; the 1962 NFL Championship between the Green Bay Packers and the New York Giants at Yankee Stadium, we took footage from that game and used it in* "**Lombardi**", *and other pieces such as* "**They Called it Pro Football**" *and the* "**Sensational Sixties**". *After a while the original film could not be located because many at the company could not remember in what show the original existed. Thus, a print of the special shot would be made and used in other productions and* ***that*** *would be used as the "original". So whenever we would produce any show where footage was needed between the years 1962 and 1987, I was on the case to track it down as would a private eye by following clues. Franco Harris's* "**Immaculate Reception**" *occurred on Saturday December 23rd, 1972. One week later, NFL Films produced* "**The Game of the Week**" *and to no one's surprise the playoff game between the Raiders and the Steelers at Pittsburgh's Three Rivers' Stadium was the subject. After showing Harris's improbable catch and run for a touchdown, the shot was moved to an NBC piece that previewed the AFC Championship Game between the Miami Dolphins and Steelers. Following the 1972 season, Films produced* "**NFL 72**" *which is a yearend show reviewing the season. Obviously, again Harris's shot is included as it was in other pieces from that season:* "**The Runners**" *which was hosted by the great Jim Brown and the Pittsburgh Steelers' Highlight film from that year. So the* "**Immaculate Reception**" *appeared in all five shows but where is the original? In 1994, while doing research for* "**75 Seasons, the story of the National Football League**", *I located the original shot in a research roll for a show we had done called;* "**Fantastic Finishes**" *that aired in 1987. It really comes down to how much time and effort is needed to find the original and how much time and effort do you want to exhaust. For me; that was satisfying.*

Billy Driber had a couple of insightful remarks; "Ace doesn't know everything, he just knows more than everyone else" and "Ace doesn't know where everything is, he just knows where everything isn't". In other words I would never spend *time doing research looking for one particular shot: If I am looking for an original shot of Gale Sayer's league leading season of 1969 and I see in a research roll that he does not have the 50th anniversary patch on the right shoulder of his uniform I won't continue or if I can see the name on the back of his jersey I know that it cannot be 1969 because it was in the year of the merger (1970) that now the NFL had both conferences be recognized not only by numbers but by their names. If I needed to find research for Mike Ditka's first year with the Eagles and saw that he is wearing number 89, I know that it cannot be 1967 (his first year with Philadelphia) because "Iron Mike" wore number 98 that year. We had a "Cheaters" program where if anyone from the company while watching television happened to see footage that they recognized as NFL Films; he or she would call the sales department and give the information concerning what station, and what time it aired. It was now up to the sales department to locate that footage from a show and once they did, we would be able to collect from that station or group that used the footage. As a reward, Films would give that employee who called it in a bonus of $75.00. An additional $75.00 was given after five "cheaters". Kevin McCoughlin was able to put $10,000 down on a home he bought while working for the company. In one instance; I was called to Jeanne Diblin's office in the hopes of being able to locate a certain shot: The only footage we had was a shot of a tight lens of a football in the air. I asked her who used it and she said it was a group out of Minnesota. I pointed out to her that the spin of the ball was from a left hander and if that's the case it probably came from the Raiders' quarterback Ken Stabler and it was probably from our production at Super Bowl XI: Raiders 32 Vikings 14.We looked at the piece and sure enough there was that same shot of the ball. We collected.*

Isn't ironic how Maine lobsters come from Maine, Lou Gehrig died from Lou Gehrig's disease and people believe that filming an NFL game in slow motion is not that hard because after all the play is moving at a speed that you can handle; and why don't the players trip over that yellow first down line that we see on TV? Yep, these are all questions that can never be answered or explained as in what is a "Gridiron Gumshoe"?

Chapter Thirty One: "Patrick and "Brookie" "Together Again" and "The Greatest Tight End Ever".

In the spring of 1995, Billy Driber and I were assigned to put together fifteen hundred questions and answers for a company from Washington D.C that wanted to include all film footage to correspond with each Q an A. The fifteen hundred would be broken down in blocks of 500 where level one was rookie, level two veterans, and level three; all pro. All would be of the multiple choice variety. The first five hundred were "no brainers": In what state do the Pittsburgh Steelers and Philadelphia Eagles play their home games? Another just as difficult: The 49ers play their home games in what city by the Bay? Remember these questions have multiple choice answers. Level two became more difficult but not impossible: Who holds the record for the most rushing yards in one game? Only two answers could be realistically chosen; Walter Payton or O.J. Simpson. The other two choices: Jan Stenerud and Joe Montana. Level three; however, was another matter: Harold "Red" Grange was more known for his exploits on the field than for his exploits off the field. In 1925 while driving with passengers; Golf Professionals' Walter Hagan and "Long Jim" Barnes a traffic officer pulled him over for speeding: How fast was the "Galloping Ghost" galloping: A − 35 miles per hour, B − 45 miles per hour, C − 55 miles per hour or D − 65 miles per hour. Answer: D. I was responsible for level three's questions and answers. One of my all time favorites: Who was the first man to throw for over 3,000 yards in a season? A − Sid Luckman, B − Frank Tripucka, C − John Unitas or D − Jack Kemp? Answer: B. The reason why this is incredible difficult and should not even be submitted as a question is that in 1960, Unitas, Kemp and Tripucka all threw for over 3,000 yards that season but Denver Broncos' quarterback Tripucka became the first because his team played on Saturday December 17th and both Kemp and Unitas played on Sunday the 18th. It was Tripucka who had the distinction of being the first.

Billy and I had three weeks to complete the video portion of the game; which meant that we had to edit the fifteen hundred questions and the fifteen hundred correct answers. More than fifty percent of the footage was on those one inch reels that physically had to be "lined up" from one reel to another and "start, stop, go and start, stop go again" to complete the edit unlike today when most of NFL Films equipment is of the digital base. It would have been impossible to "bang out" all those edits in a regular work week so we put in a total of 517 *hours in three weeks between the two of us with Billy working 260 and me 257. The difference was the three hours I took preparing a feast that included lobster, clams and shrimp the last day to celebrate our "victory". The next day; Steve handed each one of us a check for $3,000.00 for our services. I just realized why that amount: We edited fifteen hundred questions and fifteen hundred answers: Coincidence? I wish we had worked six weeks on the project.*

Prior to our insomnia, I would be directing Pat Summerall and Tom Brookshier as both would do the voice over(s) for the fifteen hundred questions and answers. At the time, Summerall was employed by the Fox Network teaming up with long time partner John Madden calling NFC Games, while Brookshier had left Broadcasting to pursue other interests. It was one of my most cherished moments working with both, remembering each as co hosts on NFL Films' **"This Week in Pro Football"** *and as CBS's number one broadcast team for six seasons 1975 – 1980. There was chemistry between the two and during their work as the voice over each displayed wit enjoying each other once again. Tom and I would continue to keep in touch until his death at the age of 78 on January 29th, 2010. Since his death I pay tribute to the former Philadelphia Eagles' defensive back by hosting his Memorial Golf Tournament at the Willow Brook Country Club in Moorestown, New Jersey. He is greatly missed.*

In 1986, NFL Films began to supply highlights for the Better Boys Foundation Mackey awards that were presented every year in Chicago: The awards are named after former Baltimore Colts' and San Diego Chargers' tight end John Mackey; who twenty years following his retirement from Pro Football was inducted at Canton, Ohio. It was there; I had the wonderful good fortune of meeting the son of a Baptist Minister and his lovely family that included his wife; Sylvia. In the summer of 1995, I had some personal business in Chicago during the awards presentation and contacted John telling him I would be in Chicago and wanted to get together. NFL Films sent representatives to the awards that included Jim Barry and Kurt Appleby to the presentation and I would meet with them that Saturday Night. First: I met John and Sylvia; at an autographed session on Friday where the Syracuse Alum and teammate of the late 1961 Heisman trophy winner Ernie Davis spent three hours happily giving his John Hancock to enthusiastic fans. One of the lovely young women working for the BBF asked if I would like to attend a party that Chicago Bulls' forward Michael Jordan was hosting. I declined with no regret: I was a Boston Celtic fan; plus I didn't like the way number 23 would stick out his tongue when he drove to the basket. My female acquaintance said she thought it was sexy.

The next day a limo picked up John, Sylvia and me and took us to Wrigley Field where John would throw out the first ball. On the way while we were stopped at a traffic light, I look to my right and see a seven foot; four inch African American man: "Hey look there's Ralph Sampson"; referring to the former NBA player who became one of the most hated players of Boston fans after his altercation with the Celtics' six foot one inch Jerry Sichting during the 1986 NBA Playoffs. Our driver asked: "how do you know that's Ralph Sampson"? Once we arrived at the field, we were taken to a luxury box area complete with once again food and drink. John's wife thought it was the greatest thing ever especially having tasted one of those little cocktail franks. I was mostly impressed with the selection of top shelf spirits. John was escorted down to the field and threw out the first ball; a little inside easily that could have been called a strike. My two co workers from NFL Films; Jim and Kurt were in the left field bleachers and Kurt had a chance to catch a home run and had to make the quick decision: should I let my beer fall and use two hands or should I try to save the 24 ounce beverage and make a left hand stab? Not being able to complete either task my friend had no idea that he would be part of ESPN's Sports Center that night. Kurt had secured his 15 minutes of fame with 14 minutes and 42 seconds to spare.

Chapter Thirty Two:
"I thought he was a Pet Detective"; "Susan" and Posthumously; Jordan and Finks.

On July 18th, 1995, ESPN flew me to the west coast to appear on the show; "Up Close". I was excited to visit "Tinsel Town" again and called my friend Caroline Carrigan whom I had met at Super Bowl XXVII. She continued to pursue an acting career and agreed to meet me for dinner at the hotel I was staying at in Beverly Hills. Feeling "on top of my game" I exuded as much confidence as anyone could stand; loving the attention I was now receiving as a celebrity. Good thing I didn't wear a hat. Drinks followed with dinner and more drinks. As much as I wanted to prepare for my interview with Chris Myers; the host of "Up Close", I couldn't focus on anything but the beautiful lady sitting across from me. She made it clear she couldn't focus on anything but the guy with the large cranium sitting across from her. Everything was perfect: I was in Hollywood appearing on a show which would air nationally, having decadent food and drink; sitting with the beautiful Caroline Carrigan, who was telling me everything I wanted to hear; plus someone found me a hat that would fit. Our hostess could see that we were into each other and asked if we had plans for the next night for dinner when she recommended a restaurant overlooking the ocean that would be perfect for the two "can't keep my eyes off of you" couple. She made reservations and guaranteed we would have the best view overlooking the Pacific. Our evening ended; but not before very small talk; actually very little talk. We couldn't wait for tomorrow.

I had made it my business to relay some interesting anecdotes concerning NFL Films and went over the latter in my mind during the limo ride to the studio. Myers and I spoke a little about what each would discuss before we would begin to record. The show opened with the perfectly thrown spiral by the Pittsburgh Steelers' Cliff Stoudt in the 1983 AFC playoff game between his team and the Los Angeles Raiders; captured by NFL Films' cinematographer Donny Marx. "One of the most perfectly thrown spirals you will ever see; that was Cliff Stoudt of the Pittsburgh Steelers against the Raiders in the 1983 AFC Playoff game; and what you will typically see from NFL Films and we welcome to the program; "Ace Cacchiotti". "Ace, I thought he was a pet detective". In response; "I'm a gridiron gumshoe a sideline shamus". I was making reference to the 1973 movie; **"Shamus"** *starring Burt Reynolds as a pool shooting; card playing' ladies man' private eye: Shamus McCoy is the main character who after getting beat up more than Reynolds has ever been in* *any other movie gets his man and the girl; Alexis Montaigne played by Dyan Cannon. I continue to almost verbatim tell the story of NFL Films and its roots as if Steve Sabol himself was sitting across from Myers. I was proud of my performance as a "mini me" Sabol and couldn't wait for the show to air which would be on July 19th.*

*Once the throngs of fans (do two people make a throng?) allowed me to enter my limo, I headed back to my hotel; calling all my friends that numbered two informing them of the air date. I was "on top of the world mom" and couldn't wait to see Caroline that evening. We had reservations for dinner at seven and the soon to be Lady Guinevere in the musical **Camelot**, Evelyn Love; the wife of James Gandolfini in the movie;* **"A Civil Action"** *from 1998 picked me up in what could only be described as "nice car"; hey a sun roof"! Once we reached our destination, the hostess who knew who we were; Caroline by an earlier description; me by my large hat, were seated. I recognized a few from the movies, including Treat Williams and as if we knew each other for years; "Hey Treat". The man who has appeared in over 90 television episodes and movies including* **"Deep Rising"** *also from 1998, who co - starred with the beautiful former model Famke Jannsan gave me an incredulous look as to say; how did you get that table overlooking the ocean? A most romantic dinner followed with a ride up and down Sunset Boulevard in Caroline's open sun roof car filled my head with intoxicating thoughts as did the two bottles of wine earlier. What followed was an intense competition: Who could out compliment the other? I let her win. With the memories of my two day stay in the "City of Angels" I headed to the airport feeling as if my feet hadn't touched the ground as high as the 30,000 feet we would eventually fly at. I immediately came back to earth: I realized I left my tickets back at the hotel: I missed my flight.*

One week before I was headed to do the show I made a phone call to Susan Majeski, someone I had never seen but wanted to meet after meeting her friends' Jay and Marianne at the Guilford Tavern in Guilford, Ct. two days before. Five months earlier, I had met both at the restaurant and struck up a conversation that eventually went in the direction of both thinking I should meet their friend; Susan. It was February 12th and I would be passing through two days later on Valentine's Day. I was hoping to meet Susan that evening but she was a no show primarily because she had been working at her lingerie store; "Intimacy" and it was "Men's Night" so I left and drove for three and a half hours until I reached NFL Films. I was to find out later that Susan had expressed doubt; "Why do I want to meet a guy name Ace that lives in Jersey and likes football"? Didn't I drive five hours from Rhode Island to south Jersey to work at NFL Films? I mean a short excursion of one and a half hours less was no big deal. Our first contact came on July 12ᵗʰ via a phone conversation. Five continuous nights we spoke and as much as two can; got to know each other. It would be a while before we actually would physically meet and it appeared the first time she would see me would be on ESPN. However, the air date was moved to August 19ᵗʰ and I couldn't wait that long. I decided I was going to surprise her and headed north to 185 Boston Post Road in Orange, Ct. I pretended I was interested in "something for my wife" and the five foot six platinum haired attractive women pointed to an area that if I decided to cross dress; even I would be excited. Finally after 20 minutes of running my hands through silky lingerie; "I've made a decision". Susan's response; "So have I Ace". As hard as I try my Rhode Island accent is with me wherever and whenever I travel. I was happy it did that day.

*Before I was to appear in Los Angeles for the show, I had reservations: My Hall of Fame pieces for the class of 1995 were to be finalized in an edit session; that Friday while I was away. I had to make a decision: Should I stay and complete the two and a half minute features for those that would be enshrined and "finish like a pro" considering the company gave me an opportunity to be part of something special and are the reason(s) for my success or think about being on a national show that would fill my head with helium. Considering NFL Films has been very generous; it was a no brainer: I left the edit session in the hands of my assistant Pete Caldes. The five that were being inducted: The Seattle Seahawks' wide receiver; Steve Largent, Lee Roy Selmon; the Tampa Bay Buccaneers' all pro defensive end, the San Diego Chargers' tight end Kellen Winslow and two others who were posthumously honored; Henry Jordan; the defensive tackle for the Green Bay Packers and Jim Finks who had served in executive positions for the Minnesota Vikings; Chicago Bears and New Orleans Saints as general manager of all three. Again; music had to be "instrumental to the mood" and the songs I selected had to be "spot on". The Jordan piece opened with NFL Music # 107 **"Rumble"** with kettle drums as Packers' players can be seen with their backs to us entering the field: Narrator Jeff Kaye begins; "Throughout the sensational sixties, Vince Lombardi's Green Bay Packers won five NFL Championships, including an NFL record three straight in the years 1965, 66, and 67". "This group of dedicated and devoted individuals dominated their decade like no other team had ever done". "One man whose individual play was pivotal to the Packers' success was defensive lineman; Henry Jordan". The piece continues with more highlights but I wanted the ending to be special: The music changes;*

and in remembrance; again Kaye narrates: "On February 21ˢᵗ, 1977, Henry Jordan departed from a world he had known for 42 years for a very special place". "And with that departure, a very special place was left in the hearts of his family and friends". 'And now 18 years later; he has found a new home; one that he will reside at forever, in again; a very special place; the Pro Football Hall of Fame". While Kaye narrates I showed a shot of Jordan and his teammate Ron Kostelnik on the bench laughing. What I didn't know at the time was that Kostelnik had died in 1993 and his wife Peggy was there with Jordan's widow; Olive. Later, the Jordan family would thank me for the wonderful piece as did Jim Finks' wife Maxine and his son Jim Jr. for what I had done for them as well. Maxine has since passed away but both Olive and Peggy have remarried and are doing well. On occasions, I speak with sons of both Jordan and Finks and we relive those most memorable moments during once again; "Pro Football's Greatest Weekend".

Chapter Thirty Three: "Turf Talk"; "The 100 Greatest Tackles" and "The Greatest Fair Catches of the Sixties".

When PolyGram became NFL Films' video distributor in 1993, they wanted to come out with a breakout video - and did with **"The One Hundred Greatest Touchdowns"** *in NFL History and one year later;* **"The One Hundred Greatest Follies".** *Now PolyGram thought since the previous two were successful why not two more in the same year and we produced;* **"Turf Talk"** *which was the one hundred greatest sound bites and* **"The One Hundred Greatest Tackles"** *simultaneously. Whenever we had to "lift" a sound bite; whether an interview or radio call from a previous production we would physically tab off from one end of magnetic tape to the other end depending on the length of the bite itself. That was time consuming but we were able to come up with another never before countdown; well for this topic anyway. We included obviously; the most recognized by previous NFL Films' pieces that included Gale Sayers' "Give me eighteen inches of daylight, that's all I need", spoken by the Chicago Bears' Hall of Fame running back. Looking through footage I found that the number of takes had reached nine before it became useable. We also faced the politically correct issue: In a previous David "Deacon" Jones piece, the man who coined the term "sack" quoted; "Whenever you go to the side of a man's head - or woman, they tend to blink; and that's all I needed". The former defensive lineman was referring to the "head slap" that we had to edit by omitting; "or woman". Lou Saban; the former head coach of the Boston Patriots, Buffalo Bills and Denver Broncos was one of our most accessible for wearing a microphone: In 1968 while coaching the Denver Broncos, he was animated during a game against the Houston Oilers and turned to one of his assistant coaches; "They're killing me Whitey, they're killing me"! Even today; my wife will use that line when she is unhappy with life or for that matter - with me; which has been more frequent since my "retirement" from NFL Films. Six years later in the 1974 season; once again we followed the now Buffalo Bills head coach in a key matchup against the Miami Dolphins. From the pre game speech in the locker room to the post game press conference after a hard to swallow 35 – 28 loss; Saban granted us access. We even hear in the post edit a familiar voice of Steve Sabol informing the Bills' head coach of a play that the officials missed; which just adds to his already; "end of the world" perspective. Another head coach who was very "agreeable" was Jerry Glanville and in 1990 while coaching the Atlanta Falcons; the man who would always leave a game ticket for Elvis Presley was upset with a rookie official, when he called him to the sidelines and made it* *clear; "This is the NFL, which stands for not for long if you keep making calls like that; "I'll be selling groceries"! In the infant stages of the company; Steve and the other producers would try to "load up" on as many interviews as possible just to give a new look and perspective for the viewers. In an interview with the "world's fastest human"; Bob Hayes, we wanted to know how the wide receiver for the Dallas Cowboys complimented his teammate; Dan Reeves? With the innocence of youth; "I'm always complimenting him because he is always during something good"! Legendary Packers' head coach Vince Lombardi initially did not want Ed Sabol's company to cover any of his practices and in one of the most humorous stories wanted to "cut the throat of the person who wrote the script for the team's 1966 highlight film;* **"A Team; A Town; A Title"**. *That happened to be Ed's son but eventually Lombardi became friends with Ed and even suggested Films do a piece on himself. The title obviously;* **"Lombardi"** *was edited by Yoshio Kitto. In many pieces involving the Packers' Hall of Fame coach, he is seen at a chalkboard illustrating the "Packer Sweep"; "If you look at this play; what we are trying to do is get a seal here – and a seal here - and run it in the alley"! Well that was staged and after the third attempt; Lombardi flips the chalk that he wrote with. That is the one we kept.*

While I was researching for; **"Turf Talk"**, *I was also looking through footage for* **"The One Hundred Greatest Tackles"**. *Although defining a great tackle would not be difficult, we still had to have reasons why this tackle is rated higher than another. The criteria: physically and athletically speaking and when in the game does it occur; and the significance of the game. I think I covered everything; I think. Some players are synonymous with hard hits: Ronnie Lott, Dick Butkus, Herb Adderely, and from the 1950's San Francisco 49ers'; Hardy Brown: Brown was a Damon Runyon type character who instilled fear in the opposition: Orphaned at four years old after he witnessed the murder of his father, he with his sisters were sent to the Texas Masonic Home; an orphanage for the children of deceased parents. While playing football for the "Mighty Mites" he led the team to the state semi finals before playing for the University of Tulsa. But it was his six year career with San Francisco that the man who would die in a state mental institution in 1991 made others' eyes roll; literally. Brown had a unique "delivery" before making a tackle: He would dip his shoulder and uncoil like a cobra knocking the ball carrier from the ball and his senses. In 1953, playing against Philadelphia, the Eagles' Toy Ledbetter recalls: "It was early in the game and I was carrying on a sweep to the right. I knew about Brown because I'd been at Oklahoma State when he was at Tulsa. I usually kept my eye on him, but this time I cut inside a block and never saw him. He caught me with the shoulder and the next thing I knew I was on the*

*ground looking for my head". Other great hits that made the production: the Giants'
Gary Reasons knocking the mouth piece from the Broncos' Bobby Humphrey in
1989 and one year later; the Bears' Richard Dent leaping over a 49ers' lineman
to sack Joe Montana. Many of the greatest to ever play the game made our top one
hundred; including Hall of Fame safety; the Cardinals' Larry Wilson who made
an ankle tackle on the Cowboys' Calvin Hill before he can escape the backfield.
Physically upset, the 1969 NFL Rookie of the year slams the ball down. One of
the tackles that wasn't actually a tackle was from the 1964 AFL Championship
Game between the Buffalo Bills and the defending champions' San Diego Chargers
who in 1963 trounced the Boston Patriots 51 – 10 when Keith Lincoln totaled
349 yards. Early in the 1964 Championship game, Chargers' quarterback Tobin
Rote threw a screen pass out to the flat for Lincoln and is "dropped" hard by the
Bills' linebacker Mike Stratton; breaking two of the Chargers' running back's
ribs. However, because Lincoln never actually had control of the ball it was ruled
incomplete and yet it couldn't "officially" be considered a tackle; otherwise it would
have been ruled a fumble. The two that wrote the script were Dave Douglas who
worked with me six years earlier on the* **"Dream Season"** *and Jim Jordan who
would go on to produce for* **NASCAR**. *Once we had gathered our one hundred,
we went into the final edit to complete another in the one hundred series: No one had
taken the time to actually decide what the countdown would be; so there we were
with a deadline and no clue what order we would list the tackles. We did agree that
number one should be; the Philadelphia Eagles' Chuck Bednarik's vicious hit on the
New York Giants' Frank Gifford which caused a fumble; that the Eagles' Chuck
Weber recovered in the game played at Yankee Stadium during the 1960 season.
Although it seemed that Bednarik was rejoicing standing over the fallen Giants'
halfback after delivering the hit; in reality he is celebrating because his teammate
recovered. Okay we now have number one: Only 99 more to go.*

*As noted earlier; when PolyGram became NFL Films' home video distributor
in 1993, we produced the* **"One Hundred Greatest Touchdowns",
"Follies", "Sound Bites"** *and* **"Tackles"**. *Michelle Valkov; who was our
Public Relations' person read one in* **GQ** *magazine when she came across one
that commented on all the "One hundred this and One hundred that" and the
next thing you know; "Steve Sabol will be producing the greatest fair catches of
the sixties". Michelle brought it to my attention and we decided to see if we could
produce such a piece. It would be not easy to actually come across fair catches
because there is nothing special about a fair catch and would not meet the criteria
of "special rolls". Thus; research would be difficult and instead of appointing two,
three or even four producers to come up with what could only be a comical feature,*

Gridiron Gumshoe

I decided to take full responsibility on the overall production that would include writing, editing and selection of music. Although it was to be an obvious tongue in cheek production I wanted to purposely write as over the top as possible leaving doubt; was I serious? I led with again some of the larger than life music telling the story how the decade of the sixties gave us some of the most memorable moments in Pro Football History; as the Packers' Bart Starr sneaks in for Green bay's third straight NFL Title and the Jets' Joe Namath leaving the Orange Bowl at Super Bowl III signaling his team is number one. The open also displays the "powerful running of the Cleveland Browns' Jim Brown, the elusiveness of Chicago's Gale Sayers and the savage ferocity of the Bears' Dick Butkus". "Viewers turned in for open mouth astonishment, wide eyed amazement and breath taking plays". From here we see fans with open mouth astonishment, wide eyed amazement, as I showed the Vikings' Fran Tarkenton elude the San Francisco 49ers for eleven seconds before he threw deep downfield where the ball is tipped by two San Francisco defenders and into the Vikings' Preston Carpenter to complete the wild 40 yard touchdown. Our own in house Narrator; Barry "Have it your way" Wolper continued; "But for sheer drama and excitement, no one play can match the heart stopping moment of the fair catch. Simple in context but so complex in execution, the fair catch proved to be the play most responsible for so many teams success during Pro Football's most exciting era"! The final shot of the open has the Baltimore Colts' Tim Brown signally for a fair catch against the Green Bay Packers from 1968. From the 96 frame shot the Title: **"The Greatest Fair Catches of the 60's"** *is shown. The countdown begins in a game played between the Broncos and Dolphins at Denver's home field; Bears' Stadium which was just a way to inform the viewer that Mile High Stadium was first known as Bears' Stadium. Sam Spence's* **"Classic Battle"** *is used with the crescendo ending with the Broncos' Floyd Little after making a fair catch is carried off the field. I also included in the script many lines that would be followed by a "what does he mean by that and I don't get it". Well; that is why the piece never saw the light of day. In the second segment in a game played between the St. Louis Cardinals and Philadelphia Eagles on opening day from 1966, Wolper begins; "In pivotal week one, the Eagles traveled to Busch Memorial Stadium to face the Cardinals". Many questions; how could week one be pivotal? This is when I realized I should keep the one copy I have for posterity. And although I did take some liberties with the final fair catch by the Vikings' Bobby Bryant who after making the catch he blows kisses to the crowd in a game played against Green Bay in 1971, I thought I had produced something special. No one had ever attempted to produce such a piece before and it is safe to say no one will ever again - especially in pivotal week one of any season.*

From the Hall of Fame
Class of 1994: Tony Dorsett
With presenter head coach
Tom Landry. Dorsett
Honored me with his recital
Of one of my lines from
My Production.

49ers' defensive back
Jimmy Johnson with
His brother Rafer
Who won the 1960
Olympic Decathalon.
And sent me a heartfelt
letter; thanking me
From His Brother's Induction
In the summer of 1994.

From Super Bowl XXIX
At the commissioner's
Party – on my right 49ers'
Owner Ed Debartolo
And former head coach
Bill Walsh on my left

Special Olympics California

501 Colorado
Suite 200
Santa Monica, CA 90401-2435
(310) 451-1162
Fax (310) 458-1029

August 4, 1994

Ace Cacchiotti
NFL Films
330 Fellowship Road
Mt. Laurel, NJ 08509

Dear Ace,

It was so good to see you at The Hall of Fame Induction Ceremonies in
Canton. Jim is so deserving of the honor and we will never forget the
feeling we had seeing him standing on the stage holding his bust that will
be placed in The Hall of Fame.

Your film and words were great as usual and added so much to the event.

When I am in the East again, I will certainly give you a call. Until then I
send my best wishes to you.

Sincerely,

Rafer Johnson
Chairman, Board of Governors

Corresponding with middle picture

On the opposite page:

The 49ers' Jimmy Johnson holding

Bust with his brother Rafer: The 1960

Decathlon Champion at the Rome Olympics.

On returning home from Canton; two days later

I received one of my most cherished letters from

A classy gentleman.

NATIONAL FOOTBALL LEAGUE

1920   1994

August 31, 1994

Mr. Ace Cacchiotti
NFL Films
330 Fellowship Road
Mt. Laurel, NJ 08054

Dear Ace:

I would like to express my thanks for your assistance in the preparation of the 1994 Rule Changes Video.

Without your complete cooperation, this project would not have been pulled off and provided us with such a tremendous product.

I look forward to working with you in years to come. Please contact me if I can ever be of assistance.

Sincerely,

JERRY SEEMAN
Director of Officiating

JS:do

From 1991 to 1993, The NFL's "Director of Officiating" and I worked together on; "The Rule Changes" for the upcoming season. It was always a "trip" working with Jerry as the word "consequently" before each explanation became his "crutch". We survived however and in 1994 I continued to work on "The Rule Changes" but now with the former 49ers' wide receiver; Gene Washington; "The Director of Football Development" for the NFL.

NATIONAL FOOTBALL LEAGUE

June 22, 1994

Ace Cacchiotti
NFL Films
330 Fellowship Rd.
Mt. Laurel, NJ 08054

Dear Ace:

Just a note to say thanks for your efforts today on the 1994 rules changes video. Having been in "the business" for several years, I know a professional when I see one. Your entire staff was a joy to work with and I really appreciate your care in making sure we produce the best product available.

Looking forward to working with you again on another project. Next time, I want the full tour of your incredible facility.

Sincerely,

Gene Washington
Director of Football Development

cc. Roger Goodell
    Jan Van Duser
    Jerry Seeman

ViCARIOUS

December 5, 1994

Three Lagoon Drive
Suite 300
Redwood City, CA 94065
Phone: 415.610.8380
Fax: 415.610.8302

Mr. Ace Cacchiotti
NFL Films
330 Fellowship Road
Mt. Laurel, NJ 08054

Dear Ace,

I just wanted to thank you personally for all the time and effort you put into our "NFL's Greatest Plays" product. All of your hard work and knowledge resulted in a first-class product. One we can all be proud of!

I enjoyed working with you and hope to work with NFL Films again in future endeavors.

Enjoy the product!

Sincerely,

Kelley Cassin

Kelley Cassin

With much apprehension; I did board an

Airline and headed west to fulfill my

Obligation to those responsible for

producing the 75 greatest plays in NFL History – and

I only consumed six Smirnoff vodkas with ice to

Reach my destination.

© ESPN, INC.
662 NORTH LA CIENEGA BLVD.
LOS ANGELES, CA 90069

August 21, 1995

Ace Cacchiotti
NFL FILMS
330 Fellowship Rd.
Mt. Laurel, NJ 08054

Dear Ace:

As promised, enclosed please find a VHS copy of your recent
interview with Chris Myers for ESPN's Up Close show.
Needless to say, the show was a tremendous success and very
well received by our viewers.

Ace, thanks again for your time. We really appreciate your
coming on the show.

Sincerely,

Cindy Katz
Talent Coordinator

My second trip to "Tinsel Town"

Enabled me to increase my hat size and spend

Time with the aspiring actress Caroline Carrigan

as we lavished in our version of "Celebrity Status" and all because

I told the producer of the show; Cindy Katz

I would be a great guest.

Chapter Thirty Four:

Yesterday was the PAST…

Tomorrow is the FUTURE…

Enjoy TODAY because it's a GIFT… That's why they

Call it…

THE PRESENT!

Sid Luckman

At Super Bowl XXX, My future third wife flew to Phoenix to meet me on the Thursday; three days before the NFL Championship Game played between the NFC's; Dallas Cowboys and the AFC's; Pittsburgh Steelers. I was excited to impress Susan and working for Satellite News for the league; once again I had free reign of Arizona's capital and all that is during a Super Bowl week. Susan arrived at the hotel that Billy Driber, our NFL Films' crew and I were staying and it was easy to see why she immediately relished her vacation sight: We had dinner at a Mexican Restaurant seated out on a patio as we enjoyed ethnic cuisine which included refried beans with everything. Our night ended with drinks at one of our hotel's many lounges making small talk with those that believed are celebrities because are recognized by being opinionated on camera. The next day, our crew covered Paul Tagliabue's press conference as I logged each question and answer so that in post edit it would be easy to find the most profound thought of the league's official fourth commissioner: And once again;"Will the league expand"? "Yes, eventually; next question". At three p.m. Pacific Standard Time my "grueling" six hour day working as a producer for the league ended and now it was time for the annual Commissioner's Party: As in Miami one year earlier, I had two tickets to the inner circle and couldn't wait to expose Susan to the different classes of people that attended. After about one hour of "Where are you from" and what do you do for a living", we decided to "escape" and find our own table commenting on everyone else's color of dress and bust size; women and men that wanted to be women as well; **(Take a walk on the wild side";** *Lou Reed 1972). As much as I make light of the night it really is an extravaganza: The NFL can really throw a*

Gridiron Gumshoe

party and I was happy to include Susan in what has always been a first class affair.

On each Saturday; one day prior to the big game, the Hall of Fame Committee announces the induction class for the upcoming season: Once again, my crew covered the press conference as John Bankert informed us: Dan Dierdorf, Joe Gibbs, Charlie Joiner, Mel Renfro and the old timers' selection of Lou Creekmur would be enshrined at Canton, Ohio. I always had a special place in my heart whenever the committee selected someone from the fifties, because it was usually long overdue and also; it was a chance to meet someone who played against the greatest from the decade. Creekmur was an offensive lineman who played from 1950 to 1959 with the Detroit Lions and was a member of three NFL Championship teams who played alongside other teammates that had been inducted at Canton: Bobby Layne, Doak Walker, Jack Christensen, Frank Gatski, Yale Lary, Joe Schmidt and Dick Labeau, who was selected for the 2010 class. I couldn't wait for that last weekend of July to meet some of those former players from the "Fabulous Fifties" as well as another Hall of Fame player from the forties; whom I would later; following the announcement: Sid Luckman had reached out to me one year earlier; asking if there was any way NFL Films could transfer some of his old footage to video tape so his family could view his highlights as a keepsake. He also had rare footage from the playoff game needed to decide the Western Division against the Green Bay Packers in 1941. The former Chicago Bears' quarterback sent me the footage and we were able to transfer the archival film for him and for us. Since then; Sid and I had become friends albeit via the phone so I was excited to meet him that Saturday afternoon at a country club in Scottsdale. That afternoon; Sid served as the celebrity spokesperson for the Mayo Clinic that is located in Rochester, Minnesota. The first man to throw for seven touchdowns in a game on November 14th, 1943 against the New York Giants was articulate, eloquent and humbled. Once he finished, Susan and I listened to this wonderful and caring man expressing heartfelt stories about his life. I have never met anyone who had such a passion for life. The three of us had a light dinner at the country club before we said goodbye. We would meet again:

My wife's mother; Audrey; had suffered a stroke on September 21st, 1993 and unfortunately her conditioned worsened as she would suffer two more. Susan was for all intents and purposes the sole caregiver of her mom who would pass away at the age of 69 at her home in Wallingford, Ct. May 15th, 1996; the same month and day that is my mom's birthday. On that Wednesday; the day of Susan's mom's passing; we had been invited to the Waldorf Astoria in New

181

York City as guests of Sid; as he was being recognized for being not just a great humanitarian but also; as a great human being as well. Susan's brother Billy told her sister there is nothing she could do until the next day concerning her mom and wanted us to continue with our plans. With a heavy heart; my wife escorted me that evening. Our good friend had provided us with an overnight stay at an impressive numbered star hotel located on Park Avenue near the Empire State Building. After checking in and having a drink at the hotel lounge, we hailed a cab and told our driver of our destination: In a scene from the movie; **"The Jerk";** *Navin Johnson played by Steve Martin is ready to face the world on his own and decided to hitchhike cross country and is picked up in front of his house by the actor Rob Reiner who is only going to the end of the fence in front of Navin's house. Navin accepts the ride. Our destination; the Waldorf Astoria is located on 301 Park Avenue, which is exactly across the street from the hotel we were staying at. We accepted the ride and I even left a five dollar tip. We sat with Sid and once again, he was comforting especially with Susan. Susan and I were married on July 12, of that year and one of the gifts we received was from Sid; a wonderful message: Yesterday was the PAST... Tomorrow is the FUTURE... Enjoy TODAY because it is a GIFT... That's why they call it... THE PRESENT! My friend also had his own clothing line and sent me two very fashionable ties: The reverse side reads as follows: "Made for a friend of Sid Luckman". We were - until his passing on July 5th, 1998 at the age of 81.*

Chapter Thirty Five:
ESPN's "Greatest Games";
and "Don't worry; the Packers' covered".

The average American spends an estimated three years of his or her life on the toilet: So I decided to become mathematical inquisitive: If 72 years of age is the average life span of an individual; then when you become 24 you have already according to this survey have spent one year on the toilet. That being true; at the age of two, one month of your life was learning to become potty trained. So once you have mastered the former you now begin to spend 4.42 percent of each day on the toilet, john, head, throne or whatever it is referred to. Well one day when I was averaging my twelve percent, I had a vision: Rhetorically speaking; "You don't think it would be anything but cool if we were able to put back in chronological order each camera angle of some of the greatest games in NFL History and show that game in its' entirety"? The first game I thought of was the New York Jets' 16 – 7 win over the Baltimore Colts at the Orange Bowl in Super Bowl III. I went into Steve's office and made the proposal and with good blessings from the "Boss" began to set out on what would become a regular viewing program on ESPN as the **"Greatest Games"**. *An incredible great deal of research would be needed to find by process of elimination each camera angle from that game and I instituted the help of Chris Willis, who at the time was an intern in my department. Chris would go on to become employed by the company as the "archivist". I was a little confused by his title but that is for another time and for another story. I had Chris go to all the special rolls from that game and also to the "wagon wheels"; a term we used to describe the large rolls of footage from each camera that had never before seen "the light of day". Meanwhile, I began to look through produced shows that might pertain to Super Bowl III such as* **"Best Ever Quarterbacks"**, **"Best Ever Coaches"** *and* **"Best Ever Teams"**. *Other shows included* **"The History of the AFL"** *and* "**To Catch the Wind**"; *a wonderful piece from the sixties on receivers. I then decided to look through other research rolls as well by utilizing the "Big Board": Located in the film vault were three; five by six feet sized plastic boards that had the title of each show produced by the company from 1962 to 1981. Many from the company thought it should have been tossed but I wanted it to stay "right where it is" because it was a lot easier to see what shows were produced by years than by clicking onto a show via computer which incidentally does not inform by date chronologically. That way I could see in 1969 following Super Bowl III we produced a season ending show for the United States' Navy and in that research I found the original shot* *of Joe Namath's number one as he left the stadium following his team's win in Miami. The shot begins with the snap of the ball as Unitas completes a pass to Willie Richardson as the final gun goes off. The camera stays on the Jets celebrating and you can see the back of some of the NFL Films' camera men wearing shirts that read AFL Films including young Sabol. As the film continues; I begin to get a little excited because I am thinking; "This might be it", this could be the Namath shot" and then I panicked; what if I rip the film"? It was the only time I had ever looked through film with any anxiety because I was about to discover the Holy Grail, the Dead Sea Scrolls and Bob Hayes' punt return from cameraman Ernie Ernst's ground end zone shot of the Cowboys' punt returner coming right at us against the Giants in 1968. (I never did because that play was damaged in post production). Well after two minutes and 37 seconds at 96 frames per second, Super Bowl III's MVP lifts that right hand and displays that index finger. I am positive many that had bet on the Colts were displaying a finger as well. Later, I was able to find the original of Namath walking to the line adjusting his shoulder pad. When* **Classic Sports** *did a feature on NFL Films in 1997, Namath hosted the feature including the segment on the film vault with me and I asked about that shot. I have always admired those that have played the game but did get a little nervous being in "Broadway Joe's" presence. I mean it actually took us two takes to complete the two minute feature. Chris and I were able to find the original camera shots from the top and top end zone and another high percentage of ground, ground end zone and long lens. Now it was time to put each play back in sequential order. Once we had, I presented it to Steve. He contacted ESPN and* **"The Greatest Games"** *series began. We needed someone to be the "play by play" guy and decided on Curt Gowdy, who did the original play by play at Super Bowl III with Al Derogatis as the "color" guy. Producer Ken Sheil was responsible for directing the shoot that would have Gowdy with no script reliving and bringing to life that incredible upset on January 12ᵗʰ, 1969. However, a problem arose when the onetime host of the* **"American Sportsman"** *wanted to know who was going to do his makeup. No one had thought of it considering Gowdy would be off camera for 99% of the show but he insisted. After a physical heated exchange with Sheil and me he agreed to have my wife Susan perform makeup artistry based on her being licensed as an aesthetician. The shoot went off with no other incidents and we were ready to present the final piece to that group located on One ESPN Boulevard in Bristol, Ct. A great deal of promotion took place and a premier was scheduled for the fall of 1997 in New York City where representatives from both companies would attend. Prior to the showing of the 74 minute production* *accolades were given to many responsible for what was a long and arduous journey. My wife became emotionally upset and left for the ladies' room when she didn't recognize any of those being praised because no one mentioned had a last name of Cacchiotti. I was upset as well: I mean again; "wasn't I responsible for not only its content and Curt Gowdy's makeup but wasn't it I who while spending 12% in that bathroom that day came up with the idea"? I finally received my due when while listening to Sabol as he was doing an interview on a local radio station the "Boss" made it clear that concerning the* **"Greatest Games"** *Series; it was an idea that was presented to him by our "Director of Archives"; Ace Cacchiotti. It may have been a little late but gee it took John Mackey 20 years following his retirement to be inducted into the Pro Football Hall of Fame and when you do the numbers it might have been another 12 percent of time spent on the toilet for the next 7,300 days if Sabol waited that same amount of time before I was mentioned as a contributor to the series. I guess I was lucky after all.*

The Hall of Fame Class that year included Mike Haynes; the defensive back for fourteen NFL seasons, playing seven each for the New England Patriots and Los Angeles Raiders, the owner of the New York Giants' and contributor to Pro Football; Wellington Mara, Don Shula; whose 347 wins is the most in NFL History as coach for the Baltimore Colts and Miami Dolphins and "Iron Mike" Webster; the Pittsburgh Steelers' center for fifteen seasons. As was the case since 1990, I was responsible for the production of the two and a half minute pieces that would be shown that Friday Night on the eve of Saturday's induction at Canton. That year NFL Films' agreed to have my friend from my W.S.N.E. radio days' Dave DiLorenzo due the voice over for those four inducted. Films paid David $250.00 for each piece and my friend with the baritone voice would also attend the festivities in Canton for four days. Gregg Pappas joined us and on Thursday July 24th, the three of us attended the cocktail reception at the downtown Hilton in Canton. While talking to some of the greatest to ever play, I heard my name being called: "Ace; come here". It was Kathy Davis; Steve Sabol's personal assistant. She was with "Deacon" Jones and introduced me. The "Deacon" wanted to know if I could assist him in what was to be his inaugural Hall of Fame Golf Classic on December 9th and 10th in Orlando, Florida. His biggest concern: would he be able to acquire film footage of the forty Hall of Fame Players that were scheduled to appear at the Buena Vista Palace and Golf Resort at Disney World? Fearing a head slap, I informed him I could definitely accommodate all his requests. From there I would be dealing with his wife Elizabeth; an attractive blond *who made an impressive appearance. While discussing details I asked "Liz" who would be the master of ceremonies that evening? "Roy Firestone". Well what happened next would change my life heading into another career: "I'll tell you what I will do": "Let me emcee and I will introduce all forty players with corresponding film footage, followed by a follies routine where I will segue from one player to another and I will also put together a ten minute piece highlighting your husband's career and tie that in with his charity". I waited for her response and before I could finish; "and tie that in with his charity" she agreed but still wanted to know if I had ever done anything like this before. I told her I was doing the same type of production for Mel Blount's 50th birthday celebration in Pittsburgh in April the following year. Actually I lied and later when Tianda; Mel's wife asked if I had done anything like I had proposed to her I told her "Yes, I am the emcee for "Deacon" Jones' inaugural Hall of Fame Golf Classic in December. Now both Tianda and Elizabeth think I have experience as an emcee. I didn't but was willing to learn. I would soon get an education in what is called being "politically correct".*

Some of the Pro Football's all time greats were going to be in attendance that December 9th: Hall of Famers; Otto Graham, Lou Groza, Marion Motley from the Cleveland Browns, Bobby Bell, Willie Lanier from the Kansas City Chiefs, and Jim Taylor and Paul Hornung from the Green Bay Packers just to name seven of the forty that were scheduled to appear. I had put my head on the chopping block and if I didn't perform the axe would come down on my supple neck. (Come on; it's been awhile since I wrote anything metaphorically!) Using some of our best music and original footage I was able to produce a thirty second highlight piece on each. Once I finished I began to look through some of the lighter moments in the careers of the forty best ever so that I could present a follies piece and finally I created a very moving tribute to arguable the NFL's best at sacking the quarterback. DiLorenzo narrated the Jones' piece and I would perform; introducing the Hall of Fame Players as well as the Follies' feature. My wife didn't want to fly alone so she agreed to be my traveling companion as we became familiar with interstate 95 South for two days until we reached our destination. The first night Jones and I were responsible for introducing the Hall of Fame Players at a local sports' bar. That went without incident but the next night; well: Friday Night was a black tie affair and all in attendance were dressed accordingly although most of the former players looked as if they were employed by a funeral parlor and at the end of the evening a couple of the former players probably wished I was a permanent resident at that same funeral parlor. It was a gala affair and now was the time *for me to introduce the night as the master of ceremonies. The most nervous I had ever been was when I fought at Jack Witchi's on May 12, 1977. (See chapter eleven). But make no mistake; I was definitely out of my comfort zone when the main light blinded me and not with science. (**Thomas Dolby 1983**). However, once I began, I introduced all forty Hall of Fame Players and settled and relaxed for only 30 seconds thinking that in one hour I would have to entertain with the follies routine. Prior to the dinner, "Deacon", Liz and I viewed the comical piece I had produced and they thought it was fine. I wanted to be careful that I wasn't going to offend anyone and made it clear to both what I would be saying as the production rolled. The last thing I wanted was forty Hall of Famers carrying my casket to my place of eternal rest. Plus, I wanted to leave everyone in a good mood for the act that followed: The Ohio based Soul and R and B group the **O'Jays** who had many hits including* **"Love Train"** *and* **"Back Stabbers"**. *When I came to the segment with Paul Hornung, I told of his exploits on and off the field as Jim Taylor explained how his Packers' teammate could score "on and off the field". I also continued; with following one year off from Professional Football, the "Golden Boy" performed magnificently. While I am showering number five with accolades the screen is telling a different story as he fumbles against Dallas in a game played in 1964 and in Keystone Cops' fashion; the ball is kicked around before the Cowboys' Warren Livingston picks it up and runs it in for a 17 yard touchdown. While the audience is laughing I explain; "No need to worry the Packers' covered": In 1963, the Detroit Lions' Alex Karras and Hornung were suspended for the season by NFL Commissioner Pete Rozelle for their involvement in gambling on NFL Games. For the longest time Karras denied doing anything wrong but the Packers' great halfback accepted punishment and was humbled by the unfortunate experience. It had always been a touchy subject for him and while I was making light of the situation it was anything but that for him. As bad as I would find out later how upset he was; he at least waited until I was finished before I would find out later his to put it mildly; disapproval: While I was doing my "act" I came across Ollie Matson in a game played in 1955 between his Chicago Cardinals and Philadelphia Eagles when Matson who is black can't handle the pitchout from quarterback Lamar McHan, he does however recover and does a two step avoiding a tackler and then laterals to teammate Dave Mann; also an African American before he throws a 13 yard touchdown pass to Don Stonesifer tying the game at 24. While this is happening I brain dead respond: "Look two brothers in the same backfield, a rarity in the 50's but this is not the Washington Redskins" as I was making reference to the team from our nation's capital who did not have* *an black player on the team until Bobby Mitchell in 1962. Owner George Preston Marshall was quoted; "We will have a black player playing for the Washington Redskins when the Harlem Globetrotters have white players." Well, as I continue, I feel the presence of another: Lem Barney is in my face on stage visibly upset. I try to diffuse the situation by telling the former Lions' defensive back that it was I who produced his Hall of Fame piece in 1992 and I would never do anything off color (did I really say that?) to offend any of the former players. He grudgingly leaves and somehow I kept it together but now the program is running late and figuratively speaking I get the hook. The O'Jays perform and I am a little shaken by the recent events and leave with my wife to the lobby where I see Marion Motley and try to explain what I believed had just happened. Motley was okay but did let me know that the next time I should be more sensitive. Saturday, the bad weather came and the Deacon Jones' Hall of Fame Golf Classic was cancelled due to a driving rainstorm; the same rainstorm my wife and I drove through on our way back home to south Jersey. Returning to work on Monday, I told Steve about the events in Orlando but he already knew because Hornung called and read my boss the riot act. In 1999, we had a round table discussion with Hornung, Jones, Michael Strahan of the New York Giants and Steve. I tried to make peace with the Packers' legend but he would have none of it and even when I had sent him highlights of his career he as a matter of fact told me he had tossed the tape in the garbage but on that Monday following the debacle at Disney World, Steve told me I should trash any ideas I had on emceeing any events because you never know who may get upset in what you have to say. As I had done on so many other occasions; I heeded my boss's word(s) and looked forward to my appearance at the Mel Blount 50th birthday bash in April.*

Chapter Thirty Six:
"It is Offensive lineman not Orfensive lineman" and "The Greatest Game Ever Played" again and again.

In the spring of 1997, Mel Blount's wife Tianda called and asked if I could come to Pittsburgh and video tape her husband's celebrity golf event and could I also orchestrate interviews with the former players that would be there and have each say something nice about Mel. Blount was a former defensive back from Southern University who played from 1970 to 1983 with the Pittsburgh Steelers. One of the best to ever play the position, number 47 was inducted into the Pro Football Hall of Fame with teammate Terry Bradshaw in 1989. I met the Blounts at Super Bowl XXVII and established a relationship with two very special people. Following his retirement from Pro Football in 1983 he founded the Mel Blount Youth home in his hometown of Vidalia, Georgia; a shelter and Christian mission for victims of child abuse and neglect. Mel knew about poverty as a child growing up on a farm. He founded his second youth home six years later in 1989 in Claysville, Pa. Each year he has a gala event that raises monies for his charity and on April 10th, 1998 he would be celebrating his 50th birthday and his wife wanted me to put something special together for his first charity event that evening. I received a list of who's who, including the master of ceremonies for the evening Bradshaw and proceeded to produce a 45 second clip on each to be used as an introduction. Tianda also asked if I could somehow put a highlight package together for her husband that would be shown introducing just him. One of those that would be attending was Jim Brown; arguably the greatest running back in NFL History. When I attempted to interview the Cleveland Browns' legend he made it clear he did not like the company I worked for because he wasn't able to get highlights of his career without "Some kind of hassle". I informed him that when I see him that April 10th; "Things will be different". He also decided that he need no prompt; "Don't tell me what to say about my brother, I've known Mel forever". **"The Mel Blount's 50th Birthday Bash"** *was to be carried live on local television station WPXI in Pittsburgh. The producer for the event asked Tianda if* **he** *could be responsible for Mel's Pro Football highlight presentation since the station was already producing the feature on his youth home. However, she made it clear that "My guy Ace from NFL Films was doing the piece". I would find out later that was a blow to the producer's ego.*

Tianda made arrangements for Susan and I to stay overnight at the Hilton in downtown Pittsburgh that Saturday night but wanted me to get there sometime in early afternoon so the local station could do a run through with me on the night's activities. After five hours on interstate 76 headed west we reached our hotel and met Tianda and the producer from WPXI. I then proceeded to rehearse with my introduction of **"Tonight's Celebrity Guests":** *Doing what now comes natural to me and in my best Steve Sabol likeness I continue through my routine: "From 1971 – 1980 number 79 played for the Steelers". After playing the position of tight end in his first five seasons he became the team's starting left offensive tackle". However, I and everyone else on the planet pronounce offensive tackle as* **or***fensive tackle and before I could finish my segment on Larry Brown, the director stops me and wants me to do it again. I do and continue: "the team's starting* **Or***fensive tackle". Once again I was* **not asked** *but* **told to stop***! By now I have to ask; "What's wrong"? The director told me that the producer has informed her that I am pronouncing the word incorrectly and it should be* **O***ffensive. I ask if the producer is kidding and is told to just continue. I do not and ask again: "Is he kidding"? The same response follows and being as diplomatic as I always have been in other uncomfortable situations; walk off the stage:* ***"I'll be ready tonight, just make sure you will be ready too"***! *Tianda who was ten months pregnant with her third child chased, pleaded with me to reconsider: "Ace, you're going to make me have the baby right here". "Please go back". I didn't and asked that she tells the producer what I have done to contribute to the event and I don't need anyone commenting on my pronunciation of "***Or***fensive" lineman. From there she explains that the producer was upset with her because she raved about the piece I had put together for her husband and called me "A genius". He took offense (or is it orfense?) to that considering it was* **"his"** *station that was responsible for the* **"whole"** *event. At game time I was ready and introduce each player without incident including Jim Brown; my best new friend after giving him one continuous hour of his career highlights. Now was the moment when Mel's highlight feature would be shown and as Dave DiLorenzo ended with: "The true measure of a man and a champion is not weighed by the sum total of his statistics but by the summation of his character; and that was never more true for the man; the Champion:" "Ladies and Gentlemen"; Mel Blount"! A standing ovation followed and as I stood between The Cleveland Brown's all time great and the Pittsburgh Steelers' owner; Dan Rooney, I applauded realizing I was being forgiven for mispronunciation.*

Gridiron Gumshoe

"Fate rarely calls upon us at a moment of our choosing". *(Optimus Prime; Transformers II: Revenge of the Fallen).*

On third down and four in the 1958 NFL Championship Game, the New York Giants' halfback Frank Gifford took the handoff from quarterback Charley Conerly and gained those four yards appearing to have made enough yardage for the first down that would have enabled the Giants to run out the clock and win the game at 17 – 14. However, on the play the Baltimore Colts' defensive tackle Eugene "Big Daddy" Lipscomb fell backwards on teammate defensive end Gino Marchetti's leg snapping it in the process. While officials scrambled to pull the players apart, the actual spot where Gifford was tackled became an issue an according to the NFL's MVP of 1956; misplaced the spot of the ball. The chains came out to measure and New York was short forcing them to punt on fourth down. Baltimore with less than two minutes remaining in the quarter proceeded to drive down the field on the passing combination of Johnny Unitas to Raymond Berry. Steve Myra's field goal sent the game into overtime; the first time ever extra time was needed to decide a winner. After another brilliant drive orchestrated by the Colts' QB that took his team to the Giants' two yard line, fullback Alan Ameche dove over for the winning touchdown as the Colts won 23 – 17 in what would be later known as the **"Greatest Game Ever Played"**! *From there; every fifth, tenth and so on anniversary year of that game played, special tribute was and continues to be made to those that played in the historic game and in the 40th anniversary ESPN wanted to showcase that game for its'* **"Greatest Games"** *series. Producer Dave Plaut and I would be responsible for its' content but unlike the previous game we had done for ESPN's Super Bowl III, NFL Films did not film the game and finding every play would be difficult. Two companies did: Tel – Ra and Winik Films. We had both companies' libraries of film and I began to come up with as many shots as possible to recreate the game. Winik shot from one side of the field from a top camera's perspective and Tel –Ra from the other side that made it possible for us to replay any pass, run and kick from the opposite side as a "reverse angle". We also got lucky: Tel – Ra had instituted a ground camera man who would later become part of the Blair Motion Pictures' and later the NFL Films' team: Art Spieller was responsible for more than a handful of 48 frames per second shots that we incorporated in the feature including the most memorable of Ameche's touchdown from the ground end zone perspective. I was able to find 113 of the actual 156 which made up the total number of plays from both teams and presented it to ESPN. With a little less than 75% of all the plays ESPN's* **"Greatest Game"** *took a look back at the 40th anniversary of the* **"Greatest Game Ever Played"**. *Interviews from the Colts' Lenny Moore and Berry and the Giants' Gifford and Pat Summerall added to the overall production. However, what was missing was a current perspective from Unitas whose interview was used from a piece Films had done in 1986. Unitas's son John Jr. was handling his father's business affairs and would not agree to an interview unless ESPN paid for the amount of his son's financial request; which they refused. Later; I would find out first hand that this seemed to be the company's policy at times concerning compensation.*

*In January of 2008, Barry Wolper called me into his office and asked if we owned all the footage pertaining to that 1958 Championship. I explained why we did and he related that info to the league head quarters in New York City. It seemed that ESPN had acquired other footage from that game from one of the Baltimore Colts' personal camera man that had filmed the game for his head coach Wilbur "Weeb" Ewbank. With that footage the Bristol, Ct. based group wanted to do a special presentation on the 50th anniversary and although it would not be the first time that an anniversary "special" was done on the game, ESPN wanted to add a new wrinkle: To colorize the game. Being very protective of the company that would give me my "release" in two months I was dead against anyone doing anything of that magnitude if the production didn't come from One NFL Films Plaza. I heard nothing concerning ESPN plans for the footage until four months later when I became an I.F.F.C. Now working as an Independent Football Film Consultant, ESPN's John Dahl informed me that the NFL had agreed to allow his company to utilize Ewbank's Film in their production as long as NFL Films would now own the actual film. I met Dahl, other representatives from ESPN and a group from Telverse Media in New York City in early June to discuss what was needed to go forth and produce the two hour special. ESPN wanted to tie in the past with the present and hoped to include interviews with players from both Giants and Colts from that game in 1958 with players from the 2006 and 2007 Super Bowl Champions; which nicely happened to be the Colts and Giants. I was asked to give information directing ESPN where as many of the original shots from the Championship Game were located at NFL Films. With a feeling that I can only describe as being; "sick to my stomach", I gave away that info reluctantly: Although I was no longer employed by NFL Films, I still felt some type of loyalty to them and also I felt that they **not** ESPN should be producing the show. I was then asked if there was any way I could contact some of the former players so that they could be interviewed for the show: Gino Marchetti, Art*

*Donovan, Raymond Berry and Lenny Moore were four that I felt were needed to add to the credibility of the production that would air in the fall. However, before I would make contact with those former Colts' players I asked: "How much are you going to pay each guy for the interview"? With an incredulous look from everyone at the table I was told it wasn't in the budget. I was then asked: "How much should we pay them"? Slipping into my Jerry ("**Show me the money**"!)Maguire mode I relayed twenty five hundred – each! They agreed and that night I called all four and informed them of the gratuity. As for me; I wanted fifteen hundred for services rendered. The agreement being; that once I had given up the information in regards to the location of the original footage I would collect my "cut" but as cut and dry as that may have sounded, it was nothing of the sorts: Before I was to be paid I needed to show four forms of identification, answer three pages of questions pertaining to my background, swear on the bible that I was an American citizen, submit to a DNA test and luckily I had someone else submit a urine sample. After all that I was still asked for a business tax identification number. At the time I did not have one and was told by Telverse Media that I could not be paid without it. Reacting in a complete "I understand matter"; I responded with: "You can keep your money"! The very next day FEDEX was at my door with a check for fifteen hundred dollars. I was given a credit on the show and can honestly say it was well done. As for those former Colts who each received twenty five hundred: Their urine samples all tested negative.*

With my assistance and good friend
Pete Caldes: The night of my 3rd
"Bachelor Party" having drinks at
His home in Philadelphia in June
Of 1996

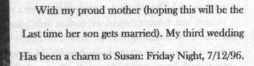

With my proud mother (hoping this will be the
Last time her son gets married). My third wedding
Has been a charm to Susan: Friday Night, 7/12/96.

Not only my best man at my marriage
To Susan but my all time main man:
I cannot find the words that would do
Justice to my friend Dan Rinaldi who
Was my biggest supporter throughout
My life; during the very few bad but
Numerous good times we shared.

Married for the third time:
To the former but still
Beautiful Susan Majeski:
Circa 1996

At an impressive country club
Resort in Phoenix
At Super Bowl XXX with
At the time my fiancé Susan
And with also one of the nicest
And most giving people I have
Ever known: The Chicago Bears'
Hall of Fame quarterback; my friend
Sid Luckman: Saturday: 1/27/1996

It was Hall of Fame
Writer and producer
Ray Didinger whose
Feature on the
"Grid Iron Gumshoe"
Launched my career
And with tongue in cheek
His as well: Circa 1997

More from
"Pro Football's
Greatest Weekend"
Gregg Pappas and I
On Saturday 7/29/97

With Hall of Fame
Colts, Packers and
Raiders' linebacker;
Ted Hendricks and
with the Packers and
Redskins' outside
Linebacker;
Dave Robinson
7/27/97

From left to right:

At Ed Sabol's retirement
Party : Bruce Lovenburgh.*
Me and Rob Alberino.
Dave "Deacon" Jones at
Canton, Ohio Summer 1998
And again left to right:
Dave DiLorenzo, me
Chris Bourquin my Canton,
Ohio buddy and his brother
At "Pro Football's
Greatest Weekend" 1997.
*Bruce passed away at the
Age of fifty in 2002.

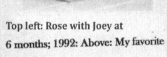

Top left: Rose with Joey at
6 months; 1992: Above: My favorite
picture of my son: Circa 2000

Middle Left to Right: Year
Unknown: My Parents
Above: "My dad" 1997
Left: At Mel Blount's
"50ᵗʰ Birthday Bash"
Pittsburgh Hilton
April 10ᵗʰ, 1999: My very
Beautiful wife Susan.

Thursday Night:
Once More at Canton;
Sitting with on my left:
The Oakland Raiders'
offensive lineman and
The Executive Director
of the NFL's Player
Union; the late Gene
Upshaw and to my left;
The Kansas City's
Middle linebacker
Willie Lanier
July 30th, 1998

Left: from the
Hall of Fame Class
Of 1998: 12 year
Veteran at receiver;
Tommy McDonald
July 30*, 1998

Chapter Thirty Seven:
Partied ... too much like it's 1999!

During the football season of 1998, I was contacted by George Soria who was involved in a small way with the retired players via his friendship with Steve Mike – Mayer; the former placekicker who played with the 49ers, Lions, Saints and Colts from 1975 – 1980. George was approached by the New York/New Jersey Chapter to see if he could organize a fund raising event for the Group; The National Alliance for Excellence: A nonprofit group that solicits money from businesses in order to award small to medium merit – based awards in their name. I was asked to emcee the event and in the process have ten Hall of Fame players appear at the fund raiser. From the Colts: Lenny Moore, Raymond Berry, Gino Marchetti and John Mackey, Yale Lary from the Detroit Lions and his teammate for three years John Henry Johnson, San Francisco's lineman; Bob St. Clair, the Kansas City Chief's linebacker; Willie Lanier, New York Giants' offensive lineman; Roosevelt Brown and soon to be inducted to Canton, Ohio, the New York Giants' former middle linebacker; Harry Carson. For each player as I had done previously at the Deacon Jones' Hall of Fame golf classic and Mel Blount's 50th birthday bash I would produce a 45 second highlight reel during his introduction. I asked for fifteen thousand which would cover the cost of the players' stipend and all travel and hotel accommodations. The affair was scheduled for Saturday night February 20th, 1999. In order for me to go forward and produce on my end, I asked for seventy five hundred initially with the remaining balance to be paid to me the night of the event. I met all parties involved including Alan Raicer who was the liaison between The Alliance and me. Alan would inform me on the progress of payment that became no progress: Although I had performed as the master of ceremony at both Deacon Jones' and Mel Blount's events, this upcoming event was my first as producer as well. It never had become an issue previously on whether or not I would be paid and as time wore on I was a little apprehensive with my involvement but now I was told by the Alliance Group if I did not continue I would be confronted with breach of contract. "What contract"? Instead of getting into a legal quarrel, I took my chances and hoped all would fulfill each initial promise. I faced a big expense that would probably cost me close to the $15,000 I asked for and now I had to have faith (although I hadn't been to church since Debbie and I married in week eight of the 1980 season) that the Alliance would come through. I continued with the preparations that included securing the Presidential Suite at the Crown Plaza Hotel across from Giants' Stadium that would be used as gathering place for the retired players

Gridiron Gumshoe

and their wives. In the room I would hook up two 36 inch television monitors to show highlights of the players and make everyone as comfortable as could be. Food and drink would also be constant throughout. Finally, with three minutes left in the fourth quarter I received a check for $7,500 and looked forward to what I perceived as a spectacular night of entertainment... On the morning of the event; my friend Eddie Skovron, his wife Nadine, my wife Susan and I checked into the Crown Plaza. It wasn't long before the nine Hall of Fame Players and Harry Carson began to filter in. I have been involved in over 30 events featuring the former players and what has been constant throughout; is the genuine camaraderie between those that have contributed to what is a very special game. It is a brotherhood, a fraternity and the glue that bonds them: Not only with the players but with the wives as well. Raymond Berry's wife Sally, Lenny Moore's wife Edie and John Mackey's wife Sylvia embraced and began to "catch up" on what each was doing with their lives. That initial greeting is priceless. All were in for a wonderful evening beginning with a pre gathering in the hotel's Presidential Suite where as mentioned earlier I had secured food, drink and entertainment for the celebrities and all ten enjoyed highlights of their careers on not two 36 inch monitors but now; one 48 inch big screen. What a sight: designated stand - up comedian Bob St. Clair "giving it" to his old rival buddies; "Look at that great block I threw for you; without it John Henry, {Johnson} you would have never scored"! St. Clair also proved to be a magician later that evening when he disappeared and returned with two new friends that he escorted back to the suite. The 49ers' big offensive lineman was very fond of the drink Jagermeister but was not able to quench his thirst with the liquor that was the team's major sponsor doing the early fifties; so he left the hotel to find a bar that did and in the process brought back with him the two wide eyed buddies who had their sights on the signed football of all ten former players. I called security (my wife) and she kept her eye on the prized possession. Now was time for the kickoff and I delivered: "From 1956 – 1967 number 24 played for the Baltimore Colts. The 1956 NFL Rookie of the year on three different occasions averaged 7 yards per carry in a season": His first year and in years 1958 and 1961. In 1964 he was voted the "**Comeback Player of the year**" *before calling it quits in 1967. Voted to Pro Football's Hall of Fame eight years later; Ladies and Gentleman, please welcome Lenny Moore"! A standing ovation for Lenny as well as for the other nine I introduced with the same fervor. The corresponding film footage enhanced each and the night continued with a speaker from the charity. I then added humor to the event with a produced piece displaying the lighter side of the players: Many remembered the New York Giants' Frank Gifford promoting the* *hair product **Vitalis** but many do not recall that the Colts' wide receiver; Raymond Berry had also showcased his on air talents. I presented each version via a split screen and continued: "Following Raymond's promo a producer for the Hollywood company MGM saw that the former player could deliver rather quite impressively his lines and he too was quite impressed; so much so he asked Raymond if he would consider playing the lead in the movie mogul's upcoming soon to be epic movie; **"Ben Hur"**. The man who was inducted into Canton, Ohio two years before his teammate Moore was gracious in his turning down the opportunity: "I have but three loves: my wife, my team and my head coach Weeb Ewbank". I continued; "Now I don't know if I have it in the correct order but I do know that MGM opted for their second choice: "Some guy named Heston"! The evening continued with a live auction followed by dancing. Now was the time for me to collect that turned into a nightmare of a time: The promoters regretfully were not going to be able to pay me the additional seventy five hundred because "we didn't make as much as we thought we would and we have other expenses to pay". I was in a real bad way because I still needed to pay each player for his appearance as well as for the cost(s) of each player's dinner. Eddie and I made it clear that a legal battle would ensue if we were "stiffed". Finally, a former offensive lineman from the Washington Redskins could see the awkwardness of the situation and wrote me a check for the remaining balance because he did not want those former players to come away from the event with a bad taste in their mouths. He would make it his business to collect from the Alliance at a later date. What began as a night to remember turned into a night I would rather forget except for what happened later: While Bob St. Clair was dancing his pacemaker started to give signs that the six foot nine disco dancer was having some discomfort. As he did in his 11 year career clearing a path for four Hall of Fame Players; the former mayor of Daly City, California (1958 – 1961) cleared a path right to the local hospital that admitted him. For one hour he lay on a table with tubes and wires hooked up to him. Finally, after numerous times asking for someone to see him, he removed himself from his prone position, left the hospital, returned to the hotel and continued to drink one of the two bottles of Jagermeister he had taken from the bar that he had visited earlier in the evening. He survived and landed in San Francisco the next day stirred but not too badly shaken.*

In 1997 both NFL Alumni and Retired Players Associations decided to honor me with membership as an associate because of my contributions to each and in early September of 1999 the Retired Players Association's annual convention *was to be held at the island of Maui. As it was in 1998's convention in New Orleans when I introduced the 113 former players in attendance via NFL Films' footage I would be responsible again for some type of presentation: I would present to the group a proposal for involvement of all 32 chapters working with each in the development of fund raising activities. The NFLPA welcomed my ideas and in turn treated my wife and me to five days in the second largest of the eight islands in our nation's 50th state. As an additional bonus my air flight was gratis. I was focused and decided to showcase what production talents I had by appearing on camera in a tuxedo presenting a black tie event for all explaining we were a first class operation. With the technology of the times I incorporated my standup with produced footage and presented a very impressive showing. Once I had finished, 16 of the 32 chapters wanted to know more. All would get an education later. Once my work was done it was time to enjoy Maui: Although I had not looked forward to the eleven hours it took to finally land on the island, I became intoxicated with the majestic surroundings. Plus; it was hard not to be impressed with the hotel suite the NFLPA had reserved for us. I had some other assignments while I was there that included the coordinating of the former players for a flag football game but overall it was a second honeymoon for Susan and me. Before I left for the 17th largest island in America(Honolulu), I put together highlights for many of the former players in attendance: Hugh "The King" McElhenny; the former halfback who played for 13 seasons from 1952 – 1964 was one of those and couldn't thank me enough for the highlight piece I gave to him. Another; was Pete Koch, the former Kansas City Chiefs' and Denver Broncos' defensive end lineman and the man who played "Swede" in the movie "**Heartbreak Ridge**" starring Clint Eastwood and Marsha Mason. Our time in Maui came to an end but not before we experienced a real live Lu Oua. Susan and I walked along the beach while experiencing the most breathtaking sight of the Pacific Ocean with our toes firmly settled in the sand as night fell. What lay ahead was the eleven hour plane ride home to South Jersey that actually took 18 hours after an emergency landing in Newark, N.J. that followed with a bus ride home to Philadelphia.*

Although our trip back to the east coast was a little unnerving, it was nothing compared to my unscheduled ill advised landing in Exeter, R.I. on May 3rd: My friend Ed Skovron contacted me in late March of 1999 and wanted to know if I had any connections with any of the former Patriots' players because a friend of his was having a celebrity golf tournament at the Alpine Country Club in Cranston, Rhode Island the first Monday of May. I did and called five *of the alum and all agreed to play. I also wanted to bring in another celebrity and got in touch with Mike Golic who following his career in Pro Football was now working for ESPN. Mike agreed and would drive east that Monday to play in the tournament. The total cost for all six was 3,500.00 and I asked for another 1,500.00 for my involvement as I would introduce each following 18 holes of golf. Golic ran into traffic on his way and arrived just in time to tee off in the last group while Eddie and I decided to have lunch. My friend for 31 years also made it clear to me that I should refrain from any alcohol because I wouldn't be needed for five hours. Once again always heeding to good advice I ordered only three Smirnoff vodkas on the rocks. We arrived back at the golf course and I started to prepare for my best Foster Brooks' impersonation; the comedian who during the sixties and seventies would appear on numerous variety shows as an inebriated fellow trying to get his point across. I was successful as I was in collecting the $5,000.00---all cash. I thanked former Patriots' Pete Brock, Ronnie Lippett, Mosi Tatupu, Roland James and Steve King as I handed each a check for their participation. $1,000.00 was paid to Golic and all of us headed for the 19th hole as day turned to evening. I always looked forward to when I can sit down and listen to "war stories" and none of the six disappointed. Evening turned to night and the "party" broke up and I headed to my parents' house. It should have taken all of twenty minutes but I would never reach 60 Foxglove Drive in Cranston, Rhode Island that night: Alpine Country Club is one of Rhode Island's finest courses situated nicely back from any major highway nestled in wooded surroundings. Although easy to find during daylight it can be treacherous at night because of the winding roads leading to and fro. When I left, I still was doing my best Brooks' impersonation and after awhile I felt I was the only person on the road looking in my rear view mirror thinking I would be abducted by aliens just as Barney and Betty Hill had been on their* **"Interrupted Journey"** *on September 19th and 20th, 1961 in the mountain regions of New Hampshire on Route 3. Finally after driving 15 miles south in the wrong direction I found an entrance to Interstate 95 and entered heading north - back to Cranston. Relieved I didn't become a statistic of the "Fourth Kind" which is the term used for alien abduction I drove as fast as I could in now what was wet conditions in a steady rain. I could see lights that happened to be owned by the vehicle only 30 feet in front of me! With cat like reflexes I swerved just in time out of the way and into the passing lane when my car decided to leave the road. Knowing I had no chance to rectify the situation, I held onto the wheel* **literally** *for dear life with my head down and braced for impact! After what seemed like only five seconds I found myself in a most precarious position unable to lift* *the car off of my left arm. The Emergency Medical Team arrived at light speed and I assured them I would be fine if they could only "lift the car off of my arm"! They did but before I was transported to Kent County Hospital in East Greenwich I made it clear; "Get my bag, there is five thousand in cash that I raised from my golf tournament"! "Excuse me sir, we're you drinking"? "Yes, but we raised five thousand dollars for charity"! I don't know if it was because the money was raised for charity that I was never asked to give blood to determine how much I had drank but I did get my bag and "settled" in for a two day stay. I was told by my immediate doctor that witnesses saw the car flip over and roll five times and that I was lucky to be alive. I guess I was and two days later, Eddie and I located the car and exclaimed; "Wow, how did I survive that"? My biggest concern before was getting my bag back but now it was getting my clothes and all my personal items from the trunk. Well it just so happened that the keys were still in the ignition and I was able to get my belongings. I took a train back to South Jersey seated in first class with my choice of food and drink. I wasn't hungry but since I had five hours before I reached my destination; I could use a drink after what I had gone through and since I didn't have my conductor's license ...... "Only Kidding"!*

Chapter Thirty Eight: "Hall of Shame", "Ground Breaking" and "My Tapes"!

*The Hall of Fame Class of 1999 added five to the list of 194 the first weekend of August: The NFL's second all time leading rusher; Eric Dickerson, Cleveland Browns' tight end; Ozzie Newsome, the Buffalo Bills' offensive lineman; Billy Shaw from the old AFL days, another stalwart on the offensive line; the Rams' Tom Mack and the man who added the word insomnia to offensive coordinators and arguably the best to ever play the linebacker position; the Giants' Lawrence "L.T." Taylor. Again, I was responsible for highlights of the five that would be presented that Friday night at the dinner and looked forward to spending time with the former players. However, 1999 would not only be the last year of the century but the last year of my involvement with those at the Hall of Fame: A group known as the Hall of Fame Foundation dedicated to raising money for the retired players had contacted the NFLPA Retired Players' Chapter in Cleveland and wanted to surprise me with a birthday party on the Saturday Night; August 7th at the Staples Sports Bar in North Canton, Ohio. George Soria whom I had met prior to the fund raising event for the National Alliance for Excellence (see previous chapter) was coordinating the birthday surprise and started to advertise in the local media weeks before the induction weekend throughout North Canton. The problem was many confused the Hall of Fame Foundation with the Hall of Fame and called the latter asking for tickets to my surprise birthday party. I couldn't understand the confusion: Hall of Fame Foundation does not sound anything like the Hall of Fame? Well maybe it does. Does it? When John Bankert; the director of the Hall of Fame got wind of this "surprise" he was furious and called my boss and wanted to know "Who the f---k does Ace think he is trying to put together a party the same night we have our own activities scheduled"? The problem was that 12 Hall of Fame Players had committed to my party which meant less Hall of Fame Players would be in attendance for Saturday Night's appearance of the group **Kool and the Gang** at Fawcett Stadium. I told Steve I had no idea of the Birthday Party but he told me that I had better cancel it because Bankert was "pissed"! I called John and let him know I had called it off and my one time good friend let it be known I was now "treading on delicate ground". Why couldn't he have just said; "Walking on thin ice"? When I arrived Thursday afternoon with my entourage that included Eddie Skovron, his son Todd; his friend Bob, Dave DiLorenzo and my wife I was informed that I wasn't going to receive all of the pass credentials I had asked for due to "some mix up". I believed Joe Horrigan and went on my way to* *somehow come up with a few more tickets to Friday Nights' dinner, which I was able to do. However, my group watched the induction ceremonies the next day at the Staples Sports' Bar hours before my surprise birthday party that included not twelve but twenty Hall of Fame Players as we watched the Tampa Ray Bandits' Wade Boggs reach the 3,000 hit plateau with a home run; the only man whose 3,000 hit came by way of a round tripper*. I might have been naïve thinking it was no big deal when I heard of the birthday party that was being planned for me: I mean I couldn't compete with* **Kool and the Gang** *- could I?*

While the world was saying goodbye to 1999 and hello to the new millennium, NFL Films would be in the process of saying so long to 330 Fellowship Road in Mt. Laurel, New Jersey and in August of the last year Films broke ground as Ed and his son documented their first dig on what would become One NFL Plaza: A 200,000 square foot facility that in two years would include state of the art equipment and an impressive tech side. The film vault would be climate control where the temperature at a constant 56% degrees perfect for storing brown bag lunches. It was an exciting time for those that had been with the company from the very beginning. From 11 employees working above a Chinese Laundromat in Philadelphia to a work force of over 300 in what in two years would be a facility worthy enough to charge people a fee for a walk through; the company had flourished. Although I was excited about having eventually our own cafeteria where food was available at any time I felt the glass would be half full with the only drinkable content located at 330 Fellowship Road. I welcome change as I much as I would a sex change: Not that there is anything wrong with that. (Okay; that's the third time I used the Seinfeld line).

In week fifteen of that season I was away that weekend spending time in Rhode Island visiting my son trying to keep up with the seven and a half year old maneuvering through the smallest of areas that were designed specifically at **Chuck "E" Cheese** *for…..seven and a half years old. I arrived back at Films on the Tuesday and heard sounds coming from the machine shop next to my office that could only be that of Jason of Friday the 13th II – X fame using a chain saw or if you are on the other end of the chainsaw; infamous. In actuality, it was the sound of a table saw cutting perfectly in half VHS of*

---

* *The New York Yankees' Derek Jeter became the second man to hit number 3,000 by way of a homerun when he connected off Tampa's David Price in the third inning on July 9th, 2011 becoming the first Yankee batsman to reach the coveted plateau.*

*NFL broadcast games. This separation was being performed by Gene and Jim; two employees on Ralph Caputo's crew and with each sacrilege the two seemed to get better at it. "What are you doing"? I couldn't contain myself. "Ace, we were told to destroy the tapes because they are not broadcast quality and who has the time to look through all seventy five cases"? "Stop"! "I'll look" and with that I began to log over 1,000 VHS tapes of broadcast games dated as far back as the broadcast of the 1961 NFL Championship between the Green Bay Packers and New York Giants. Other tapes included the 1962 AFL Championship Game; won by the Dallas Texans over the Houston Oilers 20 – 17 in quarter number six when placekicker Tommy Brooker was good from 25 yards out giving his team the win and another tape: Super Bowl III with all the commercials. I was a kid in a candy store and immediately made it known to my boss that this was an opportunity to cash in on this great treasure trove of good fortune. (Is that redundant?) The acquisition of this rivaled the film library that we had purchased from the company Tel – Ra in 1980 but the former was better because it was free but how did we come across this incredible find? It seemed that an employee from the league office had searched on the web for NFL Films' Video and incredibly another link came up. Now I am going to use the word ain't to be emphatic: There ain't no link or there shouldn't be: Films has the exclusive rights to all Pro Football content in the way of videos and any broadcast, re – broadcast without the written consent of the National Football League is definitely not nice and anyone in violation is subject to a very bad scolding from the NFL and confiscation of **ALL** seventy five cases and delivered to the "Gridiron Gumshoe" where the latter with the Peter Pan complex can look forward to each day as it was Xmas. Not only were there broadcast games with 80% of the tapes with dated commercials but also many of NFL Films' produced pieces from the companies early years and a good number of* **"This Week in Pro Football"** *with Summerall and Brookshier.* **ESPN** *continued with its* **"Greatest Games"** *series and had us produce the 1977 Playoff Game between the Oakland Raiders and Baltimore Colts at Baltimore's Memorial Stadium that took place on Xmas Eve that season. With our new acquisition we could follow the play by play and any interesting tidbits that were available which was something you couldn't get just by watching NFL Films.* **ESPN** *would add the 1986 and 1987 AFC Championship Games, 1981 NFC Championship and Super Bowl XIII in the next two years but that had to be a way where Films could utilize the Dead Sea Scrolls to a greater capacity. That would not happen for almost five years. I, on the contrary; utilized the new library to my fullest capacity: I began to make dubs of numerous games and sent them to former* *players: I sent Joe Namath Super Bowl III's NBC Broadcast with Curt Gowdy and Al Derogatis and all the commercials and **his** commercials when he was a spokesperson for the Hamilton Beach butter up popcorn popper and for the Men's cologne Brut from Fabershay. A little time later after sending the former Jets' quarterback the tapes, I received a phone call: "Ace"? "You're speaking to him". "This is Joe Namath". "Where did you get that stuff"? "My keeds loved it"! I just felt it was something that he and other former players would love to have as a keepsake. Former Packers' quarterback Bart Starr was humbled when he received the 1961 NFL Championship Game and his return letter thanking me is something I hold precious for in his writing he expressed his gratitude. ESPN's Ron Jaworski, Merril Hoge and former New England signal caller Steve Grogan are others that have received numerous broadcast games from us as well but the true value of the tapes couldn't be measured unless one took the time to watch every tape...and I did: Did you know that the Tampa Bay Buccaneers' Lee Roy Selmon* was never knocked off his feet his senior year at Oklahoma in 1975? Well, by watching one of their broadcast games an announcer mentioned that fact and in the 1980 season the Raiders' defensive back Lester Hayes recorded 13 interceptions. He actually intercepted 4 more but all were called back via penalties including one on the New York Giants' last drive in week sixteen that would have tied the record for most interceptions in one season: Rookie Rams' DB and Hall of Fame player Dick "Night Train" Lane set the mark in 1952 in just what was then a twelve game season. That type of information and other interesting facts made my viewing of the games exciting. Each day I would go about my business making copies of everything enjoying my childhood again reminiscing as the boy; "Who never wanted to grow up".*

---

* *After suffering a stroke on September 2 nd, 2011 Selmon died two days later; on September fourth. At his induction to the Pro Football Hall of Fame in 1995, I found him to be gracious and humbled. Two years later; we continued our friendship at dinner during the Deacon Jones' Hall of Fame Golf Classic. He is missed.*

Chapter Thirty Nine:
"Wow, Jim Brown has a nice house" and "Millennium Matchup".

As the 20th century headed into the new millennium, I worked on many projects; most looking back at the greatest to ever play the game: Was there anyone better at the quarterback position than John Unitas or because of Dan Marino's numbers was he considered the best to ever play? Arguably a case could be made for Joe Montana who led his 49ers to four Super Bowl Titles and would be inducted to Canton, Ohio in August of 2000. At wide receiver: From Don Hutson to Jerry Rice and all the others who made their living on catching passes, who was the best? Defensively a list of who's who: Greatest middle linebacker; Dick Butkus or Mike Singletary and at outside linebacker was it The Giants' Lawrence Taylor or the Chiefs' Derrick Thomas? Was the Eagles' and Packers' defensive lineman Reggie White more of a quarterback's nightmare than Hall of Famer "Deacon" Jones who coined the term "sack"? All mentioned were open for debate but there was no debate when it came to the question; "Who was the greatest rusher in NFL History" and in the year 2000 the NFL voted Jim Brown as not only the greatest running back of the 20th century but as its all time greatest player. Previously, I had met the former Cleveland Browns' all everything at Mel Blount's celebrity golf tournament in 1997 and after some uncomfortable moments initially, he and I became cordial towards each other and in June I received notice that he wanted to see me. He was aware of my fund raising events that had included many of his peers and hoped he could see me to thank me personally. Two acquaintances; Tim Bell and Tracy Edwards had set up the meeting and arranged a first class ticket on Continental Airlines to fly out of Newark, New Jersey to meet with the living legend at his home in Beverly Hills. Again; not being wild about flying I boarded the 727 in first class. "May I get you something sir"? "Yes two towels and twelve Smirnoff vodkas". My stewardess informed me she would do her best to get me the towels. I arrived at Los Angeles Airport just in time to meet Tim and Tracy and from there they took me to meet one of Brown's friends: Rock Johnson was a former gang leader who had turned his life around due mainly in part to the positive influence of the Cleveland Browns' legend and his Amer I can program. Johnson retold many stories that included his near death experience when he was abducted, thrown into the trunk of a car and re- emerge only to be staring down the barrel of a gun. Somehow he was able to "talk" his way out of the one way ticket to the afterlife. Since then he had devoted his life for good and became a role model for others who face trying times when influenced by others. While Johnson "entertained" us with C.S.I. stories he continued to feed fish in his very large aquarium that included some of the exotic type. The food: smaller fish that would eventually succumb to numerous bites; much like in Johnson's one time real world where only the strong survived. As I continued to do my best not to watch the impending doom of those unfortunate in the fish tank, I felt when I did look, I was seeing a metaphor. "Okay; who's hungry"?

Tracy, Tim and I had lunch at some chic café where anyone that wanted to be seen did. It was somewhere around 2.00 P.M. and we were scheduled to meet the 1957 NFL Rookie of the Year at his home at 4:30. Jim would be at his house following a round of golf. I don't remember what I ate but I do remember not wanting to consume too much alcohol because I wanted to have all my faculties when I spoke with the greatest running back of all time.

Six months earlier NFL Films had visited Brown at his home to interview him for a piece they were doing documenting the former Syracuse All American's life and in that interview Brown became a little emotional when talking about his friend; the former Washington Redskins' George Hugley who was a 20 year veteran of the San Fernando, California Police Department. Hugley was killed on February 27th, 1999 when his motorcycle was hit from behind while he was on loan to a Southern California drug task force assigned to investigate major drug traffickers. After being lifted via helicopter to Huntington Hospital in Pasadena, the 59 year old Hugley died two hours later. It was the first time anyone could remember seeing the bronze featured stoic demeanor Brown had shown all his life displaying that type of emotion. Now one half year later from that day of the interview I was about to sit down with him at his home to discuss but actually more to listen what he had to say. Brown had just returned from his day on the golf course and still had on his golf shoes when we met. I sat next to Jim on his couch and gave him a video tape of highlights of his career with sound from the perspective of the other teams' announcers. He was most appreciative as he thanked me not just for my thoughtfulness but for my thoughtfulness concerning the other players. Every once in awhile I had to come back down to earth so that I could hear what the former civil rights activist had to say. Brown can be very intimidating but not because he was voted the greatest player of the millennium but because of his knowledge of so many issues pertaining to life. I am thinking throughout my stay that here is a man that fought for everything he had; facing racial prejudice defending his and others' rights for equality. I remember when Muhammad Ali did not take the step to be inducted into the armed forces of the United States and those that supported his beliefs behind him were the Boston Celtics' Bill Russell, the U.C.L.A. Bruins' basketball star Lew Alcindor (Kareem Abdul Jabbar), singer and actor Harry Belafonte, Washington Redskins' Bobby Mitchell and seated next to Ali; Brown. All could be seen by way of film footage. Brown fought for the rights of others and that is why he supported my friends; Tracy, Tim and myself in our crusade to assist the former players. Once Jim and I had finished our conversation on the former we began to talk football and my two buddies were amazed that I held my own. Three hours had passed since my first hello and it was now to the airport where I boarded the "Red Eye" with the intent of sleeping but it never happened: I kept thinking: "Wow, Jim Brown has a nice house"!

Making reference to earlier: In 1989, Steve Sabol approached me and asked if I wanted to work on the **"Dream Season"**. *Now eleven years later; Films was about to produce the* **"Millennium Matchup"** *that would air on ESPN later during the 2000 Pro Football season. Some of the original producers from the* **"Dream Season"** *would once again lend their expertise to the project with the addition of Pete Frank whom I had something in common with: We both followed Rhode Island teams due in part to his attending college in the state. A lot had changed since last we produced that epic battle between the 1978 Pittsburgh Steelers and the 1972 Miami Dolphins: Technology mostly – and obviously for the better. Now we would focus all our attention on the teams' of the decade: The Green Bay Packers of the sixties, the seventies' Pittsburgh Steelers, four Super Bowl Titles for the San Francisco 49ers in the eighties and the 1990's Dallas Cowboys. We could now digitally place in the same frame one player from one era with another player from another; so when I found a shot of the Packers' Herb Adderley with his back to us situated a little right of the screen, I knew that a shot of the 49ers' Jerry Rice could be used with number 80 facing us situated in the left side of the screen. The other matchup would be between the Steelers and Cowboys so that anyone who played in that decade may find himself participating in the matchup of all time. Not only did I have to find footage for the project but I had to have a sharp eye and understanding of what could digitally work so that Penny Ashman and her crew could perform magic. Once again I relished the upcoming task and couldn't wait to decrease my number of hours of sleep. The first game was between the Packers of the sixties and the 49ers of the eighties. As I had mentioned in Chapter Nineteen; the fact that both teams' uniforms didn't drastically change through the years made research not too difficult. Much was the same for the other matchup: Cowboys and Steelers.*

Gridiron Gumshoe

In two hard fought games that only could be described as the most exciting outcomes in the history of mankind, the 49ers of the eighties and the Steelers of the seventies would meet to determine the "Team of the Millennium". ESPN's Joe Theisman and Mike Patrick would be doing the color and play by play respectively. I was in the final edit to "catch" any inconsistencies and initially I "got under the skin" of the two ESPN employees: On the 49ers first series; we as Network list the offensive lineup with Roger Craig number 33 and Wendell Tyler number 26 in the backfield. Patrick states; "No surprise there" and yet; the first play is a handoff to number 32 Carl Monroe. Since I am in my policeman mode I inform everyone who is listening of the mistake and innocently enough is welcomed with a "good catch Ace". Well, before the 49ers could finish their first drive it went from "good catch Ace" to "let's finish this sometime this week". Honestly, I was happy it came to that for the badge I was wearing kept sticking into my chest. With very little time left the 49ers took the lead and it appeared that San Francisco will become the greatest team to ever play on this or any other planet. The Steelers are facing incredible odds and many of us in the edit room did not know the final outcome including me. However, the last play of the game resembles; no strike that: Looks exactly like the last play of the 1972 playoff game between the Steelers and the Oakland Raiders at Three Rivers' Stadium except the Raiders are wearing San Francisco 49ers' uniforms; "And Bradshaw, rolling out of the pocket, fires downfield, and there is a collision, and … the ball is caught out the air, pulled in by Franco Harris who is running down the sidelines, Franco running… touchdown"! "I don't even know where he came from"! I do and did and so did everyone else: Technology had certainly changed and definitely for the better: Just ask Steelers' fans.

To My Right: Working with "Broadway Joe"

For Classic Sports in the NFL Films' Vault

Circa 1998

Below: 3/27/1999; At The Chuck Noll Roast

At the Pittsburgh Hilton where I

Introduced former Pittsburgh Steelers

As I had done one year earlier at

Mel Blount's 50th "Birthday Bash

On April 10th, 1998 (rt. hand corner)

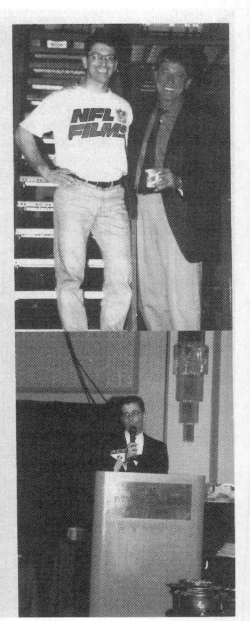

JM

Joseph W. Namath
Namanco Productions, Inc.
300 East 56t Street
New York. N.Y. 10022

Telephone: (212) 688-6310
212-758-7876

October 27, 1998

Mr. Ace Cacchiotti
NFL Films
330 Fellowship Road
Mount Laurel, New Jersey 08054

Dear Ace,

   I hope this letter finds you in good spirits and the best
of health and enjoying the NFL season.

   Please accept my apology for my failure to respond to
receiving the Super Bowl III tape. I thought I had written
to you. My children and I thank you for the happy moments we
shared looking at that memorable game.

   Ace, I can't commit to the February 20 date in Teaneck,
New Jersey, as I have family matters to attend to at that time.
I know Ed Kroke and he is a fine man and I'd like to honor him
but there are only a few D.B.'s I know that can be in two places
at once.

   If you are ever in the Palm Beach County area please let me
know and we can play a round of golf together. My office number
is 212-688-6310.

                          Sincerely,

                          JOE NAMATH

JWN:mjg

Saturday Night: 8/7/99 I celebrated my 46th Birthday with Bottom Row

L to R: Dave DiLorenzo,

Steve Mike – Mayer

"Fast Eddie" Skovron

George Soria and son

2nd Row: Lonnie Warwick

Carmine Melagnano

To my left: Chris: manager

Lenny Moore also below

Yale Lary 3rd Row: L to R:

Brian Holloway, Bob St.

Clair, Raymond Berry

And the late Roosevelt Brown

Below: The 49ers' Bob St. Clair who one year earlier; his daughter

Lynn, Susan, I and everyone else in the restaurant gazed at his

Eating of a raw flank steak (chapter 14).

Chapter Forty: "New Digs" and "Goodbye "Joe Cash"

Six decades after America came under attack by Japan's aerial aggression at the Pearl Harbor Naval Base on December 7ᵗʰ, 1941, the United States suffered the worst terrorist assault in its history: Four American airlines were hijacked and used as projectiles: Two crashed into the New York City's World Trade Center's Twin Towers, another into Washington D.C.'s Pentagon and another due to the heroic efforts of a small group on board saved thousands by sacrificing themselves overtaking control of the plane from the hijackers as United Airlines flight number 93 crashed in a field outside of southwest Pennsylvania near Shanksville some 150 miles northwest of Washington, D.C. The country wanted revenge and President George W. Bush swore America would not stop until those responsible would be brought to justice. It was determined that al – Qaeda led by Osama Bin Laden* was the terrorist group that orchestrated the unthinkable. We have been at war with Afghanistan ever since and America has never been the same. It would take some time before the country would go about their collective everyday routines but the show must go on and following a week off, Major League Baseball and the National Football League resumed their everyday schedules and twelve days from that day of infamy (9/11/01) the Giants recorded their first victory of the season: a 13 – 3 win over the Kansas City Chiefs at Arrowhead Stadium. NFL Films continued to do what they do best but in a new location: Located on One NFL Plaza in Mt. Laurel, New Jersey: stood a two hundred thousand square foot state of the art complex; designed to withstand the four seasons and an errant golf shot: (I knew I should have hit a lesser club). Those responsible for the construction of the new building did pay attention to detail. However, the man who had been responsible for the construction of NFL Films' second home on 330 Fellowship Road was not asked to be involved in the company's new building: Ralph Caputo's job was now to oversee the selling of Films' merchandise and his overall duties to the company were lessened. Eventually, he would ask for his release and "retired" with his wife Mary at the Jersey Shore. I was the last person to leave Fellowship Road and many on One NFL Plaza on more than one occasion would ask Steve; "Does Ace still work here"? Steve reassured everyone I did although I was nowhere to be seen: I was waiting for

---

* On May 3ʳᵈ, 2011 after nearly a decade of seeking vengeance for the cowardly act(s)of September 11ᵗʰ, 2001, United States Navy Seals located and killed Bin Laden in Pakistan.

the cafeteria to officially open and when it did I became a resident. Interesting note: **Aramak** the company responsible for food services at NFL Films and other corporations was also responsible for providing food to the 33 miners trapped in the San Jose mine near Copiapo, Chile under extreme conditions for over seventy days in 2010. I hoped they had a chance to sample the beef barley soup; my favorite. Although a very high percentage of employees welcomed the upgrade there were still some who felt that the company would lose that family type atmosphere that they had grown to love working at the old building. They were right: Not only did the size of the building increase by 164,000 square feet but an increase in the number of employees hired by the company. Many had just finished their tenures at different colleges excelling in no people skills. I was amazed at the number of new faces I passed in many a different hall without as so much a hello. It would have been nice if I knew who it was that didn't say "Hi". My office was located far away from the film vault because… sorry I don't have an answer for that. Eventually, I was re-located to the tech side much farther away from the film vault because… sorry I don't have an answer for that either. I found out later that Bruce Lovenburgh; the man who oversaw the daily duties of those responsible for the film processing made it clear that: "If it was up to me, Ace wouldn't touch another piece of film".
Why not just ask for Frank Sinatra to never sing another song: (I guess he had gotten his earlier wish: Sinatra died on May 14th, 1998). The company was afraid that the more people who handled film might increase the possibility of damaging the goods. Gee, our track record for the last 40 years was pretty good - wasn't it? Eventually, I was able to take my rightful place alongside Nancy Noto and Laura Gellathin in a room right across from the film vault due to an unfortunate situation: Mike Villanova took over the duties of the late Lovenburgh who passed away at the young age of 50 later that year in 2002.

Many have died before their time and with each passing so many are affected: My friend Bob Stravato who introduced me to the sport of bowling died from an incurable brain tumor at the age of 49 in February of 2002 and one month later; Mark Richmond a former drinking buddy also passed away at the age of forty. I thought of the pain and sadness their families had to endure especially when a parent outlives a child and although my father* was fortunate enough not to bury any of his children, his passing at 76 years of age was never the less still devastating.

---

* My mother buried my sister Paula on November 23rd, two thousand and ten - four days after her passing at the age of 60.

Gridiron Gumshoe

"Honey; call the rescue squad". My dad made that request two days after the Cacchiotti family celebrated what was to be my dad's last Thanksgiving in 2001. For exactly one month he continued to fight hoping to find his way back home where he could work on his jewelry but the decades of smoking **Pall Mall** *that curiously is pronounced* **Pell Mell***, would be responsible for his goodbye. Sometime in the early sixties; came the first warning from the surgeon general and from there more warnings of the threat of nicotine became more serious but since one of the warnings issued made it clear that if pregnant smoking could do harm to the fetus, I guess my dad felt since he wasn't pregnant it was okay to continue to blacken his lungs and on December 27th, 2001 he passed on. Although small in stature I always felt "Joe Cash" stood head and shoulders over anyone else's father. Always working to provide for his family, my two sisters and I never went without and XMAS was special: Even when he faced fourth down and 20 from his own two yard line late in the game, he somehow secured a first down delivering a boxful of presents right before Saint Nick ate his first cookie. My dad always came through. At 18; he and many of his brothers fought in World War II and once the war ended he married Caroline Alienello who was all of 18 at the time. "Joe Cash" worked for everything he had; nothing came easy and just when it appeared that life would get the better of him, he put a "w" in the left side of the standings. It wasn't until he was in his late forties that his arduous efforts literally paid off by being the shrewdness when it came to buying and selling jewelry. In an earlier chapter, I documented his unique "style" of buying. My dad was always there for us. Later; when I was able to secure my own identity as Ace Cacchiotti; "Director of Archives" for NFL Films, Joe Cash Jr. was no more but when eulogizing at his funeral, I made it clear; "I was most proud when I was known as "Joe Cash's" kid": Tears in my eyes as I end this chapter.*

Chapter Forty One: 'The Beginning of the End and FINISHED Like a Pro"!

The Sy – Fy, History, Weather, Food and others have their own channel and there was a buzz in the air that the National Football League was about to launch their own network ---- and did as **The National Football League Network** *on November 4ᵗʰ, 2003. Just think: more football; 36 hours a day, nine days a week including of course Wednesdays. I was one of many that couldn't wait: Here was an opportunity for NFL Films to showcase not only their wonderful and insightful pieces but because of needing to fill content on the new network, a chance to "bring to life" the history of the game by looking back at the exciting stories of the league through the camera and production eyes of NFL Films' history pieces. The "no brainer" outlook initially did not happen: TNFLN made it clear that the highest percentage of its content would gear its attention on the focus of today's game. Now we can watch three straight days of young men attempting to impress scouts at the combines and it doesn't come soon enough: Following the Super Bowl; fans of the game have to wait only three weeks before they can watch men with the highest expectations run faster and jump higher than other men that can jump higher and run faster than other men and feel the pain and sorrow for those young men that didn't run faster and jump higher than anyone else and with the new network avid fans could relive the season that ended just three weeks after the Super Bowl by watching highlights of that Pro Football Year. Exciting! Steve Bornstein, the onetime chairman of ESPN and the man who was responsible for the morning reruns of* **"Sports Center"** *on that network had made it clear initially that TNFLN would not live in the past but look to increase viewing with new and mediocre programming. I was disappointed. I felt millions had become fans of Pro Football because of NFL Films' incredible passion and devotion to the game for more than forty years. Films' perspective was visceral and moving. I just didn't think TNFLN was utilizing my employer correctly and for the first three years many agreed. Also, little subtleties began to surface: Following ESPN's* **"Sports Center"** *when special thanks were given for Pro Football content, TNFLN was credited and not NFL Films and on numerous occasions I was asked was NFL Films out of business? I then would have to explain for 20 minutes the history of the company and what has transpired since TNFLN made its debut. I decided later it was just easier to say "Yes" and whenever you would call Films and be put on hold waiting to speak with whomever you no longer were listening to Sam Spence's music but interviews from players and coaches; many who were not easily identified.*

Gridiron Gumshoe

Jeanne Diblin one of the original 21 who "retired" on "Retirement Thursday" told me that Steve Sabol was fearful that the new network would be the end of NFL Films. Now that may have been a little extreme but for all intents and purposes it was the end of the "Grid Iron Gumshoe".

Okay; I could end on the above diatribe but I would not be honest with those that have followed my journey to this point. Yes, initially The NFL Network did not air many of NFL Films' history pieces but if you have been following TNFLN, you will have experienced hundreds of nostalgia pieces by Films, including their top ten series and just recently my former landlord just produced **"The One Hundred Greatest Players"** *of all time and although I cannot find it in me to watch any of my former companies new pieces, I am sure they are well done and the latter has been verified after speaking with others that have viewed the pieces. TNFLN also has shown many past NFL Broadcasts and has done justice to the history of the game but back when it debuted there was no indication that would happen. NFL Films had always "Set the Bar High" and got the okay to produce* **"America's Game"** *in 2005 which was a look back at each Super Bowl Champion. The number reached forty following the Pittsburgh Steelers' 21 – 10 win over the Seattle Seahawks on February 5, 2006. The one hour look for each team documented their season told by three who contributed to the team's success. Again, I would be responsible for the nostalgia footage. My duties ended following Super Bowl XIX; the last year the Super Bowl was filmed in ektachrome when producer Dave Douglas asked me to locate a shot that he had asked a team of researchers to find but were not able to: San Francisco 49ers' offensive tackle Guy McIntyre lined up in his team's backfield in San Francisco's 23 – 0 win over the Chicago Bears in the 1984 NFC Championship Game. Douglas was the producer for* **"America's Game"** *Super Bowl XX Champions' Chicago Bears and asked me to find that shot of McIntyre after the Bears' Mike Singletary voiced displeasure with the 49ers using that offensive lineman in the backfield. Singletary thought it showed his team no respect and let it be known that it would be motivation to get to the Super Bowl the following year. NFL Films won acclaim for the production of* **"America's Game"** *and many felt it was one of the best they had ever produced. I tend to agree and felt satisfaction that I was able to contribute. Working closely with so many talented people had been something I relished and cherished. I loved working on nostalgia projects and* **"America's Game"** *gave me the opportunity to once again;* ***"Pay attention to detail and FINISH like a Pro!"***

Epilogue: And… "Never Be the Same Again"

The writing of **"Grid Iron Gumshoe"** *was completed after two years, eight months, two weeks, seventeen days, fourteen hours, twenty minutes and 36…37…38…39… on November 28th, 2010 – five days after we laid my sister Paula to rest but not eternally because she continues to keep in touch with us through her psychic daughter Rachel. Since that time my former "Boss" but more importantly my good friend battled brain cancer that was discovered after he suffered a seizure in Kansas City; on March 5th, 2011 while waiting to receive the Lamar Hunt award. For eighteen months he fought, until he lost his battle with the inevitable war ending an incredible career on September 18th, 2012. A Steve Sabol tribute;* **"The Guts and Glory of Pro Football"** *was scheduled for February 12th, 2013. My wife Susan and I were in attendance as was NFL Commissioner Roger Goodell, New England Patriots' owner Robert Kraft and many from the NFL Films' family and as it has always been with any production from NFL Films was no doubt quite moving but as for me in my relationship with the company; there was **no doubt** that it would; "Never be the same again".*

Goodbye; My Friend

It seemed as if there was a reason why I waited so long before I went to have this book published: Almost as if I was waiting for something. I now can.

Steve Sabol

October 2nd 1942 – September 18th, 2012

The time to say goodbye:

When is the right time to say goodbye;

No one really knows;

So we can only ask why;

Until someone or something really shows;

Us the way to leave this earth;

At the time of our choosing;

The same way we know the time of our birth;

But isn't it amusing;

That none of us can really predict;

The right time for us to leave;

And yet at birth our clock begins to tick;

So with that I say goodbye; to my friend; Steve.

My Boss; My Mentor; My friend:

The late Steve Sabol*

*Five months before his passing he paid me the highest compliment after reading
my book: In Latin; "Opus Magnum" and later referred to me as author!